FOURTH EDITION

C000172089

Psychology A Level Year 2

The Mini Companion

Mike Cardwell • Rosalind Geillis
Rachel Moody • Alison Wadeley

OXFORD
UNIVERSITY PRESS

Great Clarendon Street, Oxford, OX2 6DP, United Kingdom

Oxford University Press is a department of the University of Oxford. It furthers the University's objective of excellence in research, scholarship, and education by publishing worldwide. Oxford is a registered trade mark of Oxford University Press in the UK and in certain other countries

© Oxford University Press 2016

The moral rights of the authors have been asserted

First published in 2016

All rights reserved. No part of this publication may be reproduced, stored in a retrieval system, or transmitted, in any form or by any means, without the prior permission in writing of Oxford University Press, or as expressly permitted by law, by licence or under terms agreed with the appropriate reprographics rights organization. Enquiries concerning reproduction outside the scope of the above should be sent to the Rights Department, Oxford University Press, at the address above.

You must not circulate this work in any other form and you must impose this same condition on any acquirer

British Library Cataloguing in Publication Data
Data available

978-0-19-837529-6

10 9 8 7 6 5 4 3 2 1

Paper used in the production of this book is a natural, recyclable product made from wood grown in sustainable forests. The manufacturing process conforms to the environmental regulations of the country of origin.

Printed in Great Britain by Ashford Print and Publishing Services, Gosport

Acknowledgements
Editorial management and page layout: GreenGate Publishing Services

Cover photographer: Chris Cardwell

Links to third party websites are provided by Oxford in good faith and for information only. Oxford disclaims any responsibility for the materials contained in any third party website referenced in this work.

Contents

Introduction

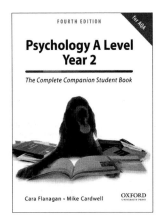

FOURTH EDITION

for AQA

Psychology A Level Year 2

The Complete Companion Student Book

Cara Flanagan · Mike Cardwell

OXFORD
UNIVERSITY PRESS

About this book

This *'Mini' Companion* is an abridged version of our main Year 2 book – *Psychology A Level Year 2: The Complete Companion Student Book*. This book covers the content for Paper 3 of the AQA A Level Psychology specification. The content for Papers 1 and 2 is covered in our AQA AS and A Level (Year 1) *Mini Companion*. Like the main textbook, the contents of *this* book are also mapped exactly onto the AQA A Level specifications. However, we have stripped down the content to leave only the essential material necessary for your exam. This *Mini Companion* is not meant to replace the main book, but to give you an additional resource that you can carry around with you – ideal for revision on the go!

This book is divided into eleven chapters that match the topics in the specification. Remember that, as with the main book, you will not have studied all of the chapters in this book. We have used the same chapter numbers as in the main book to make it easier for you to navigate around. If you are using this as a standalone text, make sure you know which chapters refer to the topic areas you have previously studied.

Most topics are covered on one page, the equivalent to a double page spread in the main textbook.

The **AO1** descriptive content for each topic is distilled down into just 200 words or so.

The **AO3** evaluative content is in the form of five (or occasionally six) points, each of the appropriate depth for 'effective' exam answers.

Key terms for each topic are explained for greater understanding.

Each page contains an **AO2** 'Apply it' feature in the form of a scenario, question and answer.

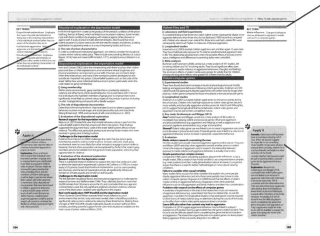

Our mini companion dog, Tofu, makes an appearance at various places in the book. He lives in a diary tin.

On the opening page of each chapter we have included the **specification** entry for that section, so you can keep an eye on what you have to know.

We have used that specification material to construct **revision lists** that you can use to keep track of your progression from a basic understanding of a topic (column 1) to complete mastery of it (column 3).

The AO2 '**Apply it**' feature that appears on research methods pages gives you the opportunity to practice exam type questions relating to each topic. And we provide **answers** to these questions!

The A Level exam

How many papers? There are three A Level papers. Papers 1 and 2 (covered in our Year 1 *Mini Companion*) are two hours each. Paper 3 (covered in this book) is also two hours.

What sort of questions? A mixture of multiple choice, short answer and extended writing questions.

How many marks? The total mark for each paper will be 96 marks.

Assessment objectives: All three sections assess AO1 (description), AO2 (application) and AO3 (evaluation).

What do these contribute to the overall A Level? Papers 1, 2 and 3 each contribute 33.3% of your overall A Level mark.

Paper 3 (7182/3)
Issues and options in psychology
This exam paper is divided into four sections, each worth 24 marks.
Section A is compulsory, and for Sections B–D you choose one topic from each.
Section A: Issues and debates in psychology
Section B: Relationships
Gender
Cognition and development
Section C: Schizophrenia
Eating behaviour
Stress
Section D: Aggression
Forensic psychology
Addiction

Chapter 1

Research methods

4.2.3 Research methods

- Content analysis and coding. Thematic analysis.
- Case studies.
- Reliability across all methods of investigation. Ways of assessing reliability: test–retest and inter-observer; improving reliability.
- Types of validity across all methods of investigation: face validity, concurrent validity, ecological validity and temporal validity. Assessment of validity. Improving validity.
- Features of science: objectivity and the empirical method; replicability and falsifiability; theory construction and hypothesis testing; paradigms and paradigm shifts.
- Reporting psychological investigations. Sections of a scientific report: abstract, introduction, method, results, discussion and referencing.
- Probability and significance: use of statistical tables and critical values in interpretation of significance; Type I and Type II errors.
- Factors affecting the choice of statistical test, including level of measurement and experimental design. When to use the following tests: Spearman's *rho*, Pearson's *r*, Wilcoxon, Mann–Whitney, related *t*-test, unrelated *t*-test and chi-squared test.

Key terms (highlight each cell when you can confidently explain each term)

Qualitative research methods	Reliability	Validity	Features of science	Probability	Inferential statistics	Statistical tests	Reporting investigations
Content analysis	Inter-observer reliability	Concurrent validity	Empirical methods	Alternative hypothesis	Calculated value	Wilcoxon	Abstract
Thematic analysis	Test–retest reliability	Ecological validity	Falsifiability	Null hypothesis	Critical value	Mann–Whitney	Introduction
Coding		Face validity	Paradigm	Probability (*p*)	Degrees of freedom	Related *t*-test	Method
Case studies		Mundane realism		Type I error	Levels of measurement	Unrelated *t*-test	Results
		Temporal validity		Type II error	One-tailed test	Spearman's *rho*	Discussion
					Significance	Pearson's *r*	References
					Test statistic	Chi-squared	
					Two-tailed test		
					Parametric		
					Non-parametric		

Content checklist
1. *In each 'describe', 'apply' and 'evaluate' cell tick when you have produced brief notes.*
2. *Once you feel you have a good grasp of the topic add a second tick to the cell.*
3. *When you feel you have complete mastery of the topic and would be able to answer an exam question without the aid of notes highlight the cell.*

I am able to …	Describe	Apply	Evaluate
Content analysis and coding			
Thematic analysis			
Case studies			
Reliability across all methods of investigation			
Ways of assessing reliability: test–retest and inter-observer			
Improving reliability			
Types of validity across all methods of investigation: face validity, concurrent validity, ecological validity and temporal validity			
Assessment of validity			
Improving validity			
Features of science: objectivity and the empirical method			
Replicability and falsifiability			
Theory construction and hypothesis testing			
Paradigms and paradigm shifts			
Reporting psychological investigations. Sections of a scientific report: abstract, introduction, method, results, discussion and referencing			
Probability and significance: use of statistical tables and critical values in interpretation of significance			
Type I and Type II errors			
Factors affecting the choice of statistical test, including level of measurement and experimental design			
When to use the following tests: Spearman's *rho*, Pearson's *r*, Wilcoxon, Mann–Whitney, related *t*-test, unrelated *t*-test and chi-squared test			

KEY TERMS

Coding Putting data in categories.

Content analysis Analysis of data from an observational study in which behaviour is usually observed indirectly in visual, written or verbal material.

Thematic analysis A technique used when analysing qualitative data. Themes or categories are identified and then data is organised according to these themes.

▼ Sample table used in a quantitative content analysis of how men and women are portrayed in TV ads

	Male	Female
Credibility basis of central character		
Product user		
Product authority		
Role of central character		
Dependent role		
Independent role		
Argument spoken by central character		
Factual		
Opinion		
Product type used by central character		
Food/drink		
Alcohol		
Body		
Household		

Content analysis

Content analysis is an indirect form of observational study, analysing materials produced by people, e.g. books, films, photographs.

◉ The process of content analysis

In a **quantitative** analysis, the instances of each coding category are tallied, and can then be represented using descriptive statistics and graphs.
The procedure involves:
1. Deciding on a sample
   e.g. TV ads over a one-week period
2. **Coding** the data using behavioural categories
   e.g. men or women using household products
3. Recording the occurrences of each coding category

In a **qualitative** analysis, examples in each category are described.

◉ Thematic analysis

Thematic analysis is a type of qualitative content analysis which summarises the data descriptively. It identifies underlying themes in the data, rather than spotting obvious words or phrases. It aims to allow themes to emerge from the data and maintain the participants' perspectives.
The steps include:
1. Reading and re-reading the data transcripts (or watching and re-watching a video)
2. Breaking the data into meaningful units
3. Assigning a label or code to each unit
4. Combining codes into larger themes
5. Ensuring that these emerging themes represent all of the data

◉ Evaluation

Content analysis is based on observations of materials produced by people in their real lives

This includes newspapers, books, paintings, photos, films and DVDs. These communications can be current and relevant to a specific research question. This gives findings high ecological validity.

Content analysis can be replicated

Materials are often publically available and can be accessed by another researcher. This means that the observations can be tested for inter-observer reliability. If several researchers identify similar themes or occurrences of coding categories, the findings are reliable.

However, content analysis is affected by observer bias

Different observers may interpret the meaning of behavioural categories differently. The language and culture of the observer will affect their interpretation of categories and themes, so content analysis is likely to be culture biased.

Content analysis summarises rich qualitative data in a simplified form

The data loses its detailed descriptive flavour. The observer may impose meaning on people's behaviour so the coding categories may lack validity, as they do not fully represent people's understanding of their own behaviour or creative output.

Thematic analysis is a very time-consuming and painstaking process

It involves examining and re-examining huge amounts of data, with themes emerging iteratively. This enables the data to be summarised and conclusions to be drawn. However, it is not always suitable when researchers have limited time available.

Apply it

Scenario. A researcher analysed children's TV programmes over a period of a week to see what kinds of programmes were available.
Explain how the researcher could have used content analysis to analyse the data he collected. (4 marks)

Application. Sample is children's TV over a week. Watch some of the programmes and choose categories such as comedy, cartoons, educational. Categories should be mutually exclusive and exhaustive, so each programme only fits into one category and all programmes are categorised. Watch all of the sample and tally the occurrences of each type of programme.

Case studies

A **case study** is a detailed study of a single individual, institution or event. Case studies provide a rich, detailed description of a person's life.

A variety of research techniques can be used to gather data, such as observations, interviews, IQ or personality tests, and even experiments to test the individual's cognitive abilities. Case studies can be longitudinal, following the individuals over time.

Findings are presented in a qualitative way, organised into themes, but can also include quantitative data like scores from tests.

◎ Case studies of individuals

Henry Molaison (HM) – his hippocampus was removed to reduce epileptic seizures, resulting in an inability to form new memories.

Clive Wearing – his memory was damaged by an infection. His wife published his story in a book called *Forever Today: A Memoir of Love and Amnesia* (2005).

Little Hans – Freud (1909) used him to illustrate the principles of psychoanalysis.

David Reimer – a boy raised as a girl, published as a success story by Money and Ehrhardt (1972) but later reinterpreted, as David was very unhappy.

Phineas Gage – in 1848 he survived an iron rod passing through his brain, but suffered changes to his personality.

◎ Case studies of events

The London riots (2011) were studied by Reicher and Stott, to re-examine explanations of 'mob' behaviour from a social psychological perspective.

Mass suicide of a cult group – Reverend Jim Jones was responsible for the deaths of 900 followers in the 1970s. This case study illustrates processes of conformity and obedience.

◎ Evaluation

Case studies provide rich, in-depth data

This can provide insight into the complex interaction of many factors. This contrasts with experiments, which aim to hold variables constant.

Case studies describe unique individuals

These people often have particular or unusual characteristics. This means that it is not possible to generalise from individual cases.

Case studies can be used to study very rare experiences

Often these could not be generated experimentally, for practical or ethical reasons. For example, individuals who have suffered extreme deprivation in early childhood, or brain damage from infection, accidents or surgery.

Ethical issues

Confidentiality and informed consent must be carefully considered in case studies. Individuals such as HM may not have been able to give informed consent. Researchers should take care not to reveal personal details that allow the person to be identified or located.

What about before?

The interest in an individual often begins after an event, such as brain damage. We cannot compare before and after. For example, we do not know how HM's epilepsy and previous drug treatments may have affected his brain prior to his surgery. This makes it difficult to draw valid conclusions.

KEY TERM

Case study A detailed study of a single individual, institution or event. Case studies provide a rich record of human experience but are hard to generalise from.

▼ Phineas Gage, the skull of the man who survived an iron rod passing through his brain.

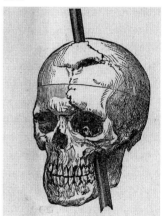

Apply it

Scenario. Louise wishes to find out about the life of a 'typical' teenager in the UK, and asks for three volunteers at a youth club.

What research methods could Louise use to find out about these teenagers' lives? Suggest how she could obtain quantitative and qualitative data for a case study. (8 marks)

Application. Quantitative: for example, age, amount of time spent on Netflix, closed questions such as Likert scales exploring preferences. Qualitative: open questions in interview or questionnaire, quotes from focus group discussion, video diaries.

KEY TERMS

Inter-observer reliability The extent to which there is agreement between two or more observers involved in observations of a behaviour.

Reliability The consistency of measurements. We would expect any measurement to produce the same data if taken on successive occasions.

Test–retest reliability The same test or interview is given to the same participants on two occasions to see if the same results are obtained.

Apply it

Scenario. Joanna is planning to research the experiences of girls in a secondary school in Uganda, to find out how they manage homework and helping with tasks in the home such as cooking and caring for younger siblings. She wants to collect quantitative and qualitative data. She is writing a questionnaire to find out their experiences, and their views of the importance of homework and helping with domestic tasks.

(a) *How could she test the reliability of the questionnaire? (3 marks)*

(b) *Why would it matter if the reliability was low? (3 marks)*

(c) *How could she improve the reliability of her questionnaire? (4 marks)*

Application. (a) By the test–retest method. She could ask a few of the girls the same questions a second time, a week later, to see if their answers were consistent.

(b) If the reliability was low, the girls may not have really understood the questions or may not have felt able to be honest, so the results would also lack validity.

(c) Joanna could write the questions in simple, clear English so they are not ambiguous. She could collect data by interviewing the girls rather than just giving them a questionnaire to complete, so that she can explain the questions or explore further to make sure the girls have understood.

Reliability

Reliability refers to how much we can depend on any particular measurement such as IQ, or the findings of a research study. We want to know whether, if we repeat the same measurement, test or study, we would get a consistent result. If not, our measurement is unreliable.

Reliability of observational techniques

The researcher records behaviour using behavioural categories.

Assessing reliability: Reliability can be assessed by comparing the data from two or more observers. This is the **inter-observer reliability** or inter-rater reliability. It is calculated as a correlation coefficient between the two sets of scores from independent observers. 'Good' reliability is +.80 or more.

Improving reliability: Reliability can be improved by making the behavioural categories clearer. Behavioural categories should be operationalised carefully so they are less subjective. Observers can improve their coding by practising or being trained in choosing categories.

Reliability of self-report techniques

These include questionnaires and interviews.

Assessing reliability: Test–retest reliability is used to assess the reliability of self-report measures. IQ tests, personality tests and other psychological tests can also be assessed for reliability in this way. The test is repeated after a short interval such as a week. Scores for each person are compared. Test–retest reliability is also calculated as a correlation coefficient, a measure of the consistency of scores for each individual. For interview data, inter-interviewer reliability could also be calculated in the same way as inter-observer reliability.

Improving reliability: Reliability can be improved by rewriting ambiguous questions. If people can interpret the same question in different ways, they may answer them differently the second time. Removing ambiguity improves reliability.

Reliability of experiments

The dependent variable (DV) in an experiment may be measured using a rating scale or behavioural categories. For example, in Bandura's (1963) Bobo doll study, the DV was the aggressive behaviours of the children. This was assessed by controlled observation, with behavioural categories such as verbal imitation. Reliability is the consistency of the way the DV is measured.

Assessing reliability: In these experiments reliability is assessed using inter-observer or test–retest methods, as above.

Improving reliability: Procedures should be standardised in any research study to improve reliability and replicability. Standardisation of procedures ensures that participants follow exactly the same procedure as each other, and other researchers can repeat the experiment.

Assessing reliability

The agreement between observers is worked out by calculating a correlation coefficient. Later in this chapter we will look at how these are calculated using statistical tests (see pages 30 and 31).

The table below shows data from two observers. The data is plotted in the scattergram. The correlation coefficient for this data (calculated with a statistical test) = +.470 This is low inter-observer reliability.

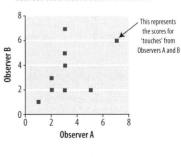

Scattergram showing correlation between observations from two observers

This represents the scores for 'touches' from Observers A and B

	Observer A	Observer B
Hits	3	7
Touches	7	6
Cuddles	3	2
Sits next to	3	5
Talks	2	3
Running about	2	2
Crying	1	1
Laughing	5	2
Smiling	3	4

Validity

◉ Internal versus external validity

Validity refers to whether an observed effect is a genuine one.

Internal validity concerns whether the researcher is measuring what they intend to, or whether the findings are affected by other factors.

Internal validity is affected by:

- Confounding variables
- Investigator effects (behaviour of the investigator that affects the participants' performance in a study)
- Demand characteristics
- Social desirability bias
- Poor operationalisation of the dependent variable or behavioural categories

External validity is how far the findings can be generalised outside the research setting, to other people (**population validity**), historical periods (historical or **temporal validity**) and settings (**ecological validity**).

◉ Ecological validity

In an experiment, the method used to measure the DV can be quite artificial, giving poor ecological validity. This could be a lab experiment, field experiment or natural experiment. We have to consider **mundane realism** – whether a study reflects real-world experiences – rather than just the location.

For example, Godden and Baddeley (1975) carried out an experiment on context-dependent forgetting. Deep sea divers learnt word lists on land or underwater, then tried to recall the words on land or underwater. The situation was 'real life' but the task was very artificial, and the divers were aware they were being studied, so may not have behaved 'naturally'.

Demand characteristics can affect ecological validity if participants are aware they are being studied, so alter their behaviour to look good (social desirability bias) or to fit what they think the researcher expects. This means they are not behaving as they would in real life.

◉ Assessing validity

A test may be reliable (see previous page) but lack validity if it does not actually measure the concept the researcher is aiming to measure.

Concurrent validity compares a new measure with an existing, validated one on the same topic. The same participants take both measures, and scores are compared.

Face validity is an intuitive, common sense judgement of whether a self-report measure appears to measure what it claims to – do the questions seem to be related to the topic?

◉ Improving validity

Face validity can be improved by replacing any irrelevant questions with new items more obviously related to the topic.

Concurrent validity can also be improved by replacing items and checking whether the validity improves.

Improving research design can deal with issues such as demand characteristics and investigator effects. For example, in a double-blind design, neither the participants nor the researcher who interacts with them knows the true aims of the study.

KEY TERMS

Concurrent validity A means of establishing validity by comparing an existing test/questionnaire with the one you are interested in.

Ecological validity The ability to generalise a research effect beyond the particular setting in which it is demonstrated to other settings.

Face validity The extent to which test items look like what the test claims to measure.

Mundane realism How a study mirrors the real world. The research environment is realistic to the degree to which experiences encountered in the research environment will occur in the real world.

Population validity The extent to which the findings of a study of a sample of participants can be generalised to other people outside the study.

Temporal validity The ability to generalise a research effect beyond the particular time period of the study.

Validity Whether an observed effect is a genuine one.

Apply it

Scenario. You have been asked to design an experiment to test whether annoying music affects children's performance in a smartphone game.

*Explain how **two** issues in the research design might affect the validity of your findings. (4 marks)*

Application. Validity issues: if the children are aware they are being studied, it might make them try much harder than normal (demand characteristics). Whether the music is 'annoying' is subjective – some children may love it. This is an extraneous variable as the music may affect children differently depending on their reaction to it.

KEY TERMS

Empirical A method of gaining knowledge which relies on direct observation or testing, not hearsay or rational argument.

Falsifiability The possibility that a statement or hypothesis can be proved wrong.

Paradigm 'A shared set of assumptions about the subject matter of a discipline and the methods appropriate to its study' (Kuhn, 1962).

Apply it

Scenario. Lauren is studying Psychology A Level. Her younger sister, Lucy, is taking GCSEs and choosing A Level courses. Lucy says, 'I don't like Science but I think Psychology sounds interesting because it's about people.' Lauren thinks she should explain to Lucy that Psychology is based on scientific principles.

Help Lauren to identify three key features of Psychology as a science that Lucy would encounter in A Level Psychology. (3 marks)

Application. Psychology is based on empirical research – A Level Psychology involves learning evidence for and against each theory. Empirical data should be objective – A Level Psychology focuses on evaluating how objective the research is, or whether it is biased. Psychological theories are built on empirical evidence and tested scientifically by coming up with testable hypotheses – A Level Psychology includes practical research where you will come up with hypotheses based on existing theory, and test them using experiments.

Features of science

Science is an evolving, systematic approach to creating knowledge.

◎ Features of science

1. **Empirical methods:** Empirical evidence is gained through direct observation or experiment. Claims can be tested and used to make predictions.
2. **Objectivity:** Objective data is collected systematically in controlled conditions, so it is not affected by the expectations of the researcher.
3. **Replicability:** Procedures are carefully recorded so that other scientists can replicate them with different groups of people to test their validity.
4. **Theory construction:** Theories are explanations of observations and findings. Theories can emerge from observation or from hypothesis testing.
5. **Hypothesis testing:** A good theory must be able to generate testable hypotheses. If the hypothesis is not supported by empirical evidence, the theory must be modified.

◎ Falsifiability

Karl Popper (1934) argued that it is only possible to disconfirm a theory. He pointed out that however many confirmed sightings of white swans there are, we cannot conclude that all swans are white; the sighting of just one black swan will disprove this theory.

Research tests the null hypothesis, e.g. 'not all swans are white'. If we are able to reject the null hypothesis (with reasonable certainty) we may accept the alternative hypothesis.

A scientific theory must have **falsifiability**. Freudian psychoanalysis can be criticised as not falsifiable.

◎ Paradigms

Thomas Kuhn (1962) proposed that scientific knowledge develops through revolutions, not the process of gradual change suggested by Popper's theory of falsification. Kuhn said that there are two main phases in science:

1. 'Normal science', in which existing theory remains dominant, while disconfirming evidence gradually accumulates.
2. **Paradigm shift:** a revolutionary overthrowing of existing theory and its replacement with a new set of assumptions and methods.

◎ Evaluation

Science is socially constructed

Kuhn's theory of paradigm shift is itself a paradigm shift from the previous way of understanding the scientific process. Scientific progress is more like a religious conversion than a systematic, logical process of hypothesis testing. This change of view also depends on social factors. Therefore, according to Kuhn, science itself is constructed through dialogue, not just a logical process of evolving theory based on empirical evidence.

Issues relating to psychology as a science

The theory of paradigm shift is debated by philosophers of science. Issues of bias in research, replicability, and the peer review process are also hot topics within psychology research. Many famous studies have proved difficult to replicate, and researchers are rigorous in criticising each other's research. Healthy debate between researchers will hopefully benefit the reputation of psychology as a valid and reliable scientific discipline.

The empirical approach requires objective evidence

A good scientist is a sceptic, and always asks, 'Where is the evidence?' Good evidence should be directly observed or collected using controlled, objective methods. This means that we can reject pseudoscientific beliefs based on weak or subjective evidence.

Probability

A hypothesis must be falsifiable (see previous page). In research, we seek to falsify the **null hypothesis**.

As we can only test a sample of the population, we have to ask 'What is the **probability** that the data collected came from a population where the null hypothesis is correct?'

If we are looking for a difference in the DV for two conditions of the IV (independent variable) in an experiment, the null hypothesis is 'there is no difference'. The **alternative hypothesis** is 'there is a difference'.

Samples may have small differences due to random variation or 'chance'. We test to see if any difference is likely to be due to these chance factors, or is large enough to represent a real difference in the populations from which the samples are drawn.

Inferential statistical tests permit us to work out how probable it is that a pattern in research data could have arisen by chance (supporting the null hypothesis). Alternatively, the effect may represent a real difference/correlation in the populations from which the samples were drawn (supporting the alternative hypothesis).

◉ Probability *(p)* levels

Psychologists generally use a probability level of 5% as the cut-off. This means there is a less than 5% chance of the results occurring if the null hypothesis is true, given as $p < 0.05$. So there is at least a 95% chance that the effect observed in the sample is a real one in the population.

In some studies, such as drug testing, researchers want to be more certain that effect is real. They may use a more stringent probability level of 1%, given as $p < 0.01$. This means there is less than 1% chance of the results occurring when there is no real difference/correlation between the populations from which the samples are drawn.

◉ Type I and Type II errors

The 5% probability level gives a good compromise between Type I and Type II errors.

A **Type I error** is a false positive: the null hypothesis is rejected when it should have been accepted.

A **Type II error** is a false negative: the null hypothesis is accepted when it should have been rejected.

In a criminal trial, there are four possible outcomes:

		Truth (which we will never know)	
		Guilty	Not guilty
Test result	Guilty verdict	True positive	False positive (guilt reported, i.e. positive) **Type I ERROR**
	Not guilty verdict	False negative (guilt not detected, i.e. negative) **Type II ERROR**	True negative

The same can be applied to a research study:

		Truth (which we will never know)	
		Alternative hypothesis H_1 true	Null hypothesis H_0 true
Test result	Reject null hypothesis	True positive	False positive **Type I ERROR**
	Accept null hypothesis	False negative **Type II ERROR**	True negative

KEY TERMS

Alternative hypothesis A testable statement about the relationship (difference, association, etc.) between two or more variables.

Null hypothesis An assumption that there is no relationship (difference, association, etc.) in the population from which a sample is taken with respect to the variables being studied.

Probability (p) A numerical measure of the likelihood or chance that certain events will occur. A statistical test gives the probability that a particular set of data did not occur by chance.

Type I error Occurs when a researcher *rejects* a null hypothesis that is true.

Type II error Occurs when a researcher *accepts* a null hypothesis that was not true.

Apply it

Scenario. A psychologist finds their results are significant at a level of significance of $p < 0.05$.

How can they be confident they have not made a Type I error in this study? Explain your answer. (3 marks)

Application. $p < 0.05$ means that there is less than 0.05 chance that the effect has occurred by chance. So there is less than 5% chance that they falsely rejected the null hypothesis (a Type I error), and they can be 95% confident that they have not made a Type I error.

KEY TERMS

Calculated value The value of a test statistic calculated for a particular data set.

Critical value In a statistical test the value of the test statistic that must be reached to show significance.

Degrees of freedom The number of values that are free to vary given that the overall total values are known.

Level of measurement Refers to the different ways of measuring items or psychological variables; the lower levels are less precise.

One-tailed test Form of test used with a directional hypothesis.

Significant A statistical term indicating that the research findings are sufficiently strong to enable a researcher to reject the null hypothesis under test and accept the research hypothesis.

Statistical test Procedure for drawing logical conclusions (inferences) about the population from which samples are drawn.

Test statistic The name given to the value calculated using a statistical test. For each test this value has a specific name such as S for the sign test.

Two-tailed test Form of test used with a non-directional hypothesis.

Statistical tests

Inferential statistics allow us to find out if results are **significant** using tables of critical values.

◉ Using statistical tests

Compare the **calculated value** of the **test statistic** with the critical value from the table of critical values.

To find the critical value, you need to know:

1. Significance level (using $p < 0.05$)
2. Kind of hypothesis: directional requires a **one-tailed test**; non-directional requires a **two-tailed test**
3. Value of N, the number of participants, or the **degrees of freedom** (df).

There is an instruction underneath the table stating how to compare the calculated value with the critical value.

◉ Parametric criteria

Parametric tests (which use the mean and standard deviation to calculate the test statistic) are more powerful than non-parametric tests (which use ranked data). This means they can detect significance in some situations where non-parametric tests can't. But they should only be used if certain criteria are met:

1. The **level of measurement** is interval or better
2. The scores (or scores of the population they represent) are **normally distributed**, and not skewed
3. The **variances** of the two samples are similar. This is not an issue with repeated measures design. For independent groups, the variance of one sample should not exceed four times the other. (Variance is the square of the standard deviation.)

Choosing an inferential **statistical test**:

| Design | Nominal | Level of measurement | |
		Ordinal	Interval
Independent groups	Chi-squared test	Mann–Whitney U test	Unrelated t-test
Repeated measures	Sign test	Wilcoxon test	Related t-test
Correlational		Spearman's *rho*	Pearson's r

Choosing a statistical test:

Sign test	◀ related ◀	Nominal data	▶ unrelated ▶	Chi-squared
		Ordinal or interval		
	Pearson's r	◀ Correlation ▶	Spearman's *rho*	
Parametric (interval data)		Tests of difference		Non-parametric (ordinal data)
	Related t-test	◀ Related ▶	Wilcoxon	
	Unrelated t-test	◀ Unrelated ▶	Mann–Whitney	

Apply it

Scenario. While researching stress, you have collected data measuring students' salivary cortisol level before an exam, to see whether this relates to the number of hours of sleep they had the previous night.

Which statistical test should you use? Explain why this test would be appropriate. (4 marks)

Application. Pearson's r. Both variables are interval data. The data is likely to be normally distributed, therefore parametric. We are looking for a correlation between two variables – salivary cortisol level and hours of sleep the previous night. Pearsons is a parametric test of correlation.

Non-parametric tests of difference

Tests of difference assess whether one set of data is significantly different from another. Related data comes from repeated measures or matched pairs experimental designs.

Unrelated data comes from independent measures experimental designs.

The Wilcoxon test is used for related samples (repeated measures or matched pairs design), and the Mann–Whitney test is used for unrelated samples (independent groups design).

To remember this: Mr and Mrs Wilcoxon are related by marriage. Mr Mann and Ms Whitney are unrelated.

◎ Wilcoxon test for related designs
Reasons for choosing:
- The hypothesis states a **difference**.
- The two sets of data are **related**.
- The data are at least **ordinal**.

If you are given the calculated value of *T*:
1. Look at the data: is the difference in the predicted direction?
2. Find critical value of *T* from table.
3. Compare calculated and critical values as instructed. (If the calculated value is equal to or less than the critical value, the result is significant.)
4. Report the conclusion, e.g. 'As the calculated value is not significant ($p < 0.05$, one-tailed, $N = 11$), we must accept the null hypothesis and conclude that there is no difference between …'

◎ Mann–Whitney test for unrelated designs
Reasons for choosing:
- The hypothesis states a **difference**.
- The two sets of data are **unrelated**.
- The data are at least **ordinal**.

If you are given the calculated value of *U*:
1. Is the difference in the right direction?
2. Find critical value of *U* from table, where the two values of *N* intersect.
3. Compare calculated and critical values.
4. Report the conclusion.

Apply it

Scenario. Suzi compared the recall of concrete words (e.g. cat, fish, table, cloud) with abstract words (e.g. beauty, truth, calm, fear). She used the same participants in each condition, and measured how many words each participant remembered. There were 23 participants, most of whom remembered more concrete words than abstract words. Four participants remembered the same number in each condition.

(a) *Write a directional hypothesis for this study. (2 marks)*

(b) *Suzi analysed the results using a Wilcoxon test. Explain why this test is suitable. (3 marks)*

(c) *The calculated value of T was 37. Use the table of critical values to decide if this is significant, and explain your decision. (3 marks)*

(d) *What can Suzi conclude? (1 mark)*

Answer. (a) People remember more concrete words than abstract words. (b) The data is at least ordinal (numbers of words recalled), it is a test of difference (concrete or abstract words) and it is a related design (same participants in both conditions, repeated measures). (c) Yes. The calculated value (37) is less than the critical value (53) ($N = 19$, $p < 0.05$, one-tailed) so it is significant. (d) The alternative hypothesis is supported – people remember more concrete words than abstract words.

▼ Table of critical vales for the Wilcoxon test.

Level of significance for a one-tailed test	0.05	0.01
Level of significance for a two-tailed test	0.10	0.02
$N = 5$	0	
6	2	0
7	3	2
8	5	3
9	8	5
10	11	8
11	13	10
12	17	13
13	21	17
14	25	21
15	30	25
16	35	29
17	41	34
18	47	40
19	53	46
20	60	52
25	100	89
30	151	137

Observed value of *T* must be EQUAL TO or LESS THAN the critical value in this table for significance to be shown.

Source: R. Meddis (1975). *Statistical Handbook for Non-statisticians*. London: McGraw Hill.

Parametric tests of difference

◉ Related *t*-test
Reasons for choosing:
- The hypothesis states a **difference**.
- The two sets of data are **related**.
- The data are **interval** level and fit the **parametric criteria** (see box).

> **Parametric criteria:**
> 1. Interval data
> 2. Normal distribution
> 3. Same variances
>
> Related data= repeated measures or matched pairs designs.
> Unrelated data= independent groups designs.

LINK

See p.14 for an explanation of how to use statistical tables.

▼ Table of critical values for the *t*-test.

Level of significance for a one-tailed test	0.05	0.01
Level of significance for a two-tailed test	0.10	0.02
df = (*N* – 2)		
1	6.314	12.706
2	2.920	4.303
3	2.353	3.182
4	2.132	2.776
5	2.015	2.571
6	1.943	2.447
7	1.895	2.365
8	1.860	2.306
9	1.833	2.262
10	1.812	2.228
11	1.796	2.201
12	1.782	2.179
13	1.771	2.160
14	1.761	2.145
15	1.753	2.131
16	1.746	2.120
17	1.740	2.110
18	1.734	2.101
19	1.729	2.093
20	1.725	2.086
25	1.708	2.060
30	1.697	2.042

Observed value of *t* must be EQUAL TO or GREATER THAN the critical value in this table for significance to be shown.

Source: abridged from R.A. Fisher and F. Yates (1982). *Statistical Tables for Biological, Agricultural and Medical Research*. (6th edition). London: Longman. Reproduced with permission by Pearson Education Limited.

Formula for *t*:

$$t = \frac{\Sigma d}{\sqrt{(N\Sigma d^2 - (\Sigma d)^2)/(N-1)}}$$

(You don't need to learn this, but should be able to use it to calculate *t*.)

If you are given the calculated value of *t*:
1. Look at the data: is the result in the right direction?
2. Find critical value of *t* from table, using *df* = *N* – 1.
3. Compare calculated and critical values as instructed.
4. Report the conclusion, e.g. 'As the calculated value (*t* = 1.8) is less than the critical value (*t* = 1.812) it is not significant (*p* < 0.05, df = 10, one-tailed). So we must accept the null hypothesis and conclude that there is no difference between …'

◉ Unrelated *t*-test
Reasons for choosing:
- The hypothesis states a **difference**.
- The two sets of data are **unrelated**.
- The data are **interval** and fit the parametric criteria. (Variances can be assumed to be the same if participants were randomly assigned to conditions.)

If you are given the calculated value of *t*:
1. Is the difference in the right direction?
2. Find critical value of *t* from the table. Use *df* = $N_A + N_B$ – 2.
3. Compare calculated and critical values of *t*.
4. Report the conclusion.

Apply it

Scenario. Mr Smith, the new principal of Angel College, is considering changing the times of the college day after reading that teenagers' sleep patterns are different from adults'. He conducts a one-week trial to see whether academic performance improves when students are able to sleep in for longer, starting the day at 10am instead of 8.30am.

Design a study that Mr Smith could carry out. Explain how he would collect data, and state an operationalised hypothesis. What experimental design is your study using? Which statistical test might be suitable to analyse the data from this study? Explain your choice. (8 marks)

Application. For example: give students tests in each subject after a week of normal working times, and after a week of later school days. IV = early or late. DV = test results. Hypothesis: students will achieve better test results after a week of starting school later than a normal week (10am instead of 8.30am). Repeated measures. Related *t*-test, because data is interval (test scores) and related, looking for a difference, and we assume it meets the parametric criterion of normal distribution. (This study could alternatively use an independent groups design; then you would use the unrelated *t*-test.)

Tests of correlation

Tests of correlation are used to determine whether the *association* (rather than a difference) between two co-variables is significant or not.

A correlation can be positive or negative, as shown in the scattergrams below. The closer the dots are to forming a diagonal line, the stronger the correlation. The strength of the correlation can be calculated as a **correlation coefficient** (−1.0 to +1.0). The sign indicates the direction of the relationship.

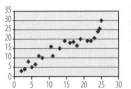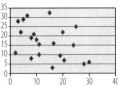

▲ The scattergrams show a strong positive correlation (+0.95) and a moderate negative correlation (−0.41).

◉ A correlation, but not significant?
Sometimes there can be a moderate or strong correlation which turns out not to be significant. This can be caused by a small sample size. The conclusion would be 'There is not a significant correlation between …' You could suggest replicating the study with a larger sample.

On the other hand, a correlation may be weak but still significant if a very large sample is tested.

◉ A non-parametric test: Spearman's *rho*
Reasons for choosing:
• The hypothesis states a **correlation** between two variables.
• The two sets of data are **related** (pairs of scores from each person).
• The data are **ordinal**.

Find calculated value of *rho* using the formula:

$$rho = 1 - \frac{6\Sigma d^2}{N(N^2 - 1)}$$

If you are given the calculated value of *rho*:
1. Is the correlation in the predicted direction? (The sign indicates a positive or negative correlation.)
2. Find critical value of *rho* from the table.
3. Compare calculated and critical values of *rho*, ignoring the sign.
4. Report the conclusion, e.g. 'As the calculated value of *rho* (−0.58) is greater than the critical value (0.564), the correlation is significant ($p < 0.05$, $N = 10$, one-tailed). This means the alternative hypothesis is supported: there is a negative correlation between … and … .'

◉ A parametric test: Pearson's *r*
Reasons for choosing:
• The hypothesis states a **correlation** between two variables.
• The two sets of data are **related** (pairs of scores from each person).
• The data are **interval** and fit the parametric criteria.

If you are given the calculated value of *r*:
1. Is the correlation in the predicted direction? (The sign indicates a positive or negative correlation.)
2. Find critical value of *r* from the table.
   Use $df = N - 2$
3. Compare calculated and critical values of *r*, ignoring the sign.
4. Report the conclusion.

KEY TERM

Correlation coefficient A number between −1 and +1 that tells us how closely the co-variables in a correlational analysis are related.

Apply it

▼ Table of critical values for Spearman's *rho*.

Level of significance for a one-tailed test	0.05	0.01
Level of significance for a two-tailed test	0.10	0.02
$N = 4$	1.000	
5	.900	1.000
6	.829	.886
7	.714	.786
8	.643	.738
9	.600	.700
10	.564	.648
11	.536	.618
12	.503	.587
13	.484	.560
14	.464	.538
15	.443	.521
16	.429	.503
17	.414	.485
18	.401	.472
19	.391	.460
20	.380	.447
25	.337	.398
30	.306	.362

Observed value of *rho* must be EQUAL TO or GREATER THAN the critical value in this table for significance to be shown.

Source: J.H. Zhar (1972). Significance testing of the Spearman rank correlation coefficient. *Journal of the American Statistical Association*, 67, 578–80. (Reproduced with kind permission of the publisher.)

Calculate Spearman's *rho* for the following studies:

(a) An investigation of the association between rating on a scale of altruism and charitable giving in the last month: $N = 15$, $\Sigma d^2 = 118$

(b) A comparison of self-report scores for attractiveness and happiness: $N = 19$, $\Sigma d^2 = 641$

Then use the table of critical values to test the significance of these correlations, assuming there was previous research which indicated you could use a directional hypothesis, and choosing an appropriate level of significance.

Answer

(a) $rho = 1 - \dfrac{708}{3360} = 0.789$.

Significant (critical value = 0.521, $p < 0.01$).

(b) $rho = 1 - \dfrac{3846}{6840} = 0.438$.

Significant at $p < 0.05$ (critical value = 0.391) but not at $p < 0.01$ (critical value = 0.460).

Chi-squared test (χ^2)

The chi-squared test can deal with **nominal** (category) data. It tests **differences** between frequencies in different categories. These can also be expressed as an **association** between variables. The data must be **independent**: no item can appear in more than one cell of the contingency table.

Reasons for choosing:
- The hypothesis states a **difference** OR an **association**.
- The data in each cell are **independent**.
- The data are **nominal**.

Contingency table

The data is displayed in a table showing frequencies in each category. There can be any number of rows and columns. A 3 × 2 contingency table would have three rows and two columns; three conditions of one variable and two of the other. A 2 × 2 contingency table has two conditions of each variable; for example:

	Left-handed	Right-handed	Totals
Left eye dominant	12 (cell A)	3	15
Right eye dominant	32	3	35
Totals	44	6	50

How to calculate chi-squared:

1. State the hypotheses.
   In the example, a non-directional alternative hypothesis could be 'There is an association between handedness and eye dominance' OR 'There is a difference between left- and right-handed people's eye dominance'.
2. Place data (observed values, **O**) in contingency table and calculate totals for each row and column.
3. Calculate expected frequency (**E**) for each cell:
   E = row × column / total
   e.g. for cell A, E = 15 × 44 / 50 = 13.2
4. Find the calculated value of χ^2 using the formula:

$$\chi^2 = \sum \frac{(E - O)^2}{E}$$

e.g. $\quad \chi^2 = \frac{(13.2 - 12)^2}{13.2} + \frac{(1.8 - 3)^2}{1.8} + \frac{(30.8 - 32)^2}{30.8} + \frac{(4.2 - 3)^2}{4.2}$

$\qquad\qquad = 0.109 + 0.8 + 0.048 + 0.343$

$\qquad\qquad = 1.31$

If you are given the calculated value of χ^2:

1. Find the critical value of χ^2,
   using $df = $ (number of rows − 1) × (number of columns − 1).
2. Compare the calculated and critical values of χ^2.
3. Report the conclusion.
   e.g. 'As the calculated value of χ^2 (1.31) is less than the critical value (3.84), there is no association between handedness and eye dominance ($p < 0.05$, $df = 1$, two-tailed).'

▼ Table of critical values for the chi-squared (χ^2) test.

Level of significance for a one-tailed test	0.10	0.05	0.025	0.01
Level of significance for a two-tailed test	0.20	0.10	0.05	0.02
df				
1	1.64	2.71	3.84	5.41
2	3.22	4.60	5.99	7.82
3	4.64	6.25	7.82	9.84
4	5.99	7.78	9.49	11.67

The observed value of χ^2 must be EQUAL TO or GREATER THAN the critical value in this table for significance to be shown.

Source: abridged from R.A. Fisher and F. Yates (1974). *Statistical Tables for Biological, Agricultural and Medical Research* (sixth edition). London: Longman.

Apply it

Scenario. Jana has researched men and women's coffee preferences. She thinks that more females drink latte or cappuccino, and more males drink Americano or espresso.

(a) *Explain why a chi-squared test would be appropriate for this data.* (3 marks)

(b) *Write a suitable directional hypothesis for this research.* (2 marks)

Answer. (a) The data is nominal, with eight categories: two genders and four coffee types. Jana is looking for an association between gender and coffee preference. The data is independent, which means that each person only appears in one cell – it is not just because people are in one gender group or the other (independent groups design), but also that each person only chooses one coffee preference.

(b) More males will prefer espresso or Americano, and more females will prefer latte or cappuccino. Alternatively, a hypothesis of association would be fine: there will be an association between gender and coffee preference, such that males will prefer espresso or Americano to latte or cappuccino, and females will have the opposite preference.

Reporting investigations

◉ Journal articles

Research studies are written up in a standard format for publication in peer-reviewed academic journals.

Abstract: A summary of the entire study in 150–200 words. One sentence for each section: aims, hypothesis, procedure, sample, results and conclusions, including implications. It enables the reader to get a quick overview of the study and decide whether to read more detail.

Introduction: This sets the context for the current research by reviewing previous research in the area, explaining the reasons for the current study. Like a funnel, starting broadly and narrowing down to focus on the aims and research hypothesis of the current research.

Method: Should contain enough information for another researcher to replicate the study. Design, sampling and procedural decisions should be justified and explained. Ethical issues may also be mentioned, as well as how they were dealt with.

Generally contains four sections:

- Design: e.g. 'repeated measures' or 'covert observation'.
- Participants: sampling methods, numbers and demographic details (age, gender, ethnicity, etc.).
- Materials: how they were made or sourced.
- Procedure: including standardised instructions, environment, order of events.

Results:

- Descriptive statistics, including tables and graphs.
- Inferential statistics.
- In qualitative research, categories and themes are described along with examples from each.

Discussion: Here the researcher interprets the study and considers implications for future research and real-world applications.

Can include:

- Summary of the findings, with some explanation of what the results show.
- Relationship to previous research.
- Methodological criticisms and suggestions for improvement.
- Implications for theory and applications.

References: All articles or books mentioned in the report are referenced in a standard format.

Apply it

Application. Write an abstract for the Stanford Prison Experiment carried out by Zimbardo and colleagues (Haney *et al.*, 1973).

Use one sentence for each section, and a maximum of 150 words. (6 marks)

Answer. This study aimed to test whether innate personality characteristics of individuals are the cause of aggressive behaviour in prisons. In a controlled observation, we investigated the behaviour of student volunteers randomly allocated to roles as guards or prisoners in a simulated prison over a two-week period, and were deindividuated by the use of uniforms, numbers and sunglasses. 'Guards' rapidly took an aggressive role, while 'prisoners' initially tried to resist but were controlled by increasingly harsh psychological means by 'guards'; two 'prisoners' became distressed and were removed early and the observation was aborted after six days. These findings support our hypothesis that situational factors determine behaviour more than innate individual differences. There are implications for the operation of prisons, as guards should be trained to keep order without abusing prisoners. (129 words)

Chapter 2

Issues and debates

Paper 3, Section A. 4.3.1 Issues and debates

- Gender and culture in psychology – universality and bias. Gender bias including androcentrism and alpha and beta bias; cultural bias, including ethnocentrism and cultural relativism.
- Free will and determinism: hard determinism and soft determinism; biological, environmental and psychic determinism. The scientific emphasis on causal explanations.
- The nature–nurture debate: the relative importance of heredity and environment in determining behaviour; the interactionist approach.
- Holism and reductionism: levels of explanation in psychology. Biological reductionism and environmental (stimulus-response) reductionism.
- Idiographic and nomothetic approaches to psychological investigation.
- Ethical implications of research studies and theory, including reference to social sensitivity.

Key terms (highlight each cell when you can confidently explain each term)

Gender and culture in psychology	Free will and determinism	The nature–nurture debate	Holism and reductionism	Idiographic and nomothetic approaches	Ethical implications of research studies and theory
Androcentrism	Hard determinism	Heredity	Levels of explanation in psychology	Idiographic approach	Ethical implications of research and theory
Alpha and beta bias	Soft determinism	Environment	Biological reductionism	Nomothetic approach	Social sensitivity
Gender bias	Biological determinism	Interactionism	Environmental (stimulus-response) reductionism		
Universality	Environmental determinism				
Cultural bias	Psychic determinism				
Cultural relativism	Science and causal explanations				
Culture					
Ethnocentrism					

Content checklist

1. *In each 'describe', 'apply' and 'evaluate' cell tick when you have produced brief notes.*
2. *Once you feel you have a good grasp of the topic add a second tick to the cell.*
3. *When you feel you have complete mastery of the topic and would be able to answer an exam question without the aid of notes highlight the cell.*

I am able to …	Describe	Apply	Evaluate
Gender and culture in psychology – universality and bias. Gender bias including androcentrism and alpha and beta bias			
Cultural bias, including ethnocentrism and cultural relativism			
Free will and determinism: hard determinism and soft determinism; biological, environmental and psychic determinism. The scientific emphasis on causal explanations			
The nature–nurture debate: the relative importance of heredity and environment in determining behaviour; the interactionist approach			
Holism and reductionism: levels of explanation in psychology. Biological reductionism and environmental (stimulus-response) reductionism			
Idiographic and nomothetic approaches to psychological investigation			
Ethical implications of research studies and theory, including reference to social sensitivity			

Gender in psychology

Gender bias
Differential treatment or representation of men and women based on stereotypes rather than real differences is known as **gender bias**. Psychology tends to be male-dominated, resulting in theories that represent a male world view (**androcentrism**). This may result in either alpha or beta bias (Hare-Mustin & Marecek, 1988).

Alpha bias
Theories with **alpha bias** exaggerate differences between men and women and devalue one gender compared to the other. This was a criticism of Freud's psychodynamic approach (Josselson, 1988); females are seen as morally inferior because they cannot fully resolve the Oedipus conflict as successfully as males do.

Beta bias
Beta bias occurs when what is assumed to be true for men is applied to women. Differences between them are erroneously minimised and the needs of one gender (usually women) may be ignored, e.g. it was assumed that the 'fight-or-flight' response to stress was universal but females are more likely to 'tend and befriend' (Taylor *et al.*, 2000).

Universality
Eradicating gender differences does not resolve gender bias and is a form of beta bias. The solution lies in **universality**: recognising differences but not the superiority of one gender over another.

Evaluation
Feminist psychology
Feminist psychologists (Gilligan, 1982) challenge androcentrism. 'Difference' psychology is thought to arise from biological explanations of behaviour. Conversely, the feminist approach aims to explain it in terms of social constructions and thus promote greater equality. Biologically based sex differences are acknowledged, but other 'differences' are more due to social stereotypes that perpetuate beliefs about women. Revision of these should facilitate change in gender roles, e.g. rather than believing women cannot be leaders, they could be trained to lead (Eagly, 1978).

Bias in research methods
If researchers believe there are gender differences, their research questions and methods may perpetuate the bias, e.g. Rosenthal (1966) found that male experimenters treated male and female participants differently, leading to better female performance. Feminists argue that findings from a controlled lab environment may not have ecological validity, e.g. in real settings women and men were judged as more similar in leadership styles compared to in lab settings (Eagly & Johnson, 1990).

Reverse alpha bias
Reverse alpha bias research challenges the male superiority stereotype. For example, Cornwell *et al.* (2013) showed that women are better at learning because they are more attentive, flexible and organised. Such findings emphasise the value of women.

Avoiding beta bias
Beta bias (minimising differences) has consequences for women, e.g. legal removal of barriers to occupational opportunities. However, assuming equality masks women's particular needs and power differences between them and men (Hare-Mustin & Marecek, 1988). For example, equal parental leave ignores the biological demands of pregnancy, childbirth and breastfeeding, therefore disadvantaging women.

Assumptions need to be examined
Examples of gender bias sometimes continue unchallenged. For example, Darwin's theory of sexual selection assumes that females are choosy, because of their relatively greater investment in reproduction, while males compete with each other. However, women can be as competitive as males: DNA evidence suggests that a good adaptive strategy for females is to mate with more than one man, thus encouraging competition with other females (Vernimmen, 2015).

Key study: Kohlberg (1969)
Moral reasoning research
How? Kohlberg's (1969) theory of moral development involved presenting participants with moral dilemmas and asking them to describe what response would be appropriate.

Showed? He suggested that male moral decisions were based on an ethic of justice. This is an example of beta bias because he assumed the male standards would apply to all people. He also found that women were less morally developed than men – a classic alpha bias outcome.

Variations of this study Gilligan (1982) pointed out that the dilemmas used by Kohlberg were biased towards justice rather than care, leading to exaggerated differences between men and women. Gilligan's own work showed that women favoured a care orientation, whereas men favoured a justice orientation; thus they differ from men, but neither gender is 'better'.

KEY TERMS
Alpha bias A tendency to exaggerate differences between men and women. The consequence is that theories devalue one gender in comparison to the other.

Androcentrism Centred or focused on men, often to the neglect or exclusion of women.

Beta bias A tendency to ignore or minimise differences between men and women. Such theories tend either to ignore questions about the lives of women, or assume that insights derived from studies of men will apply equally well to women.

Gender bias The differential treatment or representation of men and women based on stereotypes rather than real differences.

Universality The aim is to develop theories that apply to all people, which may include real differences.

Apply it
Scenario. In a report for the World Health Organization, Astbury (2001:2) wrote: 'Even when presenting with identical symptoms, women are more likely to be diagnosed as depressed than men and less likely to be diagnosed as having problems with alcohol.'

What kind of gender bias could these responses by professionals represent? Suggest two reasons why gender bias may not be a complete explanation. (3 marks)

Suggested answer. It is possible that alpha bias is responsible for stereotyping women as more susceptible to depression compared to men and seeing men as more prone than women to alcohol problems. Diagnosis is, however, complicated by the greater tendency of women to seek professional help for depression and for more men to seek help for alcohol problems. There may also be an element of self-stereotyping in that men and women are possibly more likely to acknowledge problems that seem fitting for their gender.

KEY TERMS

Cultural bias The tendency to judge all people in terms of your own cultural assumptions. This distorts or biases your judgement.

Cultural relativism The view that behaviour cannot be judged properly unless it is viewed in the context of the culture in which it originates.

Culture The rules, customs, morals, childrearing practices, etc. that bind a group of people together and define how they are likely to behave.

Ethnocentrism Seeing things from the point of view of ourselves and our social group. Evaluating other groups of people using the standards and customs of one's own culture.

Apply it

The US Army IQ test.

It's hard to believe that anyone thought the test items in the US Army IQ tests were a fair way to assess intelligence. Look at the cultural bias in the items below:

1. 'Washington is to Adams as first is to …'
2. 'Crisco is a: patent medicine, disinfectant, tooth paste, food product?'
3. 'What items are missing in these pictures?'

Answers

1. Second, because Washington was the first US president and Adams was the second.
2. It is a food product.
3. A ball is missing from the man's right hand.

Explain why these questions might be considered 'ethnocentric'. (3 marks)

Ethnocentrism refers to using one's own ethnic or cultural group as a basis for judging other groups. These three questions assess knowledge that would only be familar to American citizens. For example, Washington and Adams are US presidents, therefore it would be unrealistic to assume that lack of this knowledge among individuals from other cultural groups is a sign of low intelligence.

Culture in psychology

Cultural bias

Cultural bias is the tendency to judge all people in terms of one's own **culture** (rules, customs, morals and ways of interacting in a society). Hare-Mustin and Marecek (1988) advocated understanding of alpha and beta bias to help guard against this.

Alpha bias
Alpha biased theories assume there are differences between cultural groups. This should be carefully considered, e.g. in 15 studies of conforming tendency comparing the US (individualist) with Japan (collectivist), Takano and Osaka (1999) found only one showed greater individualism in the US, so there may no longer be a valid distinction.

Beta bias
Beta biased theories ignore or minimise cultural differences, assuming all people are the same. However, measures developed in one culture are not always suitable for another, e.g. using Western IQ tests on non-Westerners is an *imposed etic* and may make non-Westerners appear less intelligent.

Ethnocentrism

Ethnocentrism refers to using one's own ethnic or cultural group as a basis for judging other groups. The beliefs, customs and behaviours of one's own group tend to be seen as 'normal' (even superior) whereas those of other groups are 'strange' or deviant.

Alpha bias
Ethnocentrism is an example of alpha bias: one's own culture is considered to be different and better; consequently other cultures are devalued, e.g. individualist attitudes towards attachment where independence is valued and collectivist dependence is seen as undesirable.

Beta bias
Ethnocentrism can lead to beta bias if psychologists believe their world view is the only one, e.g. it was once erroneously believed that American IQ tests could be used with anyone, based on the assumption that the American standard was universal.

Cultural relativism

Cultural relativism is the idea that all cultures are worthy and that, in studying them, we must understand their world view. This could be seen as the opposite of ethnocentrism.

Alpha bias
Cultural relativism could lead to alpha bias, e.g. Mead (1935) concluded that there were significant gender differences due to culture in Papua New Guinea (but later recognised that the males were probably universally more aggressive than the women).

Beta bias
Assuming that the same rules apply universally (a beta bias) may lead to incorrect diagnosis of mental illness, e.g. 'hearing voices' may be statistically infrequent in one culture compared to another. Applying a common diagnostic system to both would do a disservice to one of them.

Evaluation

Indigenous psychologies
Indigenous psychologies counter ethnocentrism by developing theories specific to countries (an 'emic' approach), e.g. Afrocentrism disputes the universality of European values which, at worst, devalue non-European people and, at best, are irrelevant to people of African descent.

The emic–etic distinction
Emic approaches tend to be appropriate to specific cultures while 'etic' ones seek universals. One way to achieve the latter, while avoiding cultural bias, is to use indigenous researchers, e.g. Buss (1989) did this to study universal mate preference behaviour in 37 different cultures.

Bias in research methods
Henrich *et al.* (2010) suggested that a considerable amount of psychology is based on biased and universally unrepresentative middle-class, academic, often male, young adults. Such cultural bias in psychology could be addressed by sampling from different cultural groups.

Consequences of cultural bias
Just before World War I, US Army IQ tests showed that European immigrants scored slightly below white Americans and African-Americans scored the lowest. This had unwarranted, negative effects on Americans' stereotypes about the IQ of certain ethnic groups (Gould, 1981).

The worldwide psychology community
International conferences allow psychologists from different cultures to meet and exchange ideas. This should reduce ethnocentrism, encouraging understanding of cultural relativism.

Free will and determinism

◎ Determinism
Determinism is the view that human behaviour is caused by factors beyond personal control. **Hard determinism** means there is no free will whereas **soft determinism** allows for some **free will**, meaning that we can exercise choice over our behaviour.

Biological determinism
Human genome research suggests that some of our behaviours are genetically determined, e.g. high intelligence has been linked to the IGF2R gene (Hill *et al.*, 1999). Genes also influence brain structure and neurotransmitters implicated in behaviour (e.g. the dopamine hypothesis of schizophrenia).

Environmental determinism
Behaviourists believe that most behaviour is learned and unlearned via classical and operant conditioning, e.g. fear of dogs learned by being bitten; can also be unlearned through conditioning-based systematic desensitisation. Learning theory has been widely applied to many other behaviours.

Psychic determinism
Freud's psychoanalytic theory suggests that personality is determined by innate drives and early experience, e.g. the way in which parents deal with an infant's instinctively driven pleasure-seeking can shape the infant's adult personality.

Scientific determinism: emphasis on causal explanations
Scientists believe that all events are causally related. In experiments, they manipulate an independent variable (e.g. stimulus material) to observe the effect on a dependent variable (e.g. amount remembered). Observed effects are said to be caused by this manipulation.

◎ Free will
Humanistic approach
Humanistic psychologists argued that free will is necessary in order to take responsibility for and change behaviour (Rogers, 1959). Without such self-determination, personal growth and optimal psychological health cannot occur.

Moral responsibility
Moral responsibility requires that individuals exercise free will over their actions. Legally, children and the mentally ill cannot do this, but otherwise 'normal' adult behaviour is viewed as self-determined; humans are accountable for their actions, regardless of innate factors or early experience.

◎ Evaluation of determinism
Genetic determinism
It is doubtful that any behaviour is 100% genetically determined. Even genetically identical twins show variation in such things as intelligence and incidence of mental disorder, so genes do not entirely determine behaviour.

Environmental determinism
Equally, the environment cannot be the sole determinant of behaviour. At least some of the variation and similarity between identical twins must be genetically determined.

Scientific determinism
Even in physical sciences, hard determinism is unlikely (Dennett, 2003). Causal relationships are probabilistic, i.e. they increase the probability of something occurring rather than being the sole determinant. Human behaviour is complex and influenced by many factors, so a hard determinist explanation is unrealistic.

Does it matter?
Determinist explanations may be undesirable because unacceptable behaviour such as criminality is 'excused'. In the field of mental disorder, biological determinism leads to treatment targeting genes or neurotransmitters. This may discourage the consideration of potentially beneficial punishments or treatments.

◎ Evaluation of free will
The illusion of free will
Being able to decide between different courses of action may give the *illusion* of free will (Skinner, 1953). A person might 'choose' to buy a particular car or see a particular film, but these choices may be determined by previous reinforcement experiences.

Cultural relativity
'Self-determination' may be a culturally relative concept, appropriate for individualist societies only. Collectivist cultures place greater value on behaviour determined by group needs.

Research challenge to free will
Chun Siong Soon *et al.* (2008) recorded activity in the prefrontal cortex up to 10 seconds before awareness of the decision to act. However, other researchers showed that the brain activity was simply a 'readiness to act' rather than an intention to move (Trevena & Miller, 2009). For now it seems that neuroscience still supports free will.

KEY TERMS
Determinism Behaviour is controlled by external or internal factors acting upon the individual.

Free will Individuals have the power to make choices about their behaviour.

Hard determinism The view that all behaviour can be predicted and there is no free will. The two are incompatible.

Soft determinism A version of determinism that allows for some element of free will.

Apply it
Scenario. Abbie gains a place at university and starts a degree course in Business Studies with Psychology. In spite of her best efforts, she fails her first year exams. Instead of retaking them, she drops Business Studies and starts again, this time just taking Psychology. This time she is much more successful.

Using what you know about free will and determinism, discuss reasons why Abbie behaved as she did. (4 marks)

Answer. Free will means that Abbie's initial course choice and subsequent change were entirely her choice, probably based on what she thought would give her the best chance of personal growth (a humanistic concept). Hard determinism means that she would have been compelled by her reinforcement history to study her initial subjects and also would have accounted for the change of course when the initial one proved unrewarding. Soft determinism means that she would have some element of choice over her actions. Perhaps her subject choices were driven by rewarding success in them at school and approval of others, but her decision to change was entirely her own.

KEY TERMS

Environment Everything that is outside our body, which includes people, events and the physical world.

Heredity The process by which traits are passed from parents to their offspring, usually referring to genetic inheritance.

Interactionist approach With reference to the nature–nurture debate, the view that the processes of nature and nurture work together rather than in opposition.

Nature Behaviour is seen as a product of innate (biological or genetic) factors.

Nature–nurture debate The argument as to whether a person's development is mainly due to their genes or to environmental influences.

Nurture Behaviour is a product of environmental influences.

Apply it

Scenario. Pharrel is in the first year of his GCSEs but he spends more time on report than in his classes. He frequently gets into fights with the other children in his class and has recently been excluded after it was discovered he was bullying other children and stealing from them. When teachers look into his family background they discover that his father is currently in prison for aggravated burglary and his two brothers both have a history of violent assault charges.

Using your knowledge of the nature–nurture debate, outline as many possible explanations as you can for Pharrel's violent behaviour at school. (4 marks)

Answer. With regard to nature, aggressive behaviour in three close male relatives suggests genetic concordance may underlie Pharrel's aggression. In evolutionary terms, greater aggression in males relative to females, as an adaptive strategy, could also be an explanation. With regard to nurture, behaviourists would explain the aggression as a learned/conditioned response, and SLT would include aggressive role models in the family as part of the learning environment. The double bind explanation would locate the cause in dysfunctional family communication patterns.

The nature–nurture debate

The **nature–nurture debate** is an argument over the relative contribution of genetic and environmental factors in determining development.

Nature and nurture

'Nature' refers to innate influences that may be present at birth or appear through maturation. '**Nurture**' refers to influences in the **environment** that can be pre- or postnatal, physical or social. The **interactionist approach** acknowledges the importance of nature and nurture working together.

Examples of the influence of nature

Genetic explanations

Family, twin and adoption studies show that more genetically similar individuals are more similar in their behaviours, e.g. the concordance rate for schizophrenia is about 40% for identical (MZ) twins and 7% for non-identical (DZ) twins (Joseph, 2004); thus nature makes a major contribution.

Evolutionary explanations

Evolutionary explanations propose that adaptive behaviour that promotes survival and reproduction will be naturally selected, e.g. attachment behaviours mean an infant is more likely to be protected, survive and reproduce (Bowlby, 1969). Through **heredity**, attachment behaviour genes will be passed on to subsequent generations.

Examples of the influence of nurture

Behaviourism

Behaviourists assume that all behaviour is acquired through learning, e.g. attachment can be classically conditioned (the mother is associated with feeding) or operantly conditioned (food reduces hunger, so is rewarding).

Social learning theory

Bandura (1961) acknowledged that aggressive urges might be biological, but the way they are *expressed* is learned through social, environmental influences in the form of direct and indirect (vicarious) reinforcement.

Other explanations

The double bind theory of schizophrenia (Bateson *et al.*, 1956) proposes that schizophrenia develops in children who frequently receive mixed messages from their parents, e.g. love mixed with indifference prevents the child developing an internally consistent construction of reality and may lead to schizophrenia symptoms.

Evaluation

Nature and nurture cannot be separated

Asking whether nature or nurture is more important is pointless, like asking whether length or width determines a rectangle's area. For example, left untreated, the inherited disorder *phenylketonuria* leads to brain damage but, if detected at birth, damage can be averted. So is it due to nature or nurture?

Diathesis–stress

Interaction between nature and nurture is illustrated by the diathesis–stress model of mental disorder. A diathesis is a biological, genetic vulnerability (e.g. to schizophrenia) which is only triggered by an environmental stressor. Thus nature is only expressed under certain conditions of nurture.

Nature affects nurture

Reactive *gene–environment interaction* (Plomin *et al.*, 1977). The child reacts to a microenvironment caused by their own genetically influenced behaviour, e.g. a genetically aggressive child might provoke aggression in others. This becomes part of the child's environment and affects development.

Passive *influence* (Plomin *et al.*). A child's mental disorder could be due to indirect, passive effects, e.g. a parent's genetically determined mental illness creates an unsettled home environment, increasing risk of mental disorder in the child.

Active *influence* (Plomin *et al.*) or *niche picking* (Scarr & McCartney, 1983). As children mature they actively seek out experiences and environments (niches) that suit their genes. Research has shown that the influence of genes *increases* as children get older.

Nurture affects nature

Compared to controls, London taxi drivers have bigger brain regions associated with spatial memory; their hippocampi had responded to increased use (Maguire *et al.*, 2000). Their innate system was altered through experience.

Epigenetics

Epigenetics refers to the material in each body cell that acts like 'switches', turning genes on or off in response to life experiences, such as nutrition or stress. Most importantly they are hereditary, which explains why cloning doesn't produce identical copies. This means that genetics and environment are less distinct than was previously thought.

Holism and reductionism

Reductionism

Levels of explanation
Reductionist explanations of behaviour in psychology begin at the highest level and progress to simpler component elements, e.g. eye-witness memory could be explained at any of these levels:
- Highest level: cultural and social expectations affect what we remember
- Middle level: psychological explanations of personal, episodic memories
- Lower level: biological explanations about neurotransmitters' involvement in forming memories

Biological reductionism
Biological psychologists reduce behaviour to the action of neurons, neurotransmitters and hormones, e.g. it has been suggested that schizophrenia is caused by excessive activity of the neurotransmitter dopamine because drugs that block this neurotransmitter reduce symptoms.

Environmental (stimulus-response) reductionism
Behaviourist explanations suggest that all behaviour arises from learned stimulus-response links, e.g. in attachment, the mother provides food stimuli, the response is to eat and this link is reinforced by hunger reduction. The mother is rewarding and so becomes 'loved'.

Experimental reductionism
Reducing complex behaviours to variables is useful for conducting experimental research. Complex behaviours are reduced to operationalised variables that can be manipulated and measured to determine causal relationships.

Holism
Holism focuses on whole systems rather than their constituent parts. It suggests that the system is more than the sum of its individual components and that reductionist explanations are limited.

Gestalt psychology
In the first part of the twentieth century, German Gestalt psychologists focused mainly on perception, arguing that explanations for what we see only make sense through a consideration of the whole, rather than the individual elements.

Humanistic psychology
Humanistic psychologists believe that the individual reacts as an organised whole, rather than a set of stimulus-response (S-R) links. A person's sense of a unified identity is critical because lack of this 'wholeness' leads to mental disorder.

Cognitive psychology
Memory is a complex system which recently has been understood in terms of connectionist networks. These are holistic because the network as a whole behaves differently to the individual parts (e.g. neurons). Linear models (where one item links only to the next in a sequence) assume that the sum of the parts equals the whole.

Evaluation

The danger of lower levels of explanation
If lower levels are taken in isolation, the *meaning* of behaviour may be fundamentally misunderstood. Giving the amphetamine *Ritalin* to hyperactive children may miss the *real* causes of the behaviour (e.g. family or emotional problems).

Biological reductionism
Biological treatments of mental illnesses have reduced institutionalisation and removed blame from the patient. Conversely, success rates are variable; they treat symptoms not causes, and may not last. Psychological treatments, however, take more account of the whole context and function of mental illness.

Environmental (stimulus-response) reductionism (e.g. behaviourism)
The behavioural approach was developed from research using non-human animals. It may, therefore, apply less well to humans who are additionally influenced by social context, intentions, emotion and cognitions. Even non-human animals may be influenced by some of these things.

Experimental reductionism
Experimental research is precise but may not tell us about real-world situations, e.g. in eye-witness events, many factors may affect memory but cannot be recreated in an experiment; therefore findings may not reflect lived experiences.

The mind–body problem – an interactionist approach
How do mind and body/brain relate? Materialists suggest that 'mind' is reducible to the physical, e.g. dreams are electrical activity patterns in the brain. Alternatively, dualism proposes that the physical brain and non-physical 'mind' interact, e.g. psychotherapy for depression produces the same changes in levels of serotonin and norepinephrine in the brain as drug therapy (Martin *et al.*, 2001).

KEY TERMS
Holism Focuses on the whole system rather than its constituent parts and suggests that the system is more than the sum of its individual components.

Reductionism An approach that breaks complex phenomena into simpler components, implying that complex phenomena are best understood in terms of the simplest, yet complete, level of explanation.

Apply it
Scenario. Alex regards herself as addicted to smoking tobacco and seeks help which succeeds in enabling her to stop. The professional who helped her viewed smoking as a physically based substance dependence. Some weeks afterwards, Alex finds that she cannot stop eating chocolate and that it is having adverse effects on her health.
Discuss Alex's case using what you know about reductionist and holistic explanations. (6 marks)

Answer. It might be true that smoking can be reduced to an acquired dependence on nicotine which, once broken, results in complete cure. The apparent substitution of nicotine with chocolate could also be reduced to physically based substance dependence. However, the need to substitute one substance with another could be explained in a more holistic way: perhaps Alex needs some form of oral comfort to help her to control anxiety. Treatment should then address the psychological causes of the anxiety, taking into account her history, emotions and cognitions, possibly in some form of psychodynamic therapy. Finally, an interactionist approach might be taken, possibly combining cognitive behavioural therapy with medication to reduce anxiety to bring the dysfunctional behaviour under control so that Alex is restored to full health.

KEY TERMS

Idiographic approach Focuses on individuals and emphasises uniqueness; favours qualitative methods in research.

Nomothetic approach Seeks to formulate general laws of behaviour based on the study of groups and the use of statistical (quantitative) techniques. It attempts to summarise the similarities between people through generalisations.

Apply it

Scenario. Identical twin boys are brought up in very similar ways by their parents, but by the time they start infant school, their personalities have similarities but also some marked differences.

Discuss idiographic and nomothetic ways of assessing and explaining these things. (6 marks)

Answer. 'Idiographic' refers to unique characteristics in each twin, while 'nomothetic' refers to commonalities. To assess the twins, idiographic, qualitative techniques would be appropriate, e.g. case studies, using clinical interviews and observation. Nomothetic assessment might include quantitative, psychometric testing of attributes such as intelligence and personality and comparisons with norms. Behaviourists could account for similarities and differences using general conditioning principles but also unique learning histories. Similarly, a psychodynamic explanation would utilise ideas about general stages of development and common personality structure, but would also include unique experiences which shape each child differently.

The idiographic and nomothetic approach to psychological investigation

The idiographic approach

The **idiographic approach** in psychology research focuses on the individual case as a means of understanding behaviour.

Qualitative methods

The idiographic approach is qualitative because the focus is on gaining insights into human behaviour by studying unique individuals in depth rather than gaining statistical data from many individuals to determine generalities. It involves qualitative data and methods such as unstructured interviews, case studies and thematic analysis.

Examples of the idiographic approach

Freud used case studies of his patients as a way to understand human behaviour, e.g. Little Hans. Allport (1961) used his 'psychology of the individual' approach to study personality rather than using quantitative personality tests. Humanistic psychologists favour the idiographic approach because they are concerned with studying the subjective experience of the whole person.

The nomothetic approach

The **nomothetic approach** involves the study of a large number of people and then seeks to make generalisations or develop laws/theories about their behaviour. This is also the goal of the scientific approach.

Quantitative research

Quantitative research is usually nomothetic because it is based on numerical data gathered from groups of people rather than individuals, and seeks to make statistical inferences and generalisations from samples to populations.

Examples of the nomothetic approach

The biological approach seeks to understand basic principles of how the body and brain work. Behaviourists produced general laws of behaviour, specifically learning. Cognitive psychology also aims to develop general laws of behaviour, e.g. memory processes. Eysenck's (1947) psychometric approach involved measuring personality and intelligence.

Evaluation

Focus on the individual level

Humanistic and qualitative psychologists have argued that emphasis on measurement and statistics has led psychologists to lose sight of what it was to be human; thus the great strength of the idiographic approach has been to focus psychology back onto individuals.

Scientific basis

Some idiographic approaches have been criticised for being unscientific because they are subjective and lacking in generalisability. This provoked the recent growth in positive psychology which aims to make humanistic approaches more evidence-based. However, some idiographic approaches (e.g. case studies or qualitative research) already use an evidence-based approach and seek to be objective and generalisable.

Being able to make predictions

Allport (1961) argued that, like scientific approaches, the idiographic approach does allow predictions. Once extremely detailed observations of a few individuals have been assembled, they can be used to make generalisations and formulate theories. Hall and Lindzey (1970) argue that this stance makes Allport's approach basically nomothetic rather than idiographic!

Time-consuming

The idiographic approach has been criticised for being time-consuming; it involves collecting large amounts of data about one person. Nomothetic approaches involve collecting large amounts of data from groups of people, but it is relatively quick because, once a questionnaire or test has been devised, data can be generated and processed quickly.

Combined methods

Holt (1967) argued that the idiographic/nomothetic distinction is false because inevitably generalisations are made. Some approaches combine the two: Freud used idiographic case studies but used them to produce general laws about personality development. Uniqueness can result from a nomothetic approach depending on how it is defined, e.g. an individual's personality is a unique combination of commonly possessed traits.

Ethical implications: social sensitivity

Sieber and Stanley (1988) discussed research that has social consequences, i.e. socially sensitive research.

● The research process

Four aspects of research can make it socially sensitive (Sieber & Stanley, 1988):

1. **The research question.** Framing questions in particular ways, e.g. 'Is homosexuality inherited?', may damage particular groups because it offers 'scientific credibility to the prevailing prejudice' (Sieber & Stanley, 1988).
2. **Conduct of research and treatment of participants.** This mainly concerns confidentiality (e.g. if a participant confesses to a crime, should confidentiality be maintained?).
3. **The institutional context.** Research may be funded and managed by private institutions who may misuse or misunderstand the data. The media may obtain reports of such research and misreport the findings.
4. **Interpretation and application of findings.** Research findings may be used for purposes other than originally intended, e.g. in the US in the early twentieth century, IQ tests were used to demonstrate the inferiority of certain people and to identify the 'feeble-minded' who were then sterilised.

● Ethical issues in socially sensitive research

Sieber and Stanley identified 10 ethical issues that relate especially to socially sensitive research:

1. **Privacy.** A skilled researcher may extract more information from participants than expected. Some research (e.g. into AIDS) may lead to social policies that invade people's private lives (e.g. compulsory testing).
2. **Confidentiality.** If confidentiality is breached, participants may be less willing to divulge further information, thus compromising future research.
3. **Valid methodology.** Scientists may be alert to cases of poor methodology (and, therefore, invalid findings), but non-specialists may not; thus poor studies might shape social policy to the detriment of the target group.
4. **Deception.** This includes self-deception: research may encourage stereotypes (e.g. women cannot do maths), which then affects women's own performance.
5. **Informed consent.** Potential participants may not be able to consent if they do not fully comprehend what is involved.
6. **Equitable treatment.** Participants should be treated in an equitable manner, and given resources which are vital to the participants' well-being (e.g. educational opportunities), not withheld from particular groups.
7. **Scientific freedom.** Scientists have a duty to engage in research but at the same time are obliged not to harm participants or institutions in society.
8. **Ownership of data.** Some of the problems with determining ownership involve the sponsorship of the research (e.g. a university department or commercial organisation) and the public accessibility of the data.
9. **Values.** Psychologists differ in their orientation towards subjective (idiographic) and objective (scientific) approaches. Sensitive issues arise when there is a clash in such values between the scientist and recipient of the research.
10. **Risk/benefit ratio.** Risks or costs should be minimised, but problems arise in determining risk/benefit balance.

● Evaluation

The wider impact of research

With socially sensitive research in particular, there is increased potential for indirect impact on the participant's family or others that the participant represents (e.g. addicts, women, the elderly). Therefore, it is not always enough to safeguard the interests of individuals in research.

The inadequacy of current ethical guidelines

Current ethical guidelines do not require researchers to consider, as recommended by Sieber and Stanley, how their research might be used by others; therefore their advice has yet to permeate professional practice.

May disadvantage marginalised groups

It is important to represent people with disabilities, the elderly, the disadvantaged and members of minority cultures. Failure to do this means that such groups miss out on the potential benefits of research.

Should socially sensitive research just be avoided?

To avoid socially sensitive research is irresponsible. Psychologists have a duty to conduct such research.

Engaging with the public and policy-makers

Psychologists should take individual responsibility to promote their research in a socially sensitive way, as opposed to a neutral, scientific position. The BPS, recognises the importance of promoting evidence-based research responsibly to the media.

KEY TERM

Socially sensitive research Any research that might have direct social consequences for the participants in the research or the group that they represent.

Apply it

Scenario. A psychologist believes that it is possible to identify patterns of electrical activity in the brain which identify children with exceptional mathematical ability. It is claimed that this is detectable before five years of age. The psychologist wants to see if this is correct and puts forward a research proposal for funding.

Consider:

(a) *Who might be adversely affected by this research and how? (3 marks)*

(b) *Who might be positively affected by this research and how? (3 marks)*

(c) *Discuss (with others if you can) whether this research should be allowed to go ahead. (3 marks)*

Answer

(a) 'Exceptional' children may be channelled into certain types of education too early and without choice, possibly at the expense of other attributes that may have been able to develop. Parents and educators may feel obliged to assess children and respond to exceptional ability in competitive ways. Assessment may not be available to all, so some children miss out. Educational systems may focus too heavily on mathematical ability at the expense of a balanced curriculum. Unscrupulous people might try to cash in by supplying brain activity monitors.

(b) Early recognition of exceptional ability fosters its development, possibly providing a fulfilling education for the child. Parents and educators may be better informed about how to deal with the child, e.g. in ensuring they have a well-rounded education. There may be wider benefits to society in the application of superior mathematical knowledge.

(c) The implications of the research should be widely discussed with professional bodies and policy-makers in order to reach a balanced decision. There will always be costs and benefits, but no group should be disadvantaged at the expense of another. Accurate communication of research findings is essential so that they are interpreted correctly and used responsibly.

Chapter 3
Relationships

Paper 3, Section B, option 1. 4.3.2 Relationships

- The evolutionary explanations for partner preferences, including the relationship between sexual selection and human reproductive behaviour.
- Factors affecting attraction in romantic relationships: self-disclosure; physical attractiveness, including the matching hypothesis; filter theory, including social demography, similarity in attitudes and complementarity.
- Theories of romantic relationships: social exchange theory, equity theory and Rusbult's investment model of commitment, satisfaction, comparison with alternatives and investment. Duck's phase model of relationship breakdown: intrapsychic, dyadic, social and grave-dressing phases.
- Virtual relationships in social media: self-disclosure in virtual relationships; effects of absence of gating on the nature of virtual relationships.
- Parasocial relationships: levels of parasocial relationship, the absorption addiction model and the attachment theory explanation.

Key terms (highlight each cell when you can define the term confidently)

Evolutionary explanations for partner preferences	Factors affecting attraction in romantic relationships	Theories of romantic relationships	Virtual relationships in social media	Parasocial relationships
Sexual selection	Self-disclosure	Social exchange theory	Self-disclosure	Levels of parasocial relationships
Human reproductive behaviour	Physical attractiveness	Equity theory	Absence of gating	Absorption addiction model
	Matching hypothesis	Rusbult's investment model		Attachment theory explanation
	Filter theory	Duck's phase model of relationship breakdown		
	Social demography			
	Similarity in attitudes			
	Complementarity			

Content checklist
1. *In each 'describe', 'apply' and 'evaluate' cell tick when you have produced brief notes.*
2. *Once you feel you have a good grasp of the topic add a second tick to the cell.*
3. *When you feel you have complete mastery of the topic and would be able to answer an exam question without the aid of notes highlight the cell.*

I am able to ...	Describe	Apply	Evaluate
Evolutionary explanations for partner preferences, including the relationship between sexual selection and human reproductive behaviour			
Factors affecting attraction in romantic relationships – self-disclosure			
Factors affecting attraction in romantic relationships – physical attractiveness, including the matching hypothesis			
Factors affecting attraction in romantic relationships – filter theory, including social demography, similarity in attitudes and complementarity			
Theories of romantic relationships – social exchange theory			
Theories of romantic relationships – equity theory			
Theories of romantic relationships – Rusbult's investment model of commitment, satisfaction, comparison with alternatives and investment			
Duck's phase model of relationship breakdown: intrapsychic, dyadic, social and grave-dressing phases			
Virtual relationships in social media – self-disclosure in virtual relationships, effects of absence of gating on the nature of virtual relationships			
Levels of parasocial relationships, the absorption addiction model and the attachment theory explanation			

Evolutionary explanations for partner preferences

Darwin's (1871) theory of sexual selection explains the evolution of characteristics (such as physical attractiveness and intelligence) that confer a reproductive advantage as opposed to a survival advantage. Favoured mate characteristics that are, to some degree at least, inherited will then be represented more frequently in subsequent generations.

Intrasexual selection
Individuals of one sex (usually males) must compete to gain access to members of the opposite sex. The 'winners' mate and pass their genes onto the next generation. The characteristics leading to success in these same-sex competitions (e.g. strength, cunning) become widespread in the gene pool.

Intersexual selection
Members of one sex evolve preferences for desired qualities in potential mates. Members of the opposite sex who possess these desired qualities (e.g. status, attractiveness) gain a mating advantage. Preferences of one sex determine the areas in which the other sex must compete.

Sexual selection and long-term mate preference
As the genetic quality of a mate will half determine the genetic quality of any offspring, it is wise to be choosy. Low-quality mates are more likely to produce low-quality offspring. Mating with a high-quality mate ensures offspring are of high quality and an individual's genes are more likely to be passed on. Buss (1989) explored what each sex seeks in a long-term partner.

How? Over 10,000 people from 37 cultures rated 18 characteristics on importance when choosing a mate. The rating scale ran from 3 (indispensable) to 0 (irrelevant).

Showed? Women more than men desired 'good financial prospects' (resources) or qualities that would lead to future resources, e.g. ambition. Men placed more importance on fertility: seeking physical attractiveness (fertility is related to health) and youth (fertility decreases with age). Both sexes sought intelligence (linked to parenting skills) and kindness (interest in long-term commitment).

Evaluation
Cultural traditions may be just as important as evolutionary forces
Many cultures have denied women's economic and political power, which may explain their tendency to rely on men to provide security and resources. Kasser and Sharma's (1999) analysis of 37 cultures found that in cultures where women's status and educational opportunities were limited more value was placed on any potential mate's access to resources. Therefore, while there is evidence of evolutionary forces influencing preferences (Buss, 1989), social and economic factors should not be ignored.

Female preferences for high-status men may not be universal
Buller (2005) points out that the majority of studies into female mate preferences have been carried out on female undergraduates who have high educational status and expectations of high incomes. Their preference for high-status men may simply reflect their preference for men with interests, education and prospects similar to their own. As such, the evidence for a universal female mating preference is weak or non-existent.

Mate choice in real life
Studies, such as Buss (1989), only give an indication of desired characteristics rather than reflecting actual mate choice. However, in a study of actual marriages in 29 cultures, Buss (1989) found men do indeed choose younger women. In addition, questionnaires of partner preference may be a more valid measurement than real-life marriage statistics in cultures where arranged marriages are the norm.

Mate choice and the menstrual cycle
Penton-Voak *et al.* (1999) found women chose a slightly more feminised male face as 'most attractive' for a long-term relationship – their appearance implies kindness and cooperation, both valued in parental care. However, when picking a partner for a short-term sexual relationship, during the high conception risk phase of the menstrual cycle, women chose a more masculine face. Testosterone suppresses the immune system, so healthy 'masculine' males must have a highly effective immune system – a very valuable characteristic to pass onto offspring.

Is there a human equivalent of the peacock's tail?
There is support for the idea that some human traits have also evolved purely as a result of sexual selection. Nettle and Clegg (2006) compared a sample of British poets and artists and a control group of males in non-creative professions. Creative males tended to have significantly more sexual partners, and the amount of creative output was positively correlated with the number of sexual partners. Females may be motivated to choose a creative mate as creativity and ingenuity would be passed onto their offspring.

KEY TERMS
Evolutionary explanations Focus on the adaptive nature of behaviour, i.e. modern behaviours are believed to have evolved because they solved challenges faced by our distant ancestors and so become more widespread in the gene pool.

Sexual selection A key part of Darwin's theory explaining how evolution is driven by competition for mates, and the development of characteristics that ensure reproductive success.

Apply it
Scenario. Natasha is writing her online dating profile. She describes herself as young, kind and caring. She adds a photograph of herself at a recent wedding where she had her hair and make-up professionally done. Browsing through other people's profiles, she notices Billy, who describes himself as professional, ambitious and loving. She thinks he looks like a gentle person in his profile photo.

Discuss evolutionary explanations for partner preferences, making reference to Natasha and Billy in your answer. (16 marks)

Explanation extract… Natasha has promoted characteristics males would be attracted to, e.g. men seek youth and physical attractiveness (hence her choice of photo) as an indication of fertility. She is drawn to Billy's profile by his 'gentle' appearance: a desirable trait in a long-term partner, as it suggests good parenting. According to evolutionary explanations females also seek a partner with resources as they will be able to provide for any offspring resulting from the union. Both males and females seek traits such as 'kind' and 'loving' in a mate as signs of future parenting skills. Buss's (1989) survey of over 10,000 people found the traits displayed by Natasha and Billy in their dating profiles to be universal, suggesting an innate preference for certain traits. …

KEY TERM

Matching hypothesis Claims that when people look for a partner for a romantic relationship they tend to look for someone whose social desirability approximately equals their own.

Physical attractiveness

Features deemed to be physically attractive vary across cultures, but the importance of attraction does not. Men place particular importance on attractiveness as physical appearance is a clue to the woman's health and hence her fertility. Recently research (Eastwick et al., 2011) suggests women also seek physical attractiveness, more so in short-term relationships but less so in long-term relationships.

The matching hypothesis – Walster and Walster (1969)

The **matching hypothesis** suggests individuals seek out partners whose social desirability approximately equals their own. Individuals first assess their own 'value' in the eyes of a potential partner, then select the best candidates likely to be attracted to them. Opting for partners similar in social desirability to themselves (rather than someone 'out of their league') maximises chances of relationship formation.

Matching hypothesis and physical attractiveness

Matching could occur for a range of 'assets' but it has come to be associated specifically with appearance. Walster et al. referred to these matching choices as 'realistic choices'. Realistic choices consider what the other person desires, whether the other person reciprocates the feelings, whether other desirable alternatives are available for one or both of them. This means people have to settle for mating 'within their league' whether or not they want to.

Key study: Testing the matching hypothesis – Walster (1966)

How? Students at the University of Minnesota signed up to a 'computer dance' from which 177 males and 170 females were randomly selected. Four student accomplices rated the physical attractiveness as they collected their dance ticket. Participants then completed a questionnaire assessing personality, intelligence, etc. and were told their responses would be used to allocate an ideal partner for the dance (pairing was in fact random).

Showed? Regardless of their own physical attractiveness, participants responded more positively to physically attractive dates (assessed by a questionnaire completed during the dance) and were more likely to arrange subsequent dates if their date was physically attractive (assessed six months later). Factors such as personality or intelligence did not affect liking. These findings do not support the matching hypothesis.

Evaluation

Speed dating and the challenge to traditional views of attraction

Research by Eastwick and Finkel (2008) challenges the traditional views of attraction. Before a speed dating event, participants showed traditional sex differences: men emphasised the importance of physical attractiveness, women mentioned earning prospects. However, during the speed dating and follow-ups 30 days later, judgements of appearance and resources did not influence romantic interest. Instead participants' partner preferences reflected their evaluation of a specific speed-dating partner's characteristics and their romantic attraction across 17 different measurements.

Complex matching

People may compensate for a lack of physical attractiveness with other desirable qualities, e.g. charming personality, kindness, status, money. Sprecher and Hatfield (2009) refer to this 'compensation' for physical attractiveness as 'complex matching'. This might be why research often fails to find evidence of matching in terms of physical appearance.

Matching may not be that important in initial attraction

Taylor et al. (2011) found no evidence that online daters' decisions were driven by similarities in physical attractiveness. Instead, daters showed an overall preference for attractive partners, suggesting they did not take into account their own attractiveness. However, daters who did specifically target similarly attractive others were more likely to receive responses to their messages.

Sex differences in the importance of physical attractiveness

If physical attractiveness is more important for males, then research should show that males with physically attractive partners are highly satisfied with their relationship. Meltzer et al. (2014) found objective ratings of wives' attractiveness was positively related to husbands' satisfaction in the first four years of marriage. In contrast, wives' marital satisfaction was not related to objective ratings of their husbands' attractiveness. This suggests females place less importance on physical attractiveness in a long-term partner.

Implications of sex differences

If physical attractiveness plays a strong role in men's long-term relationship satisfaction then women may experience increased pressure to maintain their appearance in order to maintain their relationship (Meltzer et al., 2014). However, both sexes also desire partners who are supportive, trustworthy and warm, so those with partners who display these qualities tend to be more satisfied (Pasch & Bradbury, 1998). Accordingly, less physically attractive women who possess these qualities do not tend to have less satisfied partners.

Apply it

Scenario. Gareth has arranged to meet his blind date at a local restaurant. He arrives early and decides to wait for his date by the bar. He sees a stunning woman walk through the door and, while he hopes she is there to meet him, he tells himself she is 'out of my league'.

Outline the role of physical attractiveness in attraction. (4 marks)

Explanation. Buss's cross-cultural research found men place particular importance on physical attractiveness when choosing a mate. This is seen when Gareth immediately notices the woman's appearance as she enters the restaurant. He hopes she is there to meet him – her 'stunning' appearance makes her a desirable potential partner as her attractiveness implies health and fertility. However, Gareth worries he may not be of a similar level of attractiveness. The matching hypothesis suggests we would expect people to pair up with someone who is similar in terms of physical attractiveness, and so while Gareth may wish for a relationship with the woman she may not be so inclined.

Self-disclosure

Jourard (1971) first used the term **self-disclosure** to describe the extent to which a person reveals personal information to another person. This plays an important role in the development of romantic relationships as greater disclosure leads to greater feelings.

Self-disclosure given and self-disclosure received
The level of self-disclosure received in a romantic relationship was usually a better predictor of liking and loving than the level of self-disclosure given. Sprecher *et al.* (2013) found self-disclosure was positively related to relationship stability. Their study of 50 dating couples found the degree of disclosure was predictive of whether couples stayed together for longer than four years.

Types of self-disclosure
It is the type of information disclosed that predicts relationship satisfaction. Sprecher (1987) found disclosure of personal disappointments and accomplishments, as well as previous sexual relationships, have a greater influence on relationship satisfaction than more 'neutral' information.

Norms of self-disclosure
In the early stages of a relationship, people should engage in a moderate level of self-disclosure: not so personal as to seem indiscriminate to reveal intimate details to a relative stranger, nor so impersonal that the listener is unable to know the person better (Derlega & Grzelak, 1979). Research suggests the norm of reciprocity, i.e. people expect others to return the services they provide, applies to self-disclosure (Berg & Archer, 1980).

Key study: Sprecher *et al.* (2013)
How? 156 undergraduate students at a US university paired into two-person dyads to take part in a Skype self-disclosure task. Approximately two-thirds of the dyads were female–female and one-third male–female. In the reciprocal condition dyad members took turns asking questions and disclosing. In the non-reciprocal condition one person asked questions while the other disclosed, then they switched roles (extended reciprocity).

Showed? In the reciprocal condition assessments of liking, closeness, perceived similarity and enjoyment were higher than assessments made after the first and second non-reciprocal interactions. Turn taking self-disclosure is more likely to lead to positive interpersonal outcomes than extended reciprocity.

Evaluation
Research support for the importance of self-disclosure
Collins and Miller's (1994) meta-analysis found that those who reveal intimate information tend to be liked more than those who disclose less, and people like others as a result of having disclosed to them. They also found liking was stronger if the recipient believed the information was shared only with them.

Self-disclosure on the internet: the 'boom and bust' phenomenon
Due to the anonymous nature of communicating over the internet, people may engage in higher levels of self-disclosure than they would in face-to-face relationships. Cooper and Sportolari (1997) refer to this as the 'boom and bust' phenomenon: early self-disclosure in online relationships leads to relationships becoming intense very quickly (boom). But, the lack of underlying trust needed to support such disclosures makes it difficult to sustain the relationship (bust). Cooper and Sportolari give examples of people who have left established relationships only to find their online 'soulmate' does not turn out to be what they first seemed.

The norms of self-disclosure run deep
Research supports the fundamental importance of the 'rules' of self-disclosure. Contestants on reality TV shows tend to engage in rapid self-disclosure of intimate details. Tal-Or and Hershman-Shitrit discovered that while viewers liked characters who early on disclosed personal information, they still preferred disclosures to evolve gradually and become more intimate, as occurs in real relationships.

Self-disclosure may be greater in face-to-face than online relationships
Knop *et al.* (2016) found members of a social group disclosed personal information more often in face-to-face interactions and these disclosures were more intimate. It seems that, contrary to popular belief, people do not use the internet to disclose personal details. This may be because when disclosing information people value non-verbal cues such as eye contact and attentive silence, both of which are absent in the online environment.

Cultural differences in patterns of self-disclosure
In the West, people typically engage in more intimate self-disclosure, e.g. Americans disclose more than Chinese and Japanese (Chen, 1995). Cultural norms also shape how comfortable men and women are in self-disclosing, e.g. Japanese women prefer a lower level of personal conversation than Japanese men (Nakanishi, 1986). In contrast, Western women disclose more than Western men.

KEY TERM
Self-disclosure When a person reveals intimate personal information about themselves to another person. Through self-disclosure an individual lets themselves be known to the other person, thus 'reducing the mystery' between them.

Apply it
Scenario. Ronnie is developing feelings for the newest employee in the office. They have been spending lunchtimes together and their conversations have moved from work-related topics to personal life such as hobbies, childhood experiences and more recently past relationships.

With reference to Ronnie, outline and evaluate the role of self-disclosure in attraction. (16 marks)

Explanation extract... Collins and Miller support the suggestion that self-disclosure is an important process in the development of romantic relationships. The conclusions of their meta-analysis would suggest Ronnie has growing feelings for her work colleague as those who disclose intimate information tend to be more liked by those who disclose at lower levels. Furthermore, as only the two of them spend lunchtime together, Ronnie may feel the disclosures are for her ears only and so her attraction would continue to grow. ...

31

KEY TERMS

Complementarity of needs How well two people fit together as a couple and meet each other's needs.

Filter theory We choose romantic partners by using a series of filters that narrow down the 'field of availables' from which we might eventually make a choice.

Similarity in attitudes If people share similar attitudes, values and beliefs, communication is easier and so a relationship is likely to progress.

Social demography Refers to variables such as age, background and location, which determine the likelihood of individuals meeting in the first place.

Apply it

Scenario. Katie is describing her new partner to her friends. She says, 'We work at the same hospital and agree that people should be better informed about how to look after their health through their lifestyle choices. Both of us have similar beliefs regarding marriage and children. He can sometimes be indecisive, so he doesn't mind that I like to decide what we do at the weekend.'

Outline the filter theory of attraction. Refer to Katie's comments in your answer. (6 marks)

Explanation. The first filter the theory suggests people apply is social demography, i.e. variables such as age and geographical location. Katie and her partner work in the same hospital, so they will feel similar and more at ease with each other; this will increase the attraction felt. The second filter involves similarity of attitudes and values. This is of central importance at the start of a relationship. Through encouraging self-disclosure, Katie has learnt her partner holds similar views to her regarding marriage and children. Finally, she has assessed the complementarity of needs as she mentions she likes to make decisions while her partner can be indecisive. Katie is attracted to her new partner as his needs are harmonious with her own.

Filter theory

Kerckhoff and Davis (1962) suggest we use a series of filters when choosing a romantic partner. In the early stages demographic similarities (class, religion, location) are often most important. Later on **similarity in attitudes** and values becomes important. Finally, there is an assessment of compatibility, e.g. in terms of personality traits.

First filter: social demography

Age, social background and location reduce the range of people realistically available for us to meet. As we are more likely to come into contact with those similar to ourselves we feel more at ease with them and as a result find them more attractive. Attraction has more to do with **social demography** rather than individual characteristics.

Second filter: similarities in attitudes

Similarities in attitudes and values are of central importance at the start of a relationship and are the best predictor of the relationship becoming stable. Through self-disclosure individuals weigh up whether to continue the relationship. Partners whose attitudes and values differ greatly are 'filtered out' from the field of possible long-term partners.

Final filter: complementarity of needs

People who have opposing needs (e.g. the need to be caring and the need to be cared for) provide each other with mutual satisfaction. Finding a complementary partner ensures needs are likely to be met. Winch's (1958) study of 25 married US couples suggested social needs (such as dominance and deference) should be complementary rather than similar if marriages are to work. This is not 'opposites attract'; rather, we are attracted to people whose needs are 'harmonious' with our own.

Key study: Kerckhoff and Davis (1962)

How? 94 dating couples at Duke University completed two questionnaires assessing similarity of attitudes and values (Index of Value Consensus test) and the degree of complementarity (FIRO-B test). Seven months later, the couples completed another questionnaire to assess how close they felt to their partner now, compared to at the start of the study.

Showed? For 'short-term couples' (those dating for less than 18 months) similarity of attitudes and values was the most significant predictor of closeness. For 'long-term couples' (dating for more than 18 months), **complementarity of needs** was the only predictor of closeness.

Evaluation

Lack of research support for filter theory

Levinger et al. (1970) replicated Kerckhoff and Davis's study with 330 'steadily attached' couples. They found no evidence that similarity of attitudes and values or complementarity of needs influenced progress towards a permanent relationship. They also found no significant link between length of the relationship and the influence of these different filters. Results may have differed because the FIRO-B and Index of Value Consensus questionnaires would not have been appropriate due to changes in social values and courtship patterns that occurred since the initial study.

The real value of the filtering process

Filtering allows people to make predictions about their future interactions to avoid investing in a relationship that 'won't work' (Duck, 1973). People use a variety of strategies to gather information about each other, including encouraging self-disclosure through questioning and provoking disagreements to 'get at' the other person's real feelings. Partners decide whether to continue with a relationship or conclude it will not work and end their involvement.

Perceived similarity may be more important than actual similarity

In a speed-dating event, where decisions about attraction are made over a shorter time span, it was found that perceived but not actual similarity predicted romantic liking (Tidwell et al., 2013).

Complementarity of needs may not be that important

Dijkstra and Barelds (2008) studied 760 college-education singles on a dating site looking for a long-term mate. Each participant's own personality was measured as well as noting the personality characteristics desired in a mate. Although participants initially indicated they wanted a complementary partner rather than a similar one, there was a strong correlation between the individual's personality and their ideal partner's personality. This suggests similarity is more influential than complementarity of needs.

A problem for filter theory

Attitudes and values and an individual's needs are constantly changing. Furthermore, people are often not aware of their partner's values, needs or role preferences. Thornton and Young-DeMarco (2001) found attitudes towards relationships in young American adults changed over a period of a few decades. This included a weakened need to marry, to stay married and to have children, a more relaxed attitude towards cohabitation and more egalitarian attitudes to gender roles in marriage.

Social exchange theory

◎ Profit and loss
Thibaut and Kelley (1959) propose all social behaviour is a series of exchanges. Rewards may include companionship, being cared for and sex. Costs may include effort, financial investment and time wasted (i.e. missed opportunities with others). Rewards minus costs equal the outcome: either a profit or a loss. Commitment is dependent on the profitability of this outcome.

◎ Comparison level (CL)
Our CL is a product of our previous relationship experiences and general views of what might be expected in this particular relationship. If the profits of the new relationship exceed the CL, the relationship is judged worthwhile. If the profit is less than our CL, then a relationship with that person is seen as less attractive.

Unpleasant/unsatisfying previous relationships lead to a very low CL, meaning individuals are happy in relatively poor relationships. Previously rewarding relationships create a high CL, meaning individuals will exit a relationship that does not live up to their expectations. If the relationship exceeds the CL of both partners, there is likely to be a greater degree of solidarity.

◎ Comparison level for alternatives (CLA)
The CLA involves weighing up the potential increase in rewards from a different partner, minus any costs associated with ending the current relationship. An individual will commit to the current relationship if it is more beneficial to stay rather than seek an alternative. In contrast, if a new relationship appears to be more profitable, the current relationship will end. The more rewarding alternatives seem (e.g. friends, career, potential partner), the less dependent the individual is on the current relationship. A low degree of dependence leads to relationship instability (Kurdek, 1993). A partner may experience distress if they and/or their partner differ in their degree of dependence.

◎ Key study: Kurdek and Schmitt (1986)
How? 44 heterosexual couples, 35 co-habiting heterosexual couples, 50 same-sex male couples and 56 same-sex female couples completed a questionnaire without discussing answers with their partner.

Showed? For all couples, greater relationship satisfaction was associated with perception of many benefits of the current relationship (CL) and seeing alternatives as less attractive (CLA).

◎ Evaluation
Evidence for the influence of comparison level for alternatives
Sprecher's (2001) longitudinal study of 101 dating couples at a US university found that, when the CLA was high, commitment to and satisfaction with the current relationship was low. Sprecher also suggests those who lack alternatives are likely to remain committed (and satisfied). Those who are satisfied and committed are more likely to devalue alternatives.

The problem of costs and benefits
It is difficult to classify events in such simple terms as 'costs' or 'benefits'. For example, what may be rewarding to one person (e.g. constant attention and praise) may be punishing to another (e.g. perceived as irritating). In addition, what is seen to be a benefit at one stage of the relationship may become a cost at another stage (Littlejohn, 1989).

The problems of assessing value
Individuals must have some way of quantifying the value of costs and benefits if they are to assess whether benefits outweigh costs (Nakonezny & Denton, 2008). Social exchange theory is more typically applied to commercial and economic relationships where costs and benefits are more clearly defined. The vagueness of such terms and the difficulty in assessing their relative value in more personal relationships suggests the theory is less successfully applied to romantic relationships.

Overemphasis on costs and benefits
Social exchange theory should also consider individual differences in relational standards and beliefs. An individual's own relational beliefs may make them more tolerant of a relatively low ratio of benefits to costs, e.g. they may hold the belief 'it is selfish to focus on one's own needs' or 'for better, for worse'. This means the individual will continue to provide benefits and simply put up with the costs.

Real-world application – IBCT
Gottman and Levenson (1992) found a 5:1 ratio of positive to negative exchanges in successful relationships, compared with 1:1 or less in unsuccessful marriages. Integrated Behavioural Couples Therapy (IBCT) helps partners break the negative patterns of behaviour that cause problems so that the amount of positive exchanges increases and negative exchanges decrease. Of over 60 distressed couples treated using IBCT, about two-thirds reported significant improvements in the quality of their relationships (Christensen et al., 2004).

KEY TERM
Social exchange theory The likelihood of a person staying in a relationship is determined by an assessment of what they get out of the relationship compared to what they put in, and how the relationship measures up against what they expect and what they might achieve in a different relationship.

Apply it
Scenario. Jakub and Peter are talking about their marriages. Jakub describes his wife as his ideal companion. She is caring and always knows how to cheer him up, as well as being a wonderful mother to their children. Peter, on the other hand, fears his marriage is in difficulty. He and his wife always seem to argue and both appear more focused on spending time with friends rather than each other.

Discuss the social exchange theory of romantic relationships. Refer to Jakub and Peter's conversation in your answer. (16 marks)

Explanation extract... Jakub is describing the rewards he receives from his marriage. Social exchange theory would predict these rewards outweigh any costs incurred and so Jakub feels he is earning a 'profit'. The marriage is exceeding his comparison level and so he is committed to this relationship. Peter and his wife, however, both seem to be weighing up alternatives as they spend time with friends rather than each other. The more rewarding Peter finds this alternative, the less dependent he will be on his current relationship. The frequent arguments increase the negative exchanges in comparison to the positive exchanges. Gottman and Levenson (1992) found the ratio of positive and negative exchanges is 1:1 in unsuccessful marriages like Peter's, but successful relationships like Jakub's have a ratio of 5:1. ....

KEY TERM

Equity theory Claims that people are most comfortable when what they get out of a relationship (i.e. the benefits) is roughly equal to what they put in (i.e. the costs).

Equity theory

Inequality and dissatisfaction

An equitable relationship is one where one partner's benefits minus their costs are equal to their partner's benefits minus *their* costs. If people feel over-benefited they may experience pity, guilt and shame. If under-benefited, anger, sadness and shame are experienced. The greater the inequity, the greater the dissatisfaction and stress.

A timetable of equity and inequity in marriages

Schafer and Keith (1980) found that, during child-rearing years, wives often felt under-benefited and husbands over-benefited, creating a dip in marital satisfaction. During honeymoon and empty-nest stages, both partners were more likely to perceive equality and feel satisfied with their marriage. Hatfield and Rapson (2011) suggest that in the initial stages considerations of rewards and fairness are important. However, once deeply committed, couples become less concerned about keeping a daily score. Byers and Wang (2004) suggest those in equitable relationships are less likely to risk extramarital affairs and have longer lasting relationships.

Dealing with inequality

Hatfield and Rapson (2011) suggest equality can be restored by: *restoration of actual equality* – individuals voluntarily set things right or urge their partner to do so; *restoration of psychological equality* – individuals distort reality and convince themselves that things are perfect as they are; and *removing themselves from the inequality* – this can be physical, e.g. divorce, or emotional, e.g. falling out of love.

Key study: Stafford and Canary (2006)

How? Over 200 married couples completed measures of equality and relationship satisfaction. Each spouse also answered questions about their use of relationship maintenance strategies such as assurances (emphasising attraction, commitment), sharing tasks (household responsibilities) and positivity (upbeat and optimistic communication).

Showed? Spouses who felt their relationship was equitable showed the most satisfaction, followed by over-benefited partners. Under-benefited husbands in particular reported significantly lower levels of relationship maintenance strategies. Spouses who were treated more equitably tended to be happier and so more likely to behave in ways that contributed to their spouse's sense of equality and happiness.

Evaluation
Equality sensitivity

Not everyone experiences the same level of tension when they perceive inequality. Huseman *et al.* (1987) identified three categories of individuals: *benevolents* – 'givers' who tend to tolerate being under-rewarded; *equality sensitives* – who behave in accordance to equality theory; and *entitleds* – those who prefer to be over-rewarded and so are dissatisfied when under-rewarded or in an equitable relationship.

Gender differences in the importance of equality

Women tend to perceive themselves as more under-benefited and less over-benefited. Women are also more disturbed by being under-benefited than men (DeMaris *et al.*, 2010). Sprecher (1992) found women feel more guilt in response to being over-benefited. Women's greater relationship focus may make them more sensitive to injustices and more likely to react negatively to exploitation. An increased emphasis on gender equality in modern society may lead women to become more vigilant and reactive to inequality.

Cultural differences in the importance of equality

Equality may be less important in non-Western cultures. Aumer-Ryan *et al.* (2006) found that, in all cultures studied, equality in marriage was felt to be important but people differed in how equitable they considered their relationships to be. Men and women from the US claimed to be in the most equitable relationships, but men and (especially) women from Jamaica claimed to be in the least equitable relationships.

Evidence from non-human primates

Female capuchin monkeys became angry when denied a highly prized reward (grapes) offered in return for playing a game. If a monkey who did not play the game was then given the grapes, the capuchins became so angry they hurled food at the researcher (Bronson & de Waal, 2003). A later study found chimpanzees were most upset by injustice in casual relationships than in close, intimate ones. These findings echo evidence from human studies suggesting the perception of equality has ancient origins.

A problem of causality

Clark (1984) suggests that only when a marriage is in trouble do couples start to think in terms of rewards and equity. However, Van Yperen and Buunk (1990) found people in inequitable marriages became less satisfied over the course of the year. Hatfield and Rapson (2011) propose that in failing marriages both processes might be operating. In faltering marriages, partners become preoccupied with relationship inequalities, which then leads to relationship dissolution.

Apply it

Scenario. Greta declares the most successful relationships are ones where both partners feel equally rewarded. Tina disagrees, arguing that relationships are more complex than a simple calculation of costs and rewards.

Explain one criticism of using equity theory to explain romantic relationships. (3 marks)

Explanation. Tina may be right to disagree with Greta's statement as people may differ in their perception of equality and inequality. For example, Huseman identified benevolents (tolerate inequality), equality sensitives (strive for equality) and entitleds (seek to be over-rewarded). This casts doubt on the claims made by equity theory which are echoed in Greta's comment. If Huseman is correct then some people seek to be over-rewarded rather than to provide an equal amount of rewards as their partner (entitleds), as predicted by equality theory.

Rusbult's investment model of commitment

Relationships persist not just because of relationship satisfaction but also because of the investments made in the relationship and the absence of a better option. These three factors enable predictions about an individual's **commitment** to the relationship to be made.

Satisfaction level

The positive versus negative emotions experienced and the extent to which the individual's most important needs are fulfilled by their partner determines the level of **satisfaction** felt.

Quality of alternatives

On perceiving that their most important needs might be better fulfilled outside the current relationship, the individual may be drawn towards the alternative and away from their current partner. However, if no alternatives are present, an individual may stay with the current relationship due to the lack of options. In some cases, an attractive alternative may be having no relationship.

Investment size

Investment size is a measure of all the resources attached to the relationship which would diminish in value or be completely lost if the relationship ended, e.g. time and energy invested, shared friends and possessions. These investments are made expecting that doing so will create a strong foundation for a lasting future. Investments increase dependence, as connections with the partner, that are costly to break, increase.

Commitment level

Couples in happy relationships show a high level of commitment. Partners anticipate very little gain and high levels of loss if the relationship ends. In contrast, commitment is low when satisfaction and investment are low and the **quality of alternatives/comparison with alternatives** is high. People in satisfied relationships become dependent on the relationship because of the investments made or absence of suitable alternatives. Commitment, therefore, is a consequence of increasing dependence.

◉ Key study: Le and Agnew (2003)

How? A meta-analysis of 52 studies conducted between the late 1970s and late 1990s, producing a sample of over 11,000 participants (54% male, 46% female) from five different countries. Each study explored the components of the **investment model**.

Showed? Across all studies, commitment was highly correlated with satisfaction level (.68), quality of alternatives (−.48) and investment size (.46). The correlation between commitment and stay or leave behaviours was also significant (.47).

◉ Evaluation

Research support for the investment model

Le *et al.* (2010) analysed nearly 38,000 participants in 137 studies over a 33-year period. Commitment (or lack of it) was a particular strong predictor of whether a relationship would end. Satisfaction, quality of alternatives and investments were modest predictors of the likelihood of staying in a relationship or ending it.

Problems in measuring the variables of the model

Rusbult *et al.* (1998) developed the Investment Model Scale in an attempt to overcome the difficulty of measuring satisfaction, investment and quality of alternatives. This scale has been shown to be high in both reliability and validity, and can be used with a range of different populations. However, the scale relies on self-report and so respondents may modify answers to show themselves in a better light.

Investment in the future is also important

Goodfriend and Andrew (2008) suggest the investment model should also include the notion of partner's planned future investments. In ending a relationship an individual would not only lose investments made to date but also any future investments planned with their partner. This means some relationships may persist, not because of current investments but a desire to see future, important plans take place.

Real-world application: abusive relationships

Victims of partner abuse experience low satisfaction, which would lead us to predict they would leave the abusive partner, yet many remain. The investment model would point to a lack of alternatives and high level of investments making it too costly to leave the partner. Rusbult and Martz (1995) found alternatives and investments were a strong indication of whether abused women at a shelter remained committed to, and returned to, their partner.

The wide application of the investment model

The main claims of the investment model (e.g. that commitment is positively associated with satisfaction and investment size, and is negatively associated with quality of alternatives) have been shown to be true across different populations – research has supported the relevance of the model in the US, the Netherlands and Taiwan – and different types of relationship – marital, non-marital, gay and lesbian couples, friendships and abusive relationships.

KEY TERMS

Commitment The likelihood that an individual will persist with their current relationship. It is a product of high satisfaction and investment in the relationship and low quality of alternatives.

Investment A measure of all the resources attached to the relationship (e.g. financial, shared children), which would be lost if the relationship were to end.

Investment model An explanation of relationship stability that emphasises the importance of three factors (satisfaction, investment size and quality of alternative) in determining relationship commitment, which in turn predicts relationship stability.

Quality of alternatives/comparison with alternatives An individual's assessment of whether their needs might be better fulfilled by somebody other than their current partner.

Satisfaction A measure of the degree to which the current partner gratifies a person's important needs.

Apply it

Scenario. Tina is interviewing people in long-term relationships to determine whether there are common variables influencing the commitment each participant had to their partner.

With reference to the investment model, what variables is Tina likely to identify? (6 marks)

Explanation. Tina will probably find that people in long-term relationships experience a high level of satisfaction, e.g. the participants may report the needs that are most important to them are fulfilled by their partner. She may also find that the time and energy each participant has invested in their relationship as well as shared friends and possessions have built a strong foundation that enables the relationship to last. Finally, there may be poor quality or no alternatives to the current relationship and so the participant remains with their partner due to a lack of better options.

KEY TERMS

Duck's phase model of relationship breakdown A model of relationship breakdown that describes the different phases that people enter during the dissolution of a romantic relationship.

Intrapsychic phase An individual broods over their current relationship and considers whether they might be better off out of it. This is followed by the dyadic phase.

Dyadic phase An individual confronts their partner and discusses with them their feelings, their discontentment and the future of the relationship. This is followed by the social phase.

Social phase Discontentment spills over to friends and family, as the distress experienced by one or both partners is made public. This is followed by the grave-dressing phase.

Grave-dressing phase Partners strive to construct a representation of the failed relationship that does not paint their contribution to it in unfavourable terms.

Apply it

Scenario. Beverly is discussing a friend's recent breakup with a work colleague. Beverly says she had suspicions her friend had been unhappy in the relationship for a while. She mentions her friend had hinted that the reason the relationship ended was because she thought he was having an affair. Beverly says she always knew he couldn't be trusted.

With reference to Beverly's comments, outline and evaluate Duck's phase model of relationship breakdown. (16 marks)

Explanation extract... Beverly mentions she felt her friend was unhappy for a while before publically announcing the breakup. Duck's model would suggest the friend was in the intrapsychic phase (where she broods over her feelings towards her partner) or dyadic phase (where she shares her dissatisfaction with her partner). On telling Beverly about the breakup, her friend has entered the social phase and it seems Beverly is taking sides in saying she 'knew he couldn't be trusted'. Beverly's friend is grave-dressing by explaining the reason for ending the relationship. The mention of a possible affair justifies her actions and presents her as the loyal, trusting partner, which is a desirable trait to promote when seeking a new relationship. ...

Duck's (1982) phase model of relationship breakdown

◉ Breakdown
One partner begins to feel distress with how the relationship is conducted, e.g. inequitable relationships create dissatisfaction. On realising they are no longer willing or able to stand this dissatisfaction the individual takes the first step in the breakdown of the relationship.

◉ The intrapsychic phase
In this phase the individual considers whether they would be better off if the relationship ended. They are burdened by feelings of resentment and a sense of being under-benefited. These feelings may not be shared but expressed in other ways, e.g. in a diary or through social withdrawal. Some end the relationship without ever discussing their dissatisfaction.

◉ The dyadic phase
The individual now confronts their partner and begins to discuss their discontentment and their future as a couple. Feelings of guilt and anger surface and their partner may also share concerns. Couples become aware of what binds them (children, investments) as well as the social and economic costs of splitting up. If both partners are motivated to remain a couple, the relationship can be saved at this point, e.g. marital therapy.

◉ The social phase
The distress of one or both partners is now shared with friends and family, making it harder for the couple to deny there is a problem and bring about a reconciliation. Others may take sides, offer advice and support or even hasten dissolution through revelations about the partner's behaviour.

◉ The grave-dressing phase
Once the relationship has ended, partners attempt to justify their actions so they appear trustworthy and loyal (key attributes needed to attract a new partner). The individual has to maintain their 'social credit' to ensure future relationships are possible (La Gaipa, 1982). Individuals also reinterpret their view of their partner, e.g. the partner's 'rebellious' nature is reframed as 'being irresponsible'. Stories of betrayal or how the couple worked hard to stay together but it wasn't 'meant to be' are also a feature of this phase.

◉ Evaluation
The original model fails to reflect the possibility of personal growth
In 2006, Duck and Rollie added the final phase, 'resurrection processes', in which people move beyond any distress felt and engage in personal growth. In support of this final phase, Tashiro and Frazier (2003) found 92 undergraduates who had recently broken up with a romantic partner and who reported experiences of emotional distress and personal growth.

The impact of the social phase varies by type of relationship
The relationships of teenagers and young adults are seen as more unstable than long-term adult relationships. As a result, others may offer sympathy but no support with reconciliation as 'there are plenty more fish in the sea'. Older adults, however, have lower expectations of finding a new relationship and so the consequences of breakdown are more significant (Dickson, 1995). The social phase may then be characterised by more obvious attempts to rescue the current relationship.

Benefits of the grave-dressing phase
Monroe et al. (1999) found students whose relationship had broken down the previous year had a greater risk of developing a major depressive disorder for the first time. While research such as this shows how stressful breakdown can be, others have identified the importance of grave-dressing. For example, stories that play down personal responsibility do not threaten psychological well-being. Tashiro and Frazier (2003) found focusing on how the situation, rather than personal flaws, was responsible for the breakup helped individuals cope better.

Ethical issues in breakdown research
Participants taking part in research may experience distress when revisiting reasons for the breakdown. Privacy and confidentiality (particularly for victims of abuse) are also important issues. In all research studies, the benefits of undertaking the research must outweigh the risks, most notably the impact on participants. This is difficult when dealing with vulnerable individuals attempting to cope with the trauma and emotional distress associated with relationship breakdown.

Real-world application: implications for intervention
The model stresses the importance of communication in relationship breakdown. Paying attention to the topics discussed, what is said and how it is said can offer important insights into how the individual is thinking about the relationship. This can suggest appropriate interventions by friends and family, e.g. in the intrapsychic phase, liking for the partner could be re-established. In the social phase, people in the couple's social network may help the partners reconcile their differences.

Virtual relationships in social media

⊙ Self-disclosure in virtual relationships

Jourand's (1971) 'broadcasting self-disclosure' explains the difference between disclosure to a romantic partner and **self-disclosure** in the public domain. In private people feel more secure about sharing intimate and sensitive information; in public (e.g. on a Facebook wall) people share less private and less intimate information. People may compensate for the lack of control over the target audience by controlling what information this audience has access to.

Why do people self-disclose more on the internet?

Usually, individuals need to feel confident that what they disclose will remain confidential before sharing information. In face-to-face interactions this confidentiality may be violated or receive a negative response (ridicule or rejection). The relative anonymity of internet interactions reduces fear of disapproval and so we are more likely to self-disclose to people we don't know and probably will never see again (Rubin, 1975). Furthermore, a stranger does not have access to an individual's social circle, so the problem of confidentiality is less of an issue.

⊙ Absence of gating in virtual relationships

Gating in face-to-face relationships

Personal factors such as physical appearance and mannerisms tend to determine who we approach, and who we develop romantic relationships with. We use available features to categorise people before deciding whether we would like a relationship with them. In online relationships there is an absence of these barriers or **gates** that normally limit the opportunities for less attractive, shy or less socially skilled to form relationships in face-to-face encounters.

Absence of gating and its consequences

Removal of the traditional gating features means a person's true self is more likely to be active in internet relationships. Zhao *et al.* (2008) found that online social networks can empower 'gated' individuals to present the identities they are unable to establish face-to-face. Online interactions also allow people to 'stretch the truth' to project a more socially desirable 'self'. Yurchisin *et al.* (2005), in interviews with 11 online daters, found individuals tended to give real and better accounts of themselves. Some admitted they would steal other daters' ideas or copy others' images to increase popularity. However, most online identities were still close to the person's true self to avoid awkward real-life encounters later on.

⊙ Evaluation

The importance of the internet in romantic relationships

In a US study of 4,000 adults, Rosenfeld and Thomas (2012) found 71.8% of those with home internet access had a spouse or romantic partner compared to only 35.9% of those without internet access in their home. Taking into account age, gender, education, sexual preference and religion, individuals with internet access were twice as likely to have a partner compared to those without internet access. This suggests the internet may be displacing rather than complementing traditional ways of meeting a romantic partner.

Virtual relationships can be as strong as offline relationships

Internet relationships are often seen to be of lower quality and more temporary (Putnam, 2000). However, Rosenfeld and Thomas (2012) found no difference between the quality of online and offline relationships, nor did they find that online relationships were more fragile than those formed offline.

A biological basis for self-disclosure on Facebook

Tamir and Mitchell (2012) found increased MRI activity in the nucleus accumbens and the ventral tegmental area: two areas associated with reward. These were strongly activated when people spoke about themselves, and showed less activation when talking about someone else. Participants also experienced a greater sense of pleasure when sharing their thoughts than when they were told to keep thoughts private. This suggests the tendency to share information over social media may arise from the rewarding nature of self-disclosure.

Facebook helps shy people have better quality friendships

Baker and Oswald (2010) surveyed 207 male and female students about their shyness, Facebook usage and the quality of their friendships. For those who scored high for shyness, greater use of Facebook was associated with higher perceptions of friendship quality. In contrast, Facebook usage was not associated with perception of friendship quality for those scoring low on shyness.

Virtual relationships have consequences for offline relationships

The offline and online world should not be thought of as separate (Zhao *et al.*, 2008). The development of virtual relationships allows some individuals to bypass gating obstacles and create an identity they are unable to establish in the real world. These *digital selves* can then enhance the individual's overall self-image and as a result may increase their chances of connecting to others in their offline world.

KEY TERMS

Gates The barriers that limit opportunities for the less attractive, shy or less socially skilled to form relationships in face-to-face encounters.

Self-disclosure When a person reveals intimate personal information about themselves to another person.

Virtual relationships Relationships that are conducted through the internet rather than face to face, e.g. through social media.

Apply it

Scenario. Jimmy frequently posts on his Facebook wall. He has a large number of friends online and will happily accept new friend requests. He thinks nothing of posting his highs and lows with his online friends; from a great night out to sharing his worries. He often uses private messaging to have conversations with his online friends.

Outline the nature of self-disclosure in virtual relationships. (4 marks)

Explanation. High levels of self-disclosure in virtual relationships can be explained by the anonymity the internet provides. Jimmy is able to share personal information with less fear of disapproval or rejection than in a face-to-face relationship. As the online friends he chats to in private messages are likely to be acquaintances rather than members of his social circle, Jimmy is confident he will not see them and so confidentiality is less of a problem. Jimmy may be selective over the content he shares, e.g. posting only trivial worries in an attempt to compensate for the lack of control over those who view his profile.

KEY TERMS

Absorption addiction model Individuals can become psychologically absorbed with a celebrity to establish a sense of fulfilment. The motivational forces driving this absorption might then take on an addictive component, leading to more extreme behaviours in order to sustain the parasocial relationship.

Attachment theory An explanation of the formation of an emotional bond between two people (especially caregiver and child). It is a two-way process that endures over time. It leads to certain behaviours such as clinging and proximity-seeking.

Parasocial relationship An individual is attracted to another person (usually a celebrity), who is usually unaware of the existence of the person who has created the relationship.

Parasocial relationships (PSRs)

◉ The attachment theory explanation

PSRs with celebrities exhibit, to some degree, the fundamental properties of adult attachment identified by Weiss (1991).

- *Proximity-seeking*. Fans collect trivia about the celebrity, rearranging schedules to watch them on TV and even attempting to contact them (Leets *et al.*, 1995).
- *Secure base*. In PSRs there is little chance of rejection from the attachment figure so the individual is able to create a secure base from which to explore other relationships in a safe way.
- *Protest at disruption*. In 2015, the BBC's axing of Jeremy Clarkson from *Top Gear* was met with raw emotion typical of the loss of an attachment figure, e.g. one fan wrote, 'I want to cry.'

Attachment style

Cole and Leets (1999) found individuals with an anxious-ambivalent attachment style were most likely to enter into a PSR with their favourite TV celebrity. This attachment style is characterised by a concern that others will not reciprocate one's desire for intimacy and so forming a PSR is a means of satisfying their 'unrealistic' and often unmet relational needs. The **parasocial relationship** formed with the media figure reflects a desire for intimacy. Avoidant individuals were the least likely to enter into PSRs possibly because these people find it difficult to develop intimate relationships so avoid both real and imaginary intimacy.

◉ The absorption addiction model

PSRs may fill a void created by shyness and loneliness. This type of relationship may be appealing to some people as there is little risk of the rejection or criticism possible in real relationships (Ashe & McCutcheon, 2001). PSRs are likely to form with characters deemed to be attractive (perception of attractiveness) and similar to the viewer (perception of homophily).

Using the Celebrities Attitude Scale (CAS), Giles and Maltby (2006) identify three levels in this process:

- *Entertainment-social*: fans watch, keep up with, read and learn about the celebrity for the purposes of entertainment and gossip, e.g. 'Learning the life story of my favourite celebrity is a lot of fun.' Most people never go beyond admiring celebrities' entertainment value (McCutcheon *et al.*, 2002).
- *Intense-personal*: this represents a deeper level of involvement and includes intensive and compulsive feelings, e.g. 'I love to talk to others who admire my favourite celebrity.'
- *Borderline-pathological*: individuals empathise with the celebrity's success and failures but also over-identify with the celebrity and engage in uncontrollable behaviours and fantasies, e.g. 'If I walked through the door of the celebrity's house, they would be happy to see me.'

From absorption to addiction

An introverted nature, difficult social circumstances and lack of meaningful relationships may lead some adolescents to become 'absorbed' by the lives of the celebrity (McCutcheon *et al.*, 2002). Absorption leads fans to believe they have a special relationship with the celebrity, motivating them to learn more about the celebrity. These motivational forces may become addictive, leading to more extreme (and delusional) behaviours to sustain satisfaction with the PSR. At the borderline-pathological level, progressively stronger involvement is required to stay 'connected' to the celebrity.

◉ Evaluation

Research support for factors involved in parasocial relationships

Schiappa *et al.*'s (2007) meta-analysis found people with higher levels of PSRs also watched more TV. Their analysis also showed a significant positive relationship between the degree to which a person perceived TV characters as real and their tendency to form PSRs. They also found evidence to support the claim that the likelihood of forming a PSR with TV characters was linked to characters seen as attractive and similarity to the viewer.

Are parasocial relationships linked to loneliness?

While some research has found PSRs may develop as a way of dealing with loneliness or loss, other research has found no relationship between intensity of loneliness and intensity of PSRs. Eyal and Cohen (2006), in a study of 279 students who were fans of the TV show *Friends*, found the intensity of their PSR with their favourite character was the strongest predictor of feelings of loneliness after the final episode was broadcast. This suggests the loss of a PSR can *create* feelings of loneliness.

The absorption addiction model: links to mental health

Using the Eysenck Personality Questionnaire (EPQ), Maltby *et al.* (2003) found the *entertainment-social* level was associated with extraversion (lively, sociable, active), while the *intense-personal* level was associated with neuroticism (tense, emotional, moody). Neuroticism is related to anxiety and depression, and so provides a clear explanation of why higher levels of PSRs are associated with poorer mental health. Further research could explore the implications of a reported connection between psychoticism (impulsive, anti-social, egocentric) and the *borderline-pathological* level.

Loss of a parasocial relationship is linked to attachment style

Three hundred and eighty-one Israeli adults completed questionnaires that included questions about their PSRs with their favourite TV characters, how they would feel if those characters were taken off air, and their attachment styles. Viewers expected to feel sadness, anger and loneliness if their favourite character was no longer on TV (feelings similar to those experienced after the loss of a close personal relationship). These reactions were related to both PSR intensity and the viewer's attachment style, with anxious-ambivalently attached participants anticipating the most negative reactions (Cohen, 2004).

Cultural similarities in parasocial relationships

Schmid and Klimmt (2011) investigated whether differences existed between the PSRs formed with Harry Potter by fans in Germany (individualistic culture) and Mexico (collectivist culture). Despite cultural differences, fans from both countries showed similar patterns of PSRs with Harry Potter and other characters in the franchise. Their online survey revealed the fans admired Harry Potter and found similarities between their own lives and those portrayed in the books and films. This demonstrates the universal influence of mainstream media cultures.

Apply it

Scenario. Tammi loves One Direction. She is a regular user of fan pages and has seen them in concert four times. She enjoys discussing the band members and their music with her friend. Verity is 'in love' with one of the members of the band; she becomes angry if she reads he is dating another celebrity and thinks if she just had an opportunity to meet him he would realise they were meant to be together. She spends a lot of her time alone watching their music videos.

With reference to Tammi and Verity, discuss explanations of parasocial relationships. (16 marks)

Explanation extract... The absorption addiction model would place Tammi at the entertainment-social level as her interest in the band provides entertainment and gossip with her friends. Verity, however, has a more intense PSR; she seems to be borderline-pathological as she holds unrealistic fantasies about what would happen if she met the band member she 'loves'. Verity seems isolated from others ('she spends a lot of her time alone'), and so this loneliness may have led her to form a PSR. However, Chory-Assad and Yanen (2005) found no relationship between intensity of PSRs and intensity of loneliness. ...

Chapter 4

Gender

- Sex and gender. Sex-role stereotypes. Androgyny and measuring androgyny including the Bem Sex Role Inventory.
- The role of chromosomes and hormones (testosterone, oestrogen and oxytocin) in sex and gender. Atypical sex chromosome patterns: Klinefelter's syndrome and Turner's syndrome.
- Cognitive explanations of gender development, Kohlberg's theory, gender identity, gender stability and gender constancy; gender schema theory.
- Psychodynamic explanation of gender development, Freud's psychoanalytic theory, Oedipus complex, Electra complex, identification and internalisation.
- Social learning theory as applied to gender development. The influence of culture and media on gender roles.
- Atypical gender development: gender identity disorder; biological and social explanations for gender identity disorder.

Key terms (highlight each cell when you can confidently explain each term)

Androgyny (Bem)	Biological explanations	Cognitive explanations (Kohlberg)	Psychodynamic explanations (Freud)	Social learning theory	Culture and media influences	Atypical gender development
Sex-role stereotypes	Chromosomes	Gender constancy	Oedipus complex	Reinforcement	Cultural differences	Gender dysphoria
Gender	Hormones	Conservation	Electra complex	Modelling	Counter-stereotyping	Transgender
Sex	Intersex	Pre-operational	Identification			Gender identity disorder
	Klinefelter's syndrome	Gender schemas	Internalisation			
	Turner's syndrome					

Content checklist

1. In each 'describe', 'apply' and 'evaluate' cell tick when you have produced brief notes.
2. Once you feel you have a good grasp of the topic add a second tick to the cell.
3. When you feel you have complete mastery of the topic and would be able to answer an exam question without the aid of notes highlight the cell.

I am able to ...	Describe	Apply	Evaluate
Sex and gender. Sex-role stereotypes			
Androgyny and measuring androgyny including the Bem Sex Role Inventory			
The role of chromosomes in sex and gender			
The role of hormones (testosterone, oestrogen and oxytocin) in sex and gender			
Atypical sex chromosome patterns: Klinefelter's syndrome and Turner's syndrome			
Cognitive explanations of gender development, Kohlberg's theory, gender identity, gender stability and gender constancy			
Gender schema theory			
Psychodynamic explanation of gender development, Freud's psychoanalytic theory			
Oedipus complex, Electra complex, identification and internalisation			
Social learning theory as applied to gender development			
The influence of culture and media on gender roles			
Atypical gender development: gender identity disorder			
Biological and social explanations for gender identity disorder			

Sex and gender

Sex is a biological fact – whether a person is a genetic male or female. **Gender** refers to a person's sense of maleness or femaleness. The development of gender is due in part to biology (nature) and in part to life experiences (nurture).

Sex-role stereotypes

Sex-role stereotypes (also called gender stereotypes) are a set of social norms about how men and women should behave. Learnt from **explicit** teaching by parents, teachers and others, e.g. 'Boys don't cry' or 'Girls like pink'.

Also **implicit** learning from same-sex models by imitation (see 'Social learning theory', p.46).

Androgyny

The term **androgyny** was introduced by Sandra Bem in the 1970s. She argued that it is psychologically healthy to avoid fixed sex-role stereotypes. People should be free to adopt a variety of typically masculine or feminine behaviours.

Bem Sex Role Inventory (BSRI)

One hundred US undergraduates rated 200 personality traits as desirable for men or women, and these were narrowed down to 40. The BSRI includes 60 items: 20 masculine traits, 20 feminine and 20 neutral. The BSRI includes items such as: 'independent', 'ambitious' (masculine items); 'compassionate', 'affectionate' (feminine items). Individuals rate themselves on a 7-point Likert scale, from 'never or almost never true' to 'almost always true'. Scores for masculinity and femininity are calculated.

Individuals may be categorised as masculine (high masculine score, low feminine score), feminine (high feminine score, low masculine score), androgynous (high scores for both) or undifferentiated (low scores for both).

○ Evaluation

Research support for parental influence
Smith and Lloyd (1978) **observed** women playing with babies (not their own) dressed as a boy or a girl. If a mother thought she was playing with a boy, she encouraged more motor activity and offered gender-appropriate toys (e.g. squeaky hammer rather than doll).

Support for the relationship between androgyny and psychological health
Prakash et al. (2010) tested 100 married women in India using a personal attribute scale to measure androgyny. Women with higher masculinity scores had lower scores for depression, anxiety, stress and physical health issues. Women with high femininity scores had higher depression scores. This fits Bem's prediction.

Real-world application
If androgyny is better for psychological and physical health, parents could raise children free from sex-role stereotypes. Some parents have done this, but others protest that it is equivalent to child abuse, showing their persistent belief that stereotypes are important for healthy development.

Reliability of the BSRI
Test–retest reliability over a four-week period ranges from 0.76 to 0.94. A short form of the scale with 30 items has better internal reliability. Less socially desirable terms such as 'gullible' have been removed.

Validity of the BSRI
People with higher self-esteem score higher overall, so the scale may measure self-esteem rather than androgyny. Also, the adjectives used in the BSRI were selected in the 1970s; Hoffman and Borders (2001) found only 'masculine' and 'feminine' were still endorsed as masculine or feminine. Attitudes have changed and the BSRI has poor temporal validity.

KEY TERMS

Androgyny A combination of male and female characteristics.

Gender A person's sense of maleness or femaleness, a psychological/social construct.

Sex Being genetically male (XY) or female (XX).

Sex-role stereotypes A set of shared expectations within a social group about what men and women should do and think.

Apply it

Scenario. Adam was given a toy toolkit for his sixth birthday. His younger sister, Evie, said she wanted one too because when she grows up she wants to be a builder. Adam laughed at Evie and said, 'You can't be a builder. You're a girl.'

Explain what is meant by a sex-role stereotype. Refer to Adam and Evie as part of your answer. (4 marks)

Explanation. A sex-role stereotype is a set of shared expectations within a social group about what men and women should do and think. The society we live in teaches us expectations about how men and women should behave, such as expectations that men are doctors and women are nurses. Adam has a fixed sex-role stereotype about girls because he thinks they can't be builders. Evie does not hold the same stereotypes as her brother. She is more flexible in her thinking about what boys and girls can do. This may be because she has had different experiences from Adam, or it may be that her stereotypes are still forming as she is younger.

KEY TERMS

Chromosomes The X-shaped bodies that carry all the genetic information (DNA) for an organism.

Hormones The body's chemical messengers. They travel through the bloodstream, influencing many processes including the stress response, maternal bonding and mood.

Intersex An individual who is not distinctly male or female due to mismatch between chromosomes and genitals.

The role of chromosomes and hormones in sex and gender

Genes determine biological sex and also determine the production of sex hormones, which influence gender identity.

The role of chromosomes

Typical chromosome patterns

Humans have 23 pairs of **chromosomes**. The sex chromosomes, XX (female) or XY (male), usually determine the sex of an individual. Every foetus first develops female external genitalia. After three months, the external and internal genitalia differentiate into vulva, vagina, uterus and ovaries or penis and testes.

Atypical sex chromosome patterns

Klinefelter's syndrome (XXY) affects 1/1,000 males. They have reduced testosterone, are often infertile and have less muscle, less facial hair and broader hips than typical males.

Turner's syndrome (XO, a missing X chromosome) affects 1/2,000 females. They have a vagina and uterus but underdeveloped ovaries, so do not menstruate.

The role of hormones

Most gender development is governed by **hormones**.

Testosterone is produced by the adrenal glands in both sexes. More testosterone is produced in male foetuses, causing genitalia to develop. From about three months, male foetuses produce testosterone in the testes. The surge of testosterone during puberty produces secondary sexual characteristics (deepening voice, body hair). Genetic males with androgen insensitivity syndrome (AIS) may appear female. Testosterone affects brain development prenatally: XX females exposed to male hormones before birth later showed more tomboyish behaviour (Berenbaum & Bailey, 2003).

Oxytocin promotes feelings of bonding and contentment and causes milk to flow in a lactating mother, and has a role in orgasm in both sexes.

Oestrogen promotes secondary sexual characteristics (breasts, body hair) in females and directs the menstrual cycle, preparing the uterus for pregnancy.

Evaluation

Challenging biological determinism

Money (Money & Ehrhardt, 1972) claimed that **intersex** individuals could be raised as either a boy or a girl. David Reimer's penis was damaged as a baby and he was raised as a girl, but he was unhappy and transitioned to male as a teenager. This suggests that chromosomal sex, not just upbringing, influences gender identity.

Unpredictable outcomes of intersex gender development

XX females with congenital adrenal hyperplasia have unusually high levels of androgens and may be assigned male gender at birth. Some accept their assigned gender and some do not. So gender development is affected by a combination of biology, experience, personality and socialisation.

The nature–nurture interaction

Imperato-McGinley *et al.* (1974) described four XY males born with female genitalia, due to androgen insensitivity, and raised as girls, who developed male genitalia during puberty. They adjusted easily to their new male role. This shows an interaction of testosterone and culture.

Treatment of intersex babies and those with Turner's syndrome

Research on intersexual individuals has influenced the nature of therapeutic support they are offered. Intersex babies are not now treated surgically until they can make an informed decision. Girls with Turner's syndrome can be given growth hormone so they reach normal height. Oestrogen therapy helps them develop secondary sexual characteristics, and also benefits their heart and bone health.

Apply it

Scenario. Jolanta is 13, and her mother has taken her to see the GP as she is worried about her. She is very short compared to her friends and has not started to develop breasts. Her mother says that Jolanta talks fluently, and is doing fine at school. However, the doctor suspects that Jolanta may have Turner's syndrome.

Why does the doctor suspect Turner's syndrome, and how could she confirm this? What advice can she give to Jolanta and her mother? (4 marks)

Application. As Jolanta is short and has no sign of developing secondary sexual characteristics, the doctor suspects she may have Turner's syndrome. The doctor may have spotted other physical signs such as short neck, low-set ears, etc. The doctor will have to do a chromosome test to find out. It may be too late to treat Jolanta with growth hormone, but she could be given oestrogen replacement therapy so she develops female characteristics, and this will protect her bones and heart too.

Kohlberg's theory of gender development

Kohlberg (1966) proposed that children gradually develop the ability to think about gender, progressing through stages, as they become capable of more complex and abstract thought. This is a **cognitive developmental approach**, like Piaget's theory of cognitive development, which proposes that brain maturation and experience interact to enable children's thinking to develop.

◉ Stage 1: Gender labelling
Age two to three. Children label themselves and others as boy/girl or man/woman, based on outward appearance (clothes, hairstyle). Children change the labels as appearances change: 'He has long hair now, so he must be a girl.' This is pre-operational thinking.

◉ Stage 2: Gender stability
Age four to seven. Children recognise that gender is stable over time (girls grow into women) but not over situations. They are still swayed by outward appearances. McConaghy (1979) found that young children thought a doll in a dress was female even when male genitals were visible.

◉ Stage 3: Gender constancy
Age six. Children realise gender shows **conservation** across time and situations, and realise their gender will not change. At this stage of **gender constancy**, children start to learn gender-appropriate behaviour by paying more attention to same-sex models.

◉ Evaluation
Research evidence supports Kohlberg's theory
Slaby and Frey (1975) asked young children questions like 'Were you a little girl or a little boy when you were a baby?' Children didn't recognise gender stability until three to four years old. Children who scored highly on stability and constancy showed greater interest in same-sex models.

Methodological criticism of studies with young children
Martin and Halverson (1983) re-examined the responses, concluding that the children were in 'pretend' mode. Bem (1989) argued that children use the cues that are most relevant in our society, such as clothes, and that many children didn't actually know what opposite-gender genitals look like.

The ages of the different stages may need adjusting
Slaby and Frey found that gender constancy appeared as young as age five. This may be because children have a lot more exposure to gender information nowadays, e.g. through the media. So the age bands may be younger than Kohlberg proposed.

Gender differences in development
Slaby and Frey found that boys tend to exhibit gender constancy before girls. This may be because boys are more likely to identify with same-gender role models than girls, as men are more powerful in society (see 'Social learning theory', p.46). Boys are more likely to be punished for gender-inappropriate behaviour than girls.

Gender stereotypes without constancy
Martin and Little (1990) showed that children under four display strong stereotypes about male and female behaviour. They had strong beliefs about what boys and girls were permitted to do, before they had developed gender stability, let alone gender constancy.

KEY TERMS
Conservation The ability to understand that, despite superficial changes in appearance, basic properties of an object remain unchanged. This ability appears around the age of six or seven.

Gender constancy The recognition that your gender is a constant, not just across your lifetime but also in different situations.

Pre-operational A stage in Piaget's theory of cognitive development where a child's logic lacks internal consistency.

Apply it
Scenario. Jason's father is a soldier. He is worried that Jason is not behaving like a proper boy. Jason likes wearing fairy dresses and prefers drawing pictures to fighting. However, Jason's mother thinks Jason will grow out of this phase. Jason is four years old.

Based on Kohlberg's theory of gender development, what advice could you give to Jason's parents? (4 marks)

Application. As Jason is only four, he has not reached the stage of gender constancy, so may not realise that his behaviour is unusual for a male. He will probably change his tastes in clothes as he grows up and sees that men do not wear fairy dresses. If he is given opportunities to observe men fighting he may well imitate this behaviour as he learns to identify with men.

KEY TERM

Schema A cognitive framework that helps organise and interpret information in the brain. Schemas are usually constructed from previous experience, and used to generate future expectations. They can be behavioural or cognitive.

Apply it

Scenario. Oli's parents both go out to work. Oli's mum likes doing DIY jobs at weekends, like assembling flat-pack furniture, and his dad never uses power tools but prefers to read a book. However, when Oli is shown a drill, and asked, 'Who would use this, Mummy or Daddy?', he replies, 'Daddy.' And when he is asked what Mummy and Daddy do all day, he says, 'Daddy goes to work and Mummy cleans the house.'

How does gender schema theory explain Oli's answers? (4 marks)

Application. Oli has acquired his schema from films or stories or from other families in which the father goes out to work and the mother stays at home and carries out domestic tasks. He sees a power drill as a 'boy's toy' because of advertising or other factors, like the labelling of loud, powerful objects as masculine. He sees his mum and dad contradicting these gender schemas in their behaviour, but his schemas stay intact, and he answers according to the schemas rather than his observations.

Gender schema theory (GST)

Martin and Halverson (1981) developed this cognitive approach, in which a child seeks to acquire information about their own gender.

A key difference from Kohlberg's theory is that gender labelling is sufficient for a child to pay attention to gender-appropriate behaviours. Kohlberg claimed this did not happen until after gender constancy was established.

A second difference is that GST explains how **schemas** influence memory and attention, which then affect behaviour.

◎ Schemas
Schemas are mental representations of concepts. Children learn gender schemas at about age three, from interaction with other children and adults, and from the media. Gender schemas relate to cultural norms, and 'appropriate' behaviour for men and women.

◎ Ingroup and outgroup schemas
Children identify with an ingroup: boys or girls. This leads to positive evaluation of the ingroup and negative evaluation of the outgroup: 'Boys are better than girls.' This enhances self-esteem. They actively seek information about their ingroup, to acquire gender schemas. They actively avoid outgroup behaviours.

◎ Resilience of gender beliefs
Children ignore information that is inconsistent with gender schemas, so it is very difficult to change stereotypes using counter-stereotypes. Gender beliefs can be very fixed.

◎ Peer relationships
Children believe that same-sex peers are 'like me' and share the same interests, and are therefore more fun to play with. They learn to avoid negative consequences of ignoring the schemas, such as being teased for playing with opposite-sex children.

◎ Evaluation
Research supports gender schemas forming before gender stability is reached
Martin and Little (1990) found children under four had strong gender stereotypes about what boys and girls are allowed to do. They hadn't developed gender stability or constancy. Kohlberg's theory would require children to develop constancy before understanding gender roles, at about age six.

Recent research indicates that gender identity forms even earlier
Zosuls *et al.* (2009) observed children playing, and concluded that they were using gender labels by 19 months. However, children may show gender-typed preferences even earlier than this, before gender identity, challenging gender schema theory.

Gender schemas organise memory and affect attention
Martin and Halverson (1983) found that children under six recalled more gender-consistent pictures (male firefighter, female teacher) than gender-inconsistent ones (female chemist, male nurse). Bradbard (1986) found that four- to nine-year-olds took a greater interest in toys labelled as ingroup (boys' toys) and remembered more details about them.

Gender schemas may distort information
In Martin and Halverson's study, schemas even caused distortion of memories, so that children shown a boy holding a doll (inconsistent, or counter-stereotypical) described him as a girl. A consequence of these distorted memories is that they maintain ingroup and outgroup gender schema.

Resilience of children's gender stereotypes
GST explains why children are frequently highly sexist, despite the efforts of parents and teachers to provide counter-stereotypes. However, Hoffman (1998) reported that children whose mothers work have less stereotyped views of what men do. This suggests that children are not entirely fixed in their views but are receptive to some gender-inconsistent ideas.

Psychodynamic explanation of gender development

This explanation includes the cognitive elements of **identification** and internalisation.

● Freud's psychoanalytic theory

Freud (1905) proposed that, during the phallic stage (age three to six), boys experience the **Oedipus complex**:

1. Desire their mother and want her whole attention.
2. See their father as a rival and wish he was dead.
3. Develop anxiety about their wish for their father to die. This leads to castration fear, which is repressed.
4. Eventually resolve the conflict by identification with the father, and internalisation of the father's gender identity (attitudes and behaviours).

Jung (1913) proposed that girls experience a similar process, the **Electra complex**:

1. Initially attracted to their mother, but discover she doesn't have a penis.
2. Transfer their sexual desires to their father.
3. Girls blame their mother for their lack of a penis, believing they were castrated.
4. This penis envy is later converted into a wish to have a baby, resolving anger against the mother. Eventually identify with the mother and internalise her gender behaviours.

Unresolved phallic stage

Frustration and/or overindulgence may lead to fixation at the phallic stage, and an individual who is not capable of intimacy. Freud also claimed that fixation could be a root cause of amoral behaviour and homosexuality.

● Evaluation

Support from case studies

Freud based his theory on case studies, such as Little Hans who developed a phobia of horses due to repressing his desires for his mother. Levin (1921) reported on 32 patients with bipolar disorder; 22 had unresolved Electra complex or penis envy. However, case studies can be subjectively interpreted by researchers.

Children's sexual awareness

The Oedipus and Electra complexes depend on the child having an awareness of genitals. A study by Bem (1989) found that many children aged three to five did not know what opposite-sex genitalia looked like, which would make it impossible for the Oedipus/Electra complex to develop in the way described by Freud.

The theory lacks predictive validity

It predicts that children in one-parent families or with same-sex parents would have difficulty acquiring a gender identity. Patterson (2004) found that children of lesbian parents develop gender identities in similar ways to children of heterosexual parents, and have normal social relationships.

Alternative psychodynamic explanations

Chodorow (1994) suggested that mothers and daughters are closer because they are the same sex, whereas boys become more independent. This is supported by observations that mother–daughter pairs play more closely than mother–son pairs (Goldberg & Lewis, 1969).

Gender bias in Freud's theory

Feminists dismiss Freud's idea of inferior female development due to penis envy. Freud admitted he didn't really understand women. Many people also object to the idea that young children experience sexual drives. However, Lacan (1966) suggested that penis envy can be considered as a symbolic envy of male power in a male-dominated society.

KEY TERMS

Electra complex A stage in girls' gender development according to psychodynamic theory.

Identification An individual adopts an attitude or behaviour because they want to be associated with a particular person or group.

Internalisation An individual accepts the attitudes or behaviour of another.

Oedipus complex A stage in boys' gender development according to Freudian theory.

Apply it

Scenario (from Freud's case study of Little Hans). At three years old, Hans was interested in his penis and liked playing with it, but his mother didn't like this behaviour and threatened to get a doctor to cut it off. At four, Hans developed a phobia of horses, which became generalised anxiety about leaving the house, and Hans's father started objecting to Hans climbing into his parents' bed in the morning to cuddle his mother.

Using this information, and your knowledge of Freud's psychoanalytic theory, how would Freud interpret the causes of Hans's phobia? (4 marks)

Application. Interested in his penis: phallic stage age three to six, libido focused on the genitals.

Mother threatened to cut it off: castration anxiety.

Phobia of horses: horse represented his father, who he wished was dead (a rival for his mother's love). General anxiety from repressing his wish to kill his father.

Wanted to cuddle his mother in bed: sexual desire for his mother.

His father objected: reinforced the rivalry.

KEY TERM

Social learning theory Learning through observing others and imitating behaviours that are rewarded.

Social learning theory (SLT) as applied to gender development

Bandura explained that we learn indirectly from other people (models) by observing and imitating their behaviour, as well as directly through classical and operant conditioning (association and reinforcement). Gender role development is the result of learning from social agents who model and reinforce gender role behaviours (Bandura, 1991).

Indirect reinforcement

Children observe the gender behaviour of others from home, school and the media. They learn, from the consequences, whether the behaviour is worth repeating (**vicarious reinforcement**). Girls **identify** with other females and are more likely to **imitate** their behaviour. Boys may also observe their mother's behaviour at home but are less likely to imitate it.

The role of mediational processes

Bandura called **social learning theory** a social cognitive theory. Children store information about reinforcements as mental representations which create an expectancy of future outcomes. They will then display the behaviour if the expectation of reward is greater than the expectation of punishment.

Direct reinforcement

Reinforcement (e.g. praise) of gender behaviour increases the likelihood that a child will repeat it; punishment (e.g. disparaging remarks) reduces it.

Direct tuition

When children acquire linguistic skills, they learn appropriate gender behaviour through explicit instructions such as 'Be ladylike'.

Self-direction

Bandura believed that people internalise gender-appropriate behaviours, then actively direct their own behaviour. He called this environmental determinism. Behaviour has been **internalised** and is no longer dependent on external reinforcement.

Evaluation

Evidence to support modelling

Bandura's Bobo dolls studies (1961) showed children's imitation of adults' aggressive behaviour. Perry and Bussey (1979) found that children preferentially selected the fruit they had observed a same-sex model choosing. Children only imitated behaviour if it didn't contradict stereotypes (e.g. a man wearing a dress).

Direct tuition may be more effective than modelling

Martin *et al.* (1995) found that boys played with toys labelled 'boys' toys' even if they saw girls playing with them. They didn't play with 'girls' toys' even when they saw boys playing with them. Adults' behaviour sometimes contradicts their direct tuition, which weakens the effect of teaching (Hildebrandt, 1973).

Peers as gender influences

Lamb and Roopnarine (1979) observed that reinforcement of male-type behaviour in pre-school girls was less long-lasting than reinforcement of male-type behaviour in boys. And later in childhood, peers may simply reinforce existing stereotypes. This suggests that the role of peers is more as a reminder of existing gender-role stereotypes rather than replacing them with new ones.

Self-direction

Bussey and Bandura (1992) showed children (aged three to four) videos of other children playing with masculine or feminine toys. The younger children disapproved of others but not themselves for gender-inconsistent behaviour, whereas older children disapproved of both. These evaluations were confirmed by the children's actual choices of toys in play.

Too much emphasis on social process

Social learning theory largely ignores the role of biological influences in shaping gender role. For example, research has shown that testosterone during prenatal development creates a more 'masculine' brain and a tendency to certain types of behaviour. Cross-cultural research (e.g. Buss' research on partner choice) also indicates there are universals in the way that men and women behave which in turn supports the role of biology. Such universal similarities suggest that biology plays an important role in shaping gender behaviour, and that social factors merely refine it.

Apply it

Scenario. Annabelle, age 16, is often told by her parents that she is not being ladylike, and that she should wear a skirt when they go out as a family, not jeans. However, her friends rarely wear skirts and seem to have lots of fun.

Use social learning theory to explain how this might affect Annabelle's behaviour. (16 marks)

Application extract. Annabelle receives direct tuition from her parents, 'should wear a skirt', and also direct punishment – the criticism 'not being ladylike'. However, she also receives modelling from peers of wearing jeans, and vicarious reinforcement as they seem to be having fun. There is a conflict between these two influences; she is old enough to make her own choice and weigh up the likely punishment from her mother vs the expectation of reward she has gained from observing peers.

Evidence from research by Martin *et al.* suggests that Annabelle may be more affected by direct tuition. Lamb and Roopnarine's research suggests that peers merely reinforce existing gender-role stereotypes, so Annabelle's peers may have less influence over her behaviour than she imagines.

Cultural and media influences on gender roles

Gender roles are the different behaviours, jobs, tasks and duties that men and women take on.

◎ Cultural influences

The gender rules of a **culture** underlie stereotypes. They influence peer and parental reinforcement via social learning. Gender rules relate to customs, morals, childrearing practices and relationships.

Cultural differences: Mead (1935) found **cultural role differences** between three social groups in Papua New Guinea; Arapesh men and women were gentle and cooperative, Mundugumor men and women were violent and competitive, whereas Tchambuli women were dominant.

People across cultures believe that women are more conformist than men, but conformity actually varies (Berry *et al.*, 2002), and is highest in tight, sedentary (non-nomadic) societies.

Cultures can change with time, e.g. UK women perform more domestic duties than men but the gender gap is decreasing.

Some cultures recognise a third gender, such as the hijras in India.

◎ The influence of the media

Media **role models** perpetuate gender stereotypes. **Vicarious reinforcement** affects people's self-efficacy about their ability to master gender-consistent or inconsistent activities.

On the other hand, the media can present counter-stereotypes which reduce children's adherence to stereotypes (Pingree, 1978).

Usually, men are portrayed as independent and directive, whereas women are shown as dependent, unambitious and emotional (Bussey & Bandura, 1999). Men are more likely than women to be shown controlling events (Hodges *et al.*, 1981) and women in adverts are shown as more flawless and passive than men (Conley & Ramsey, 2011).

◎ Evaluation

Cultural differences

The evidence for cultural differences shows how culture influences gender roles, but there is contrasting evidence that shows that biology is at least as important. For example, social role theory (Eagly & Wood, 1999) argues that the biologically based physical differences between men and women allow them to perform certain tasks more efficiently. This suggests that although cultural influences are important in the development of gender roles, they are not the only influence.

Cross-cultural research may suffer from observer bias and subjective interpretation

Freeman (1984) criticised Mead's research as invalid, as the indigenous people had given a false picture of their behaviour. Mead later changed her conclusions, noting that there were more similarities than differences between males and females. This weakens the support of her research for cultural differences in gender roles.

Research evidence supporting the role of media influence

The Notel study by Williams (1985) compared children's stereotypes before and after the introduction of TV to their remote Canadian valley. After TV arrived, the children's views had become significantly more sex-stereotyped.

Media effects may be insignificant

Research suggests that simply exposing children to gender stereotypes is not sufficient to change attitudes. It seems that the media's effect is simply to reinforce the status quo. For example, Signorelli and Bacue (1999) examined the effects of over 30 years of TV programming and found very little change in gender stereotypes as a result of media exposure.

Counter-stereotyping and backlash

Counter-stereotypes can change expectations about gender role. However, Pingree (1978) found that pre-adolescent boys display stronger stereotypes after exposure to non-traditional models. In addition, gender-inconsistent messages are mis-remembered (Martin & Halverson, 1983). This can make it difficult to use the media to change stereotypes.

KEY TERMS

Culture The rules, customs, morals, childrearing practices, etc. that bind a group of people together and define how they are likely to behave.

Media Tools used to store and distribute information, e.g. books, films, TV, commercials.

Apply it

Scenario. A study of Harvard Law School classrooms found that, in a class with a male instructor, men spoke two and a half times longer than their female classmates. However, when a female instructor led the classroom, they had 'an inspiring effect on female students', leading women to speak three times as much as they did with a male instructor.

Suggest why the difference occurs with a female instructor, and what the effects of this could be. (6 marks)

Application. The female instructor 'had an inspiring effect' on the female students, as she was a counter-stereotypical role model, a confident professional woman who took a lead and talked to the class a lot. As the instructor, she would probably be talking more than the students. This challenges stereotypes of female reticence or shyness, and enables female students to identify with her and imitate her behaviour. In contrast, male students may identify less with a female instructor and therefore be quieter. Also, there is the possibility that the female instructor was deliberately encouraging female students to talk, by targeting them with questions or by direct tuition, telling them that they need to practise talking to be successful lawyers.

KEY TERM

Gender identity disorder Individuals experience gender dysphoria (confusion), with strong persistent identification with the opposite gender and discomfort with their own.

Atypical gender development

Gender identity disorder (GID) is a condition listed in *DSM-V*, also known as gender dysphoria, transgender and transsexual, and characterised by discomfort with one's assigned gender. Male to female (MtF) outnumber female to male (FtM) by about 5:1. GID does *not* include intersex conditions where abnormal chromosomes or hormones cause a mismatch between gender identity and sexual characteristics.

◉ Biological explanations of GID
The brain-sex theory suggests that transsexuals' brains do not match their genetic sex. For example, the BSTc area of the thalamus is larger in men than women, and its size correlates with preferred gender rather than biological sex (Zhou *et al.*, 1995).

A 'transsexual gene', a longer version of the androgen receptor gene, reduces sensitivity to testosterone and may under-masculinise the brain. MtF transsexuals are more likely to have this gene (Hare *et al.*, 2009).

Ramachandran (2008) suggested that GID is due to innate **cross-wiring**, in which the sensory cortex is connected differently. So two-thirds of FtM transsexuals report the sensation of a phantom penis.

Some **environmental pollutants**, such as pesticides, contain oestrogens, which could affect foetal development. Vreugdenhil *et al.* (2002) found that boys with mothers who had been exposed to dioxins displayed feminised play.

◉ Social explanations of GID
Overly close **mother–son relationships** could lead to greater female identification in boys. Stoller (1975) observed overly close and enmeshed mother–son relationships in males with GID.

Females with poor **father–daughter relationships** could identify as males, unconsciously hoping to gain acceptance from their father.

Another explanation is **childhood trauma** or maladaptive upbringing at a critical stage of gender development.

◉ Evaluation
Criticisms of the brain-sex theory
Chung *et al.* (2002) noted that the BSTc is the same size in males and females until adulthood, whereas most transsexuals report their gender dysphoria as starting in early childhood. Also, people in the BSTc studies had received hormone therapy, which could have affected their BSTc size.

Support for cross-wiring
Ramachandran and McGeoch (2007) report that 60% of non-GID men and only 30% of GID men experience a phantom penis after penis amputation (e.g. for cancer). In addition, only 10% of FtM patients experience phantom breasts after surgery to remove breasts.

Support for social explanations
Zucker *et al.* (1996) found that 64% of boys with GID also had separation anxiety disorder, compared to 38% of boys with some gender concerns but not diagnosed with GID. However, Cole *et al.* (1997) found no more psychiatric conditions in 435 people with GID than in a normal population.

More than one explanation is needed
Furuhashi (2011) studied 27 Japanese males; some experienced GID since childhood, and others only since adolescence. Blanchard (1985) identified 'homosexual transsexuals' and 'non-homosexual transsexuals', who are aroused by the fantasy of themselves as a woman. There may be different explanations for different types of GID.

Social consequences of GID diagnosis
There are potential social consequences for individuals with GID, if causes are found. If a biological cause is identified, it might also help society to be more accepting for those identified as possessing this biological vulnerability. Either way, researchers should be sensitive to potential social consequences for individuals with GID.

Apply it

Scenario. Nina is 12 years old. Ever since she can remember, she has much preferred socialising with boys rather than girls. Most of her hobbies are typically masculine, and she is often mistaken for a boy because of the way that she dresses. She has recently told her parents that she wants to rename herself Nathan, and wants to be referred to as 'he'.

Discuss both biological and social explanations of gender identity disorder. Refer to the case of Nina as part of your answer. (16 marks)

Explanation extract. Nina may have biological differences causing her to identify as a boy: differences in brain areas, or 'cross-wiring', so that she has the sensation of a phantom penis (Ramachandran). According to a social psychological explanation, she may have a poor father–daughter relationship and feel rejected by her father as a girl, hoping to be more affirmed as 'Nathan'. Or it may be a social/cultural explanation, that she feels she doesn't fit cultural stereotypes of femaleness because of her typically masculine hobbies and clothing, and gets on better with boys, so she identifies more with boys and wants to be one. …

Chapter 5

Cognition and development

Paper 3, Section B, option 3. 4.3.4 Cognition and development
- Piaget's theory of cognitive development: schemas, assimilation, accommodation, equilibration, stages of intellectual development. Characteristics of these stages, including object permanence, conservation, egocentrism and class inclusion.
- Vygotsky's theory of cognitive development, including the zone of proximal development and scaffolding.
- Baillargeon's explanation of early infant abilities, including knowledge of the physical world; violation of expectation research.
- The development of social cognition: Selman's levels of perspective-taking; theory of mind, including theory of mind as an explanation for autism; the Sally–Anne study. The role of the mirror neuron system in social cognition.

Key terms (highlight each cell when you can define the term confidently)

Piaget's theory	Piaget's stages of intellectual development	Vygotsky's theory	Baillargeon's theory	Selman's levels of perspective-taking	Role of the mirror neuron system
Accommodation	Class inclusion	Scaffolding	*False belief*	*Perspective-taking*	Mirror neurons
Assimilation	Conservation	Zone of proximal development	*Nativist approach*	*Social cognition*	
Cognitive development	Egocentrism		*Physical reasoning system*	Autism	
Equilibration	Object permanence		Violation of expectation research	Sally–Anne test	
Schema				Theory of mind	

Content checklist

1. *In each 'describe', 'apply' and 'evaluate' cell tick when you have produced brief notes.*
2. *Once you feel you have a good grasp of the topic add a second tick to the cell.*
3. *When you feel you have complete mastery of the topic and would be able to answer an exam question without the aid of notes highlight the cell.*

I am able to …	Describe	Apply	Evaluate
Piaget's theory of cognitive development: schemas, assimilation, accommodation, equilibration			
Piaget's stages of intellectual development and characteristics of these stages, including object permanence, conservation, egocentrism and class inclusion			
Vygotsky's theory of cognitive development, including the zone of proximal development and scaffolding			
Baillargeon's explanation of early infant abilities, including knowledge of the physical world			
Baillargeon's violation of expectation research			
The development of social cognition: Selman's levels of perspective-taking			
Theory of mind, including theory of mind as an explanation for autism; the Sally–Anne study			
The role of the mirror neuron system in social cognition			

KEY TERMS

Accommodation The process of adjusting or changing existing schemas because new, conflicting information creates disequilibrium.

Assimilation The process of fitting new experiences into an existing schema without making any change to the schema.

Cognitive development The process by which our mental processes change as we age.

Equilibration Experiencing a balance between existing schemas and new experiences.

Schema A cognitive framework that helps organise and interpret information in the brain. Schemas are usually constructed from previous experience, and used to generate future expectations. They can be behavioural or cognitive.

Apply it

Scenario. Alisha takes her two nephews, aged three and six, to the zoo. Her youngest nephew shouts out 'cat' whenever he sees animals with four legs, fur and a long tail. Her older nephew, who has been to the zoo before, is able to distinguish between lions, tigers and leopards.

How might Piaget's theory of cognitive development explain the difference between Alisha's two nephews?
(4 marks)

Explanation. Alisha's younger nephew has a schema for 'cat' which he is using to understand the new animals he meets at the zoo. As these animals also have four legs, fur and a long tail, he can assimilate them into his existing schema. Alisha's older nephew's previous visit to the zoo led to his existing 'cat' schema changing to accommodate new information, e.g. mane = lion, stripes = tiger and spots = leopard. When he began to notice the difference between the creatures, a state of imbalance would have been experienced. Equilibration is the experience of balance between existing schema and new experiences which was achieved when the 'cat' schema was changed to accommodate different species of 'big cats'.

Piaget's theory of cognitive development

Piaget believed **cognitive development** resulted from *maturation* – with age, certain mental operations become possible – and *environment* – through interactions understanding of the world becomes more complex.

Mechanisms of cognitive development

◯ Schemas

Children are born with a few **schemas** such as the grasping reflex and mental representation of the human face. From birth onwards schemas develop as a result of environmental interactions. New experiences lead to the development of new schemas, e.g. learning separate schemas for the different faces of family members and learning to distinguish between cats and dogs.

◯ Assimilation, accommodation and equilibration

Assimilation: When trying to understand new information the existing schema is applied. When new information can be incorporated into the existing schema assimilation occurs, e.g. an infant may suck a new teddy in the same way it already sucked their rattle.

Accommodation: The process of changing the existing schema when new information cannot be assimilated, e.g. a child may have the schema 'four legs and fur = dog'. Every new creature with the same features is assimilated into the schema. One day someone uses the word 'cat' for a four-legged, furry animal which challenges the current schema (it cannot be assimilated). A new schema is developed: 'four legs, fur and a tail that doesn't wag = cat'.

Equilibration: If an experience cannot be assimilated into existing schemas, an unpleasant state of imbalance occurs. The individual seeks to restore balance through equilibration. Cognitive development is the result of adaptation between the existing schema and the environment's 'demands' for change.

Lifespan learning
Throughout our life new experiences are either assimilated or accommodated by creating new schemas. However, a young child cannot always accommodate new experiences because his or her mind is simply not mature enough (see p.51 for stages of cognitive development).

◯ Evaluation

Research shows that face schemas are innate
Fantz (1961) showed four-day-old infants preferred a schematic face over a face where the same features were jumbled up. This suggests infants chose the unique configuration of facial features over a complex pattern; however, it is not clear whether this is just due to a preference for symmetry. An innate face preference would have an adaptive advantage – a newborn who can recognise and respond to its own species will better elicit attachment and caring.

Equilibration is difficult to demonstrate
Inhelder *et al.* (1974) demonstrated that mild conflict between what is expected and what happened helped children's learning. Bryant (1995) criticises this research, arguing this wasn't the sort of conflict Piaget was describing – Piaget's conflict was a more major discord between two things. This is a general issue with Piaget's theory – some theoretical aspects are not really testable because concepts are difficult to operationalise.

Important implications for education
Piaget (1970) stated, 'Each time one prematurely teaches a child something he could have discovered for himself, that child is kept from inventing it and consequently from understanding it completely.' In contrast, Bennett (1976) found that children taught via formal methods performed better on reading, maths and English. The lack of success of 'discovery learning' may be because more time is spent on core topics and discovery learning requires sensitive teachers who know how to guide students.

The role of language
Piaget argued cognitive maturity is a prerequisite for linguistic development. This was supported by Sinclair-de-Zwart (1969) who demonstrated language differences in 'non-conservers' and 'conservers'. Non-conservers tended to use absolute terms (e.g. big) rather than comparative terms (e.g. larger). They also used a single term for different dimensions, such as 'small' to mean 'short', 'thin' or 'few'. When non-conservers were taught verbal skills, 90% were still unable to conserve. This contradicts Vygotsky's view that language is fundamental to cognitive development (see p.52).

A comprehensive theory
Piaget produced the first comprehensive theory of children's cognitive development. It has been more extensively developed than any other theory and has had a general influence on educational practice. His theory has been widely researched and is valued for its combination of nature (biological maturation) and nurture (experience). Piaget's concept of nurture focused on the physical environment while Vygotsky emphasised the importance of the social environment (see p.52).

Piaget's stages of intellectual development

◉ Stage 1: Sensorimotor stage (0–2 years)
The infant first learns how to co-ordinate sensory input with motor actions. 'Circular reactions' describe how an infant repeats actions over and over to test sensorimotor relationships. Around eight months children gain **object permanence**. Previously, very young infants lose interest in an object when it is hidden behind a pillow as they assume it ceases to exist.

◉ Stage 2: Pre-operational stage (2–7 years)
'Operations' describe internally consistent logical mental rules. Pre-operational children lack logic-based reasoning, meaning they rely on appearance rather than reality. In **conservation** tasks, a pre-operational child fails to see the logic that volume cannot change (they fail to 'conserve' volume), e.g. when shown two rows of six counters and then one row is spread out to look longer, the children do not realise they still contain the same amount.

Thinking is **egocentric**. The three mountains task revealed children could not select the picture that represented the doll's perspective, choosing the picture showing their own view instead.

Another quality of thinking at this stage relates to **class inclusion**. Children can classify objects into categories but have difficulty considering sub-groups. For example, Piaget showed children four toy cows – three black and one white. When asked, 'Are there more black cows or more cows?', the children answered, 'More black cows.'

◉ Stage 3: Concrete operational stage (7–11 years)
Children acquire the basics of logical reasoning. Conservation is the single most important achievement at this stage because it provides evidence of the child's command of logical operations. What children lack is the ability to think abstractly.

◉ Stage 4: Formal operational stage (11+ years)
Children can now solve abstract problems using hypothetico-deductive reasoning. They think like a scientist: developing hypotheses and testing them to determine causal relationships. Children also display idealistic thinking – they are no longer limited to how things are but can imagine how things might be if certain changes were made.

◉ Evaluation
Piaget's methods may have made children appear less capable
While Bryant (1995) described Piaget's tasks as simple yet ingenious investigations of quite complex topics, critics argue their design may have confused children. McGarrigle and Donaldson (1974) showed that when 'naughty teddy' messed up the counters making one row longer, young children coped better because the change was explained by teddy's behaviour. In Piaget's version, the deliberate transformation implied that an alternative response to 'Are they the same?' was required. Hughes (1975) asked children to suggest where a naughty doll could hide from the policeman in a version of the three mountains task. In this more realistic task, children were able to take another's perspective.

The idea of biologically driven stages is correct
Piaget may have underestimated young children's abilities, and overestimated the ability to use abstract logic. (Dasen (1994) claims only a third of adults ever reach the formal operational stage.) However, evidence still supports qualitative changes in thinking linked to maturation. While the notion of fixed stages may be too rigid, it could be viewed as a useful model for understanding behaviour and generating research.

Piaget's theory may not be universally applicable
Piaget came from a middle-class European background and studied children from European academic families who valued academic abilities. This might be why he placed considerable value on the role of logical operations in cognitive development. Other cultures and classes may place greater value on a more basic level of concrete operations, e.g. making things rather than abstract thinking.

Important applications for education
For real learning to take place, Piaget suggests activities should be at the appropriate level for the child's age. If an activity is pitched above the child's current level, then any learning taking place will be superficial at best. The Plowden Report (1967) drew extensively on this view and led to major changes in UK primary education. The assumption that development of cognitive structures is related to maturity, meaning practice should not improve performance, has received some research support. In contrast, Bryant and Trabasso (1995) found that training could improve performance.

Alternative explanations and conclusions
Vygotsky provides a useful counterpoint to Piaget's theory (see p.52), suggesting that development can be explained in terms of social rather than individual factors. Nonetheless, Piaget's theory has had an enormous influence on education practices and psychological research. Bryant (1995) reminds us that Piaget's key contribution was to highlight the radical differences in thinking between young children and adults.

KEY TERMS
Class inclusion The relation between two classes where all members of one class are included in the other, e.g. the category 'animal' includes sub-groups such as cats and dogs, which can further be divided into breeds.

Conservation The ability to understand that, despite superficial changes in appearance, basic properties of an object remain unchanged. This ability appears around the age of six or seven.

Egocentrism Seeing things from your own viewpoint and being unaware of other possible viewpoints.

Object permanence A child's understanding that objects that are no longer visible nevertheless continue to exist.

Apply it
Scenario. Last year Mr Sampa taught the Year 6 class at Merrydale Primary School. This year he has taken over the school's Reception class. By his own admission he sometimes finds he overestimates the Reception children's abilities and has had to re-plan a number of his lessons.

With reference to Mr Sampa's experience, discuss Piaget's stages of intellectual development. (16 marks)

Explanation extract… The children in Mr Sampa's Year 6 class would be at the concrete operational stage of intellectual development (7–11 years) and so would be able to understand the basics of logical reasoning. For example, if Mr Sampa showed the class two glasses each containing the same amount of water, then poured one of the glasses into a tall, thin glass, the children would know the new glass still holds the same amount of water. The children in Reception class would not be able to understand this conservation task as they are in the pre-operational stage (2–7 years), meaning their reasoning is based on what they see rather than what is reality. Mr Sampa has to re-plan his lessons as, according to Piaget, children are not biologically ready to be taught certain concepts until they have reached a certain age. …

KEY TERMS

Scaffolding An approach to instruction that aims to support a learner only when absolutely necessary, i.e. to provide a support framework (scaffold) to assist the learning process. Scaffolding describes the process whereby a learner is assisted through their ZPD.

Semiotics The signs and symbols developed within a particular culture, e.g. language and mathematical symbols.

Zone of proximal development The 'region' between a person's current ability, which they can perform with no assistance, and their potential capabilities, which they can be helped to achieve with the assistance of 'experts'.

Vygotsky's theory

Vygotsky agreed with Piaget that a child's thinking is qualitatively different from adults. However, he placed much greater emphasis on the importance of culture influences (interactions with others and language).

Elementary and higher mental functions

Children are born with *elementary* mental functions, e.g. memory, perception. The role of culture is to transform these basic, biological functions into *higher* mental functions, e.g. use of mathematical systems.

The role of others: experts

Experts are individuals who possess greater knowledge than the child. The child learns through sharing problem-solving experiences with the expert. Initially the expert guides the activity, but gradually the responsibility transfers to the child.

The role of language

Experts transmit culture to the child using **semiotics**. Initally, language takes the form of shared dialogues between the adult and child (pre-intellectual speech), but as the child develops mental representation, he or she is able to communicate with themselves to enable intellectual development.

The social and individual level

Every function in the child's cognitive development appears first on the social level (between the expert and the child) and then on the individual level (inside the child). The social experience enables the development of higher mental functions. Both social and individual experiences depend on the use of semiotics.

The zone of proximal development (ZPD)

Learning does not occur in the current area of development, as nothing new would be learned. Nor does it take place too far ahead of what the child can already do independently, as the new challenges would be too far from the child's current knowledge to be useful. Learning occurs in the ZPD between these two positions.

Scaffolding

The expert creates a 'scaffold' (temporary support) which is gradually withdrawn. Wood and Middleton (1975) observed mothers supporting their three- to four-year-old in assembling a 3D pyramid puzzle (a task beyond the child's current abilities). Mothers provided more explicit instructions if the child experienced failure and less explicit instructions when the child was successful. Successful scaffolding depends on 'contingent regulations': the teaching needs to adjust according to the learner's response.

Evaluation

Evidence for the role of culture

Vygotsky's claims about the role of culture in cognitive development have been supported in cross-cultural research. For example, Gredler (1992) pointed to the primitive counting system used in Papua New Guinea as an example of how culture can limit cognitive development. This system, which uses the thumb, fingers and arm, makes it very difficult to add and subtract large numbers, a limiting factor for cognitive development in this culture.

Evidence for the role of language

Carmichael *et al.* (1932) support the suggestion that the acquisition of a new word is the beginning of the development of a concept. Participants were given one of two labels for certain drawings, e.g. a kidney shape was labelled as either a kidney bean or a canoe. When later asked to draw the shape, the images produced represented the label seen. On the other hand, Sinclair-de-Zwart (1969) found teaching children who could not conserve comparative terms like 'bigger' and 'shorter' did not improve their ability to conserve, challenging the view that language leads to cognitive development.

Experts adjust input according to the learners' ZPD

McNaughton and Leyland (1990) observed young children and their mothers working on increasingly difficult puzzles. Mothers offered little help if the puzzle was too easy (below the child's ZPD). If the puzzle was of moderate difficulty (within the ZPD), the child was supported to solve the puzzle themselves. A puzzle that was too difficult (beyond the ZPD) increased rate of intervention.

Relatively little research support

Compared to the wealth of research into Piaget's theory, there is relatively little research relating to Vygotsky's ideas. Vygotsky's concepts are more difficult to operationalise and so the theory does not lend itself to experimentation.

Vygotsky may have overplayed the importance of the social environment

If all that was needed was social input we would expect learning to be a lot faster. The emphasis on social factors also means biological factors are largely ignored. Finally, the theory is criticised for lacking detail, although this is partly because Vygotsky died at a young age and did not have time to develop his theory (Lindblom & Ziemke, 2003).

Apply it

Scenario. Terry is helping his daughter learn to ride a bike. She can ride easily with stabilisers, but now that Terry has removed them she is really struggling. Terry decides to hold the back of the bike seat with one hand and the handle bars with the other to help his daughter understand the need to balance. When she is able to pedal in a straight line he tries just holding the back of the seat.

Using your knowledge of Vygotsky's theory, explain how Terry is supporting his daughter's cognitive development. (3 marks)

Explanation. Terry would be seen as an expert as he understands how to ride a bike. His daughter can ride a bike with stabilisers (her current area of development) but cannot yet ride without assistance (this is beyond what she can do independently). Terry is scaffolding her learning as he is assisting her through her zone of proximal development. Terry knows balance is important when riding, so he uses strategies that will help his daughter develop her balance. She is learning about the importance of maintaining her balance before she develops this skill for herself.

Baillargeon's research

Baillargeon suggested the reason why young infants did not show object permanence was not because of a lack of mental ability, but because they could not plan and execute the motor abilities needed to search for the hidden object.

● Key study: Violation of expectation (VOE)

Baillargeon and DeVos (1991) proposed an impossible event will elicit surprise in infants – violation of expectation research.

How? A large or small carrot travelled along a track, at one point being hidden by a screen with a large window cut into it. The top half of the large carrot should be visible in the screen's window while the small carrot would not be seen. The impossible event would be a large carrot passing behind the screen but not appearing in the window.

Showed? Children as young as three months demonstrated object permanence, something Piaget states doesn't develop until around eight months. The infants looked longer at the large carrot as if they expected to see it in the window – they understood the principle of occlusion (what happens when an object is obstructed by another).

KEY TERMS

False belief The understanding that others may hold and act on mistaken (false) beliefs.

Nativist approach A theory that suggests humans are born with innate abilities.

Physical reasoning system An innate system that provides a framework for reasoning about the displacements and interactions of physical objects.

Violation of expectation research A method of conducting research with infants using their surprise as a measure of whether what they see is not what they expect to see. Thus we know what their expectations are.

Habituation events

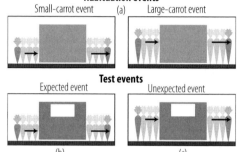

Small-carrot event · (a) · Large-carrot event

Test events

Expected event · Unexpected event

(b) · (c)

▲ An example of a violation of expectation task. The infant is first shown the carrots moving along the track in the habituation events (first row labelled (a)) to get used to the activity.

In the test events (second row), the infant sees a small or large carrot going past a window (b) and (c). If the child understands object permanence, he/she should be surprised when the large carrot does not appear in the window in picture (c).

● Explaining an infant's knowledge of the physical world

Baillargeon *et al.* (2009) suggested infants are born with a **physical reasoning system** (PRS) that helps them interpret and learn from experience. Initially, reasoning about a novel phenomenon takes the form of an all-or-nothing concept. Later, variables that may affect the concept are added. In the case of the unveiling phenomenon (covering principle), Baillargeon (1994) suggests the following developmental sequence:

1. Infants form the concept that a protuberance indicates an object, e.g. infants aged nine and a half months show surprise when a cover with a protuberance showing is removed and no object is seen but are not surprised if an object smaller than the protuberance is revealed.

2. Later they identify a variable that affects this relationship, e.g. by 12.5 months the mismatch between size of the protuberance and object revealed elicits surprise.

The process of initial understanding of a concept and then later incorporation of variables occurs for all other physical relations, demonstrating the application of innate learning mechanisms.

● An infant's knowledge of the psychological world

Song and Baillargeon (2008) used VOE to test **false beliefs** in very young children. Children watched a woman repeatedly reach for a doll with blue pigtails when offered a choice between this toy and toy skunk (implying a preference for the doll). Out of the sight of the woman the skunk was placed in a box that had blue hair protruding from it while the doll was placed in a plain box. The infant knew where the doll was, but could they predict where the woman would think the doll was? Infants as young as 14.5 months showed surprise when the woman opened the box without blue hair, suggesting they expected the woman to hold a false belief (that the doll was in the box with the blue hair showing).

Apply it

Scenario. Sami is planning a violation of expectation study to investigate whether infants have an understanding of object permanence.

What advice would you offer Sami to improve the validity of his research? (4 marks)

Explanation. First, Sami needs to avoid a biased sample. For example, Piaget is criticised for using infants from middle-class families. Sami could approach families who place birth announcements in newspapers to obtain a more diverse sample. Second, Sami needs to reduce the possibility of parents unconsciously communicating cues to the child during the VOE procedure. He should instruct parents to close their eyes and not to talk to their child. Finally, he should use a double-blind study. The observers should only see the infant's face when judging whether surprise is shown, and they should not be able to see the event the child can see so that they do not know whether it is possible or impossible, as this knowledge may bias their observations.

Evaluation

Carefully controlled research

Baillargeon and DeVos used birth announcements in the local paper to produce a less biased sample (compared to Piaget's middle-class sample). To avoid parents communicating cues to the child on their lap, parents shut their eyes and did not interact with the child. Finally, each trial had two observers noting the level of interest shown by the child in a double-blind design – the observers were not aware of the event occurring (possible or impossible) to avoid their judgements being biased.

Internal validity of the VOE method may be low

Is the VOE method actually measuring surprise? Infants may look longer at an impossible event because it contains one or more features that are interesting, not because the event violates expectations. Schlesinger and Casey (2003) found that infants' gaze was different during possible and impossible tasks. This suggests interest in impossible tasks is better explained by perceptual interest rather than interest being due to an unexpected occurrence.

Alternative explanations of infants' knowledge of the physical world

Baillargeon's **nativist approach** proposes infants are born with innate mechanisms allowing rapid acquisition of knowledge. Spelke, another nativist, offers a contrasting explanation: rather than innate mechanisms, she proposes infants are born with substantial knowledge regarding objects – *innate principles*. Spelke *et al.* (1992) argue that infants are born with core knowledge which includes a basic understanding of the physical world. Baillargeon criticises this suggestion, arguing that innate principles would mean infants should demonstrate expectations about all events relating to one core principle (e.g. occlusion) at the same time, but this is not supported by research evidence.

Was Piaget right after all?

Bremner (2013) points out that infants' surprise and interest does not necessarily mean they understand the principle of object permanence. Piaget saw cognitive development as not simply acting in accordance with the principle but rather being able to understand the principle. Furthermore, while Baillargeon's research might suggest Piaget underestimated infants' abilities, it does not challenge the assumption that certain mental abilities appear with maturation.

The effect of different experiences

The suggestion that infants possess innate mechanisms driving development could be tested by considering the abilities of children from different cultures. If such research showed that different experiences lead to different rates of development, then Baillargeon's approach would be challenged. While Baillargeon herself did not study the effect of experience on development, her inventive methods for studying infants' abilities have enabled further research in this field.

Selman's levels of perspective-taking

Selman's perspective-taking dilemmas

Selman (1971) presented children with dilemmas. For example, Holly is an eight-year-old girl who likes to climb trees. After falling out of a tree her father makes her promise to stop climbing. Later that day she and her friends see a kitten stuck in a tree. Only Holly is able to climb well enough to rescue the cat but she remembers the promise to her father. Selman then asked children, 'If Holly climbs the tree should she be punished?', 'Will her father understand if she climbs the tree?', 'Will her friend Sean understand if Holly refuses to help the kitten?'

Selman's five stage theory

Selman's analysis of children's responses revealed a pattern of age-related reasoning, leading him to construct a developmental model of perspective-taking. A key feature is the progression from egocentrism to the ability to consider multiple perspectives and social norms.

Stage 0 – Undifferentiated perspective-taking. Approx. age 3–6 years	Able to distinguish between self and others but largely governed by own perspective, e.g. Holly's dad will not be mad as he will think the same as Holly.
Stage 1 – Social informational perspective-taking. Approx. age 6–8 years	Aware of different perspectives but assume this is because others are aware of different information, e.g. Holly's dad wouldn't be mad if Holly shows him the kitten, he will change his mind.
Stage 2 – Self-reflective perspective-taking. Approx. age 8–10 years	Now able to view their own thoughts and feelings from another's perspective and recognise that others do the same, e.g. Holly's dad will understand why Holly saved the kitten.
Stage 3 – Mutual perspective-taking. Approx. age 10–12 years	Can imagine how the self and others would be viewed from a third, impartial party. Can consider two viewpoints at once, e.g. Holly's dad will be able to understand his and her viewpoint.
Stage 4 – Societal perspective-taking. Approx. age 12–15+ years	Personal decisions are made with reference to social conventions, e.g. Holly's dad will not be mad because it is important to treat animals humanely.

Relation to deception (planting a false belief in another's mind)

Deception is an outcome of perspective-taking that children usually master around the age of three, e.g. Cole (1986) found that at this age children could hide their disappointment at receiving the worst present when watched by others but did show disappointment when filmed covertly.

Evaluation

Research support for stage theory

Selman's (1971) original sample of 225 participants had an age range of 4 ½ to 32 years of age. Two years later, 48 of the boys were re-interviewed by Cooney and Selman (published 1978) who found 40 of the boys had made gains in their level of perspective-taking and none had regressed. Three years later, analysis of 41 boys again showed no regression or skipping stages (Gurucharri & Selman, published 1982). This sequence may be due to the stages being closely related to the stages of development proposed by Piaget (Keating & Clarke, 1980).

Research support for the role of experience

Even if stages of development are biologically driven, the role of experience is well supported. FitzGerald and White (2003) found children showed more development when parents encouraged them to take the perspective of the victim in cases where the child may have caused harm to another. This implies that the development of perspective-taking is also related to social interaction.

The importance of perspective-taking skills

FitzGerald and White (2003) found that maturity of perspective-taking was negatively related to aggression and positively related to pro-social behaviour. Selman et al. (1977) found children who were poor at perspective-taking had more difficulty forming and maintaining relationships and were less popular. Such research suggests perspective-taking skills lead to important social developments and may explain the lack of social development in some individuals.

Correlation, not causation

Correlational research means we cannot claim perspective-taking skills cause higher levels of social competence. Maybe, more popular children interact more with others and these experiences develop their perspective-taking skills. If so, then perspective-taking skills are simply an indication of how socially developed a child is.

Real-world application

Evidence that perspective-taking abilities can be improved with experience has important implications for schools, therapy and treatment of criminals. Selman (2003) believes facilitation of perspective-taking is one of the fundamental missions of primary education, and so should be central to daily activities, e.g. play is a natural way to learn perspective-taking (Smith & Pellegrini, 2008). Social skills training (SST) has been used with older children as well as in therapeutic sessions for people with mental disorders or emotional problems. SST programmes have been developed to teach perspective-taking skills to prisoners to develop their empathetic concern for others and increase pro-social behaviour on release from prison.

KEY TERMS

Perspective-taking A central dynamic of social development that involves being able to view a situation or emotions from another person's viewpoint (also called role-taking).

Social cognition Refers to how our mental state (cognition) moderates our interaction with other people (social behaviour).

Apply it

Scenario. Freddie was recently involved in a playground fight and would not apologise to the other boy. His parents were called and Freddie was asked to explain his actions. Freddie knew his parents would be disappointed in him but felt when they knew that the other boy was bullying his friend they would understand why he was fighting.

With reference to Freddie's behaviour, discuss Selman's levels of perspective-taking. (16 marks)

Explanation extract... Freddie seems aware that others may hold a different view to him (he expects his parents to be disappointed when he feels it was acceptable to fight) but that this may be because they do not realise the other boy was a bully. This suggests Freddie is at stage 1, social informational perspective-taking, and we could presume he is aged between six and eight. Research suggests a progressive age-related developmental sequence with children moving from egocentrism to deeper levels of insight into the feelings of others. While this may be biologically driven, social experiences also play a role (FitzGerald & White, 2003), e.g. if Freddie's parents had previously encouraged Freddie to take the perspective of the victim when he harmed another, he might show some remorse towards the boy he was fighting with. …

KEY TERMS

Autism A mental disorder which usually appears in early childhood and typically involves avoidance of social contact, abnormal language and so-called 'stereotypic' or bizarre behaviours.

False belief The understanding that others may hold and act on mistaken (false) beliefs.

Sally–Anne test A story about two dolls (Sally and Anne). Sally doesn't know that the ball she placed in a basket has been moved to a box by Anne – the audience sees Anne do this. Where will Sally look for her ball: where she left it or where it has moved to? The story is used to test theory of mind in children.

Theory of mind (ToM) An individual's understanding that other people have separate mental states (beliefs, intentions, emotions) and that others see the world from a different point of view to their own.

Theory of mind (ToM)

Early development
Seventy-two-hours-old newborns show understanding of others in their ability to imitate facial expressions such as tongue and lip protrusions (Meltzoff & Moore, 1977, 1983). Around the age of three months infants will follow a person's gaze to nearby objects, indicating an understanding of communicative intent (D'Entremont et al., 1997). Infants are capable of social interaction, but it isn't until theory of mind (ToM) appears around the age of three or four years that social relationships develop. Around this age, children start using terms like 'think' and 'know' when referring to others.

Key study: Assessing theory of mind
Wimmer and Perner (1983) devised a false belief task to assess ToM.

How? Researchers act out the following story using dolls and matchboxes: Maxi sees his mother put some chocolate in a blue cupboard. When Maxi goes out to play his mother uses the chocolate to make a cake, putting the leftover chocolate in a green cupboard. When Maxi returns he wants some chocolate. Children are then asked, 'Which cupboard will Maxi look in?'

Showed? Nearly all three-year-olds tested said Maxi would look in the green cupboard. Some four-year-olds understood that while they knew where the chocolate was, Maxi would look in the blue cupboard. By the age of six all children could answer correctly.

Theory of mind as an explanation of autism
The social interaction difficulties autistic individuals face may be explained by an inability to understand the mental states of others and to predict and adjust to the behaviour of others. Baron-Cohen et al. (1985) adapted the Maxi task to create the Sally–Anne test.

How? 20 autistic children (mean age about 12), 14 children with Down's syndrome (same chronological age but lower mental age) and 27 'normal' children (mean age around four and a half) viewed the Sally–Anne scenario. They were asked control questions to check they had seen Anne move the marble, then asked the 'belief' question about where Sally would believe the ball to be.

Showed? 85% of 'normal' children correctly answered the false belief question. The same was true for the children with Down's syndrome. Only 20% of autistic children answered correctly.

Later research with adults
As autistic adults can pass the Sally–Anne test, Baron-Cohen et al. (1997) devised the Eyes task to test whether high-functioning individuals might have ToM. Participants are shown pictures of people's eyes and asked to select one of two emotions that might be represented, e.g. attraction versus repulsion. Adults on the autistic spectrum had a mean score of 16.3 (range 13–23) compared to 'normal' participants (mean score 20.3 out of 25, range 16–25) suggesting, in general, there was an impairment in autistic individuals.

Biological basis
The fact ToM develops at a particular age and is likely to be absent in people with autism led Baron-Cohen (1995) to propose a theory of mind module (ToMM): a specific brain mechanism that matures around the age of four and explains our ability to understand the mental states of others.

Evaluation
Relationship between understanding intentions and ToM
Carpenter et al. (2001) found autistic children aged two-and-a-half to five years could follow someone else's gaze and also looked where someone pointed. This behaviour was much the same as 'normal' children, which suggests the understanding of intention is a separate ability to ToM.

Evidence for the role of experience and biology
Perner et al. (1994) report that ToM appears earlier in children from large families, as having a large family, especially one with older siblings, means the child is challenged to think about the feelings of others when resolving conflicts. Sabbagh and Callanan (1998) found that discussion about motives and other mental states promotes ToM development. In addition, Liu et al. (2004) found a similar developmental sequence in 300 Chinese and North American children but the timing differed by as much as two years. Such research suggests biology has a role (ToM occurred in both cultures), as does the social environment.

Baron-Cohen's Eyes task may have low internal validity
Baron-Cohen claimed the Eyes task measures mind reading, which is essentially the same as ToM. However, Wellman and Woolley (1990) argue there is a difference between knowing another's internal state and understanding their experience of the world. The Sally–Anne test measures ToM (as the child is asked to consider Sally's experience) but the Eyes task may not.

ToM as an explanation for autism

If a lack of ToM was a central aspect of autism then we would expect all autistic individuals to show this impairment. However, research suggests only some autistic individuals lack ToM. Furthermore, children with autism may not develop ToM because their condition prevents them communicating and engaging with others. They may lack the appropriate social experiences that lead to ToM rather than ToM leading to poor social interaction. Research studies into autism are often quasi-experiments (the IV (autism) is not controlled by the researcher) so causal conclusions are not justified.

Cultural bias

Baron-Cohen studied British people, and his approach to understanding autism has a very Western perspective. Maguire (2013) suggests the Western view of social interaction has led to higher rates of diagnosis in the West compared to other cultures where symptoms associated with autism may not be considered abnormal.

Apply it

Scenario. Tanya and her friend Tilly were using plastic counters to work on maths problems. As it was nearly break time the teacher said the quickest group to tidy up could be the first out to play. Tilly hid the counters under the maths books so they could go out to play. When the teacher realised this she called Tilly back into the classroom to put the counters in the box where they should have been stored. Where would autistic children suggest Tanya should look for the counters after play time?

Explain your answer with reference to theory of mind research. (4 marks)

Explanation. Autistic children would expect Tanya to look in the box the counters had been moved to as they would not realise that Tanya would hold a false belief – the counters were still under the maths books. This scenario is similar to the Sally–Anne task which showed the majority of 'normal' and Down's syndrome children understood the concept of false beliefs but only 20% of autistic children did. Research such as this suggests autistic children do not have theory of mind: they do not understand that others may see the world from a different point of view than their own and so would not realise that Tanya would still believe the counters to be under the maths books as she did not know Tilly had moved them.

KEY TERM

Mirror neuron Neurons in the brain that react when a person performs an action and also when another individual performs the same action. This means that an observer experiences the actions of another as if it were their own. It encodes the action of another as if the observer were carrying out the same action.

The role of the mirror neuron (MN) system

The accidental discovery of mirror neurons

Rizzolatti et al. (1996) found that when macaque monkeys watched another monkey perform an action certain neurons in the F5 area of the premotor cortex became active. These neurons were also active when the monkey repeated the action. They had discovered a system that explains how one individual imitates another.

Imitation

Imitation is important in acquiring skilled behaviours (Meltzoff & Moore; see p.56). Behavioural regulation is another aspect of imitation. MN response is generally 'off-line' – the response doesn't result in imitation as the observation-response link is 'off'. On-line behaviour results in immediate imitation of observed behaviour because the observation-response link is 'on'. Lhermitte et al. (1986) found that individuals who have frontal cortex damage (the area involved in inhibitory control) display compulsive imitation, presumably because the link is 'on' when it should be 'off'.

Understanding intention

Lacoboni et al. (2005) showed participants three movie clips: context clip – before/after tea; action clip – hand grasps cup to drink/to clear away; and intention clip – combined content and action. MN activity was highest in the inferior frontal cortex during the intention clip, suggesting this area is concerned with why a person behaves as they do.

Perspective-taking and ToM

MNs may be seen as 'a part of, or a precursor to, a more general mind reading ability' because they enable us to experience someone else's actions as if they are our own (Gallese & Goldman, 1998). This suggests MNs are the mechanism underlying ToM and may also lead to the development of empathy – to understanding how others are feeling.

Language acquisition

It is likely MNs are involved in the imitation of speech sounds at the beginning of learning language (Rizzolatti & Arbib, 1998). Binkofski et al. (2000) found evidence of MNs in Broca's area involved in speech production, which is the human equivalent of the F5 area in macaque monkeys.

The basis of human uniqueness

Ramachandran (2000) proposed MNs are especially developed in humans, enabling us to excel in social relationships: this is the evolutionary basis of the success of the human species.

Evaluation

Research evidence from individual neurons

fMRI studies only tell us about the activity of thousands of neurons. However, Mukamel et al. (2010) were able to record activity in the single neurons of 21 epilepsy patients. Some neurons were active when a task was observed and, when it was performed, these neurons were located in expected areas (the premotor cortex) and unexpectedly in the medial temporal lobe (an area involved in memory function). Neurons with anti-mirror properties were also identified – these allow us to think about the actions of others without performing the action ourselves.

Research evidence from disruption of MNs

We would expect that damage to MN areas would result in deficits in performance. Research suggests this does seem to be the case, e.g. Tranel et al. (2003) found participants with damage to the left premotor area (and associated regions) could identify pictures of motor actions but not retrieve words for these actions.

Gender differences

Women have been shown to have greater social sensitivity than men. If MNs underlie social sensitivity, we would expect to find gender differences in MN activity. Cheung et al. (2009) compared EEG activity in men and women watching a moving dot or hand actions. MN activity in both genders was only recorded when watching hand actions, with women showing a significantly stronger response.

Explaining autism

MN abnormalities may underlie the fact that autistic people often find it difficult to copy actions (Williams et al. 2001). Dapretto et al. (2006) studied activity in autistic and non-autistic children as they watched faces showing anger, fear, happiness, sadness or no emotion. Autistic children showed reduced activity in the inferior frontal gyrus (part of the MN system). Activities that strengthen MNs through tasks involving the imitation of others may help autistic individuals (Slack, 2007).

The role of mirror neurons may have been exaggerated

Churchland (2011) suggests all MNs do is report information to higher-level neural circuits which then establish the intentions and thoughts of others – MNs are simply neurons that fire in response to an action. Heyes (2009) proposes MNs develop through experience (associative learning) rather than being innate (evolutionary adaptation). Neurons become paired as they are simultaneously excited or because one regularly precedes the other.

Apply it

Scenario. Researchers studying neural activity in humans found the same patterns of activity in certain brain areas when participants watched an origami demonstration and when they later made the origami figures themselves.

With reference to this example, discuss the role of mirror neurons in social cognition. (16 marks)

Explanation extract... The patterns of brain activity are likely to have been located in the premotor cortex, a brain area identified by researchers as containing mirror neurons. For example, Rizzolatti et al. (1996) recorded neural activity in the F5 area of the premotor cortex in macaque monkeys when they observed another monkey tear up paper. The same neural activity was seen when the monkeys then performed the action. The participants watching the origami did not imitate the paper-folding actions as they occurred, as the MN response is off-line, meaning the observation-response link is 'off'. If one of the participants had damage to their frontal cortex the researchers could predict they would display compulsive imitation because the observation-response link is 'on' (Lhermitte et al., 1986). MNs have a role in social cognition as the ability to imitate is important in skill development, e.g. Meltzoff and Moore found newborns were able to imitate the facial movements of adults. ...

Chapter 6

Schizophrenia

Paper 3, Section C, option 1. 4.3.5 Schizophrenia

- Classification of schizophrenia. Positive symptoms of schizophrenia, including hallucinations and delusions. Negative symptoms of schizophrenia, including speech poverty and avolition. Reliability and validity in diagnosis and classification of schizophrenia, including reference to co-morbidity, culture and gender bias and symptom overlap.
- Biological explanations for schizophrenia: genetics, the dopamine hypothesis and neural correlates.
- Psychological explanations for schizophrenia: family dysfunction and cognitive explanations, including dysfunctional thought processing.
- Drug therapy: typical and atypical antipsychotics.
- Cognitive behaviour therapy and family therapy as used in the treatment of schizophrenia. Token economies as used in the management of schizophrenia.
- The importance of an interactionist approach in explaining and treating schizophrenia; the diathesis–stress model.

Key terms (highlight each cell when you can confidently explain each term)

Classification	Reliability and validity in diagnosis and classification	Biological explanations	Psychological explanations	Drug therapy	Psychological therapies	Interactionist approach
Avolition	Co-morbidity	Dopamine hypothesis	Cognitive explanations	Atypical antipsychotics	Cognitive behavioural therapy	Diathesis–stress model
Delusions	Culture	Genetics	Dysfunctional thought processing	Typical antipsychotics	Family therapy	
Hallucinations	Gender bias	Neural correlates	Family dysfunction		Token economy	
Negative symptoms	Reliability					
Positive symptoms	Symptom overlap					
Schizophrenia	Validity					
Speech poverty						

Content checklist

1. In each 'describe', 'apply' and 'evaluate' cell tick when you have produced brief notes.
2. Once you feel you have a good grasp of the topic add a second tick to the cell.
3. When you feel you have complete mastery of the topic and would be able to answer an exam question without the aid of notes highlight the cell.

I am able to ...	Describe	Apply	Evaluate
Classification of schizophrenia			
Positive symptoms of schizophrenia, including hallucinations and delusions			
Negative symptoms of schizophrenia, including speech poverty and avolition			
Reliability and validity in diagnosis and classification of schizophrenia, including reference to co-morbidity, culture and gender bias and symptom overlap			
Biological explanations for schizophrenia: genetics			
Biological explanations: dopamine hypothesis			
Biological explanations for schizophrenia: neural correlates			
Psychological explanations for schizophrenia: family dysfunction			
Cognitive explanations including dysfunctional thought processing			
Drug therapy: typical antipsychotics			
Atypical antipsychotics			
Cognitive behaviour therapy as used in the treatment of schizophrenia			
Family therapy as used in the treatment of schizophrenia			
Token economies as used in the management of schizophrenia			
The importance of an interactionist approach in explaining and treating schizophrenia; the diathesis–stress model			

KEY TERMS

Avolition   The reduction, difficulty or inability to initiate and persist in goal-directed behaviour, often mistaken for apparent disinterest.

Delusions   Firmly held erroneous beliefs that are caused by distortions of reasoning or misinterpretations of perceptions or experiences.

Hallucinations   Distortions or exaggerations of perception in any of the senses, most notably auditory hallucinations.

Negative symptoms   Appear to reflect a diminution or loss of normal functioning.

Positive symptoms   Appear to reflect an excess or distortion of normal functioning.

Schizophrenia   A type of psychosis characterised by a profound disruption of cognition and emotion.

Speech poverty   The lessening of speech fluency and productivity, which reflects slowing or blocked thoughts.

Classification of schizophrenia

Schizophrenia is the most common type of psychosis, affecting about 1% of people at some point in their life. It is characterised by a profound disruption of cognition and emotion and loss of contact with external reality.

Positive symptoms

Hallucinations: perceptual distortions or exaggerations. Auditory hallucinations are the most common: hearing a voice (or voices) telling the person how to behave or commenting on their behaviour.

Delusions: firmly held, but erroneous, beliefs caused by distortions of reasoning, or misinterpretations of perceptions or experiences. Paranoid delusions involve the belief that a person is being conspired against (e.g. being followed by MI5). Delusions of grandeur involve inflated beliefs about the person's power and importance (e.g. believing oneself to be Jesus Christ).

Disorganised speech: problems in organising thoughts appropriately. In 'derailment', the individual shifts topics as new associations arise, and fails to form coherent and logical thoughts.

Grossly disorganised or catatonic behaviour: being unable or not motivated to initiate or complete a task. Poor functioning in everyday life (e.g. lack of personal hygiene). Catatonic behaviours involve a reduced reaction to the immediate environment, rigid postures or aimless motor activity.

Negative symptoms

People with schizophrenia are often unaware of these **negative symptoms** and less concerned by them than others are, but cannot manage their life without help.

Speech poverty (or alogia): deficits in verbal fluency and productivity, and less complex syntax. Speech poverty is believed to reflect slowing or blocked thoughts.

Avolition: a reduction of self-initiated involvement in interests and desires, as well as an inability to begin and persist with tasks. Schizophrenics will sit for hours on end doing nothing.

Affective flattening: a reduction in the range, and intensity, of different forms of emotional expression (e.g. body language). During speech, schizophrenics may show a deficit in prosody, the non-linguistic features such as intonation, which give listeners cues about emotional content.

Anhedonia: a loss of interest or pleasure in physical or social activities, or a lack of reactivity to normally pleasurable stimuli. Social anhedonia (e.g. not experiencing pleasure from interpersonal situations) overlaps with disorders like depression, whereas physical anhedonia (e.g. not experiencing pleasure from things like bodily contact) doesn't.

Diagnosing schizophrenia

Schizophrenia is most often diagnosed between the ages of 15 and 35. Men and women are equally likely to be diagnosed as schizophrenic.

DSM-V (2013) requires a person to show two or more 'Criterion A' symptoms: delusions, hallucinations, disorganised speech, grossly disorganised or catatonic behaviour, negative symptoms. Only one of these is required if delusions are 'bizarre', or hallucinations involve a voice offering a running commentary about the person, *or* several voices in conversation.

DSM-V also requires the person to display social/occupational dysfunction in one or more major areas of functioning. These are 'Criterion B' symptoms. These include work, interpersonal relations and self-care.

'Criterion C' symptoms refer to duration. Continuous signs of disturbance must have persisted for at least six months, including one month or more of 'Criterion A' symptoms.

Apply it

Scenario. Joel is studying Chemistry at university. For the last month or so, his family and friends have noticed him behaving increasingly bizarrely and talking to himself in whispers even though there was nobody there. Lately, he has refused to answer or make calls on his mobile phone, claiming that, if he does, it will activate a chip in his brain that was implanted by the security forces. Then he stopped leaving his flat for days on end.

Using your knowledge of the classification of schizophrenia, explain why Joel would be likely to be given a diagnosis of schizophrenia. (6 marks)

Application. Joel's behaviour shows some positive symptoms of schizophrenia: talking to himself could mean he is hearing voices (auditory hallucinations); he has delusions about a chip in his brain; and his behaviour appears bizarre. This is Criterion A. He has had these symptoms for a month, which is Criterion C. He also has negative symptoms: stopping leaving his flat could be a sign of avolition or anhedonia, and shows that he is not functioning, as he is meant to be studying. This is Criterion B.

Reliability and validity in diagnosis and classification

◉ Reliability

Test–retest reliability: the consistency of measurements taken by a single clinician at several points in time. Inter-rater reliability refers to the consistency of measurement between different clinicians at the same time.

◉ Validity

Validity of diagnosis: extent to which a diagnosis reflects an actual disorder, that is, whether a diagnostic system such as *DSM-V* measures what it says it measures. Reliability is a pre-condition for validity. A diagnosis cannot be valid if it is not reliable.

Differences in culture: in diagnosis and experience of schizophrenia. Copeland (1971) gave psychiatrists a description of a patient; 69% of US and only 2% of British psychiatrists diagnosed schizophrenia. Luhrmann *et al.* (2015) found that many African and Indian people with schizophrenia experienced their voices as playful or helpful, whereas US patients mostly heard harsh, violent voices.

Gender bias in diagnosis occurs when its accuracy depends on an individual's gender. Broverman *et al.* (1970) found that American clinicians equated mentally healthy 'adult' behaviour with mentally healthy 'male' behaviour, so women were perceived as less mentally healthy.

Symptom overlap: most people diagnosed with schizophrenia have sufficient symptoms of other disorders that they could also receive at least one other diagnosis (Read, 2004).

Co-morbidity: 50% of patients with schizophrenia also have depression, and 47% substance abuse (Buckley *et al.*, 2009). 1% of the population develop schizophrenia and 2–3% develop OCD, but 12% of patients with schizophrenia also fulfil the diagnostic criteria for OCD.

◉ Evaluation

Lack of inter-rater reliability

Inter-rater reliability correlations in the diagnosis of schizophrenia are as low as 0.11 (Whaley, 2001). Psychiatrists asked to differentiate between 'bizarre' and 'non-bizarre' delusions also disagreed in their judgements, with inter-rater reliability for this aspect of diagnosis of just 0.40 (Mojtabi & Nicholson, 1995).

The ethnic culture hypothesis

Ethnic minority groups may protect members from distress associated with mental disorders. Brekke and Barrio (1997) found that non-white minority group members (Afro-American and Latino) were *less* symptomatic than majority (white American) group members. Ethnic minority cultures have better social structures than majority group cultures, suggesting that the development of the disorder is linked to the cultural background of the individual.

Differences in prognosis

A diagnosis of schizophrenia has poor predictive validity: 20% recover their previous level of functioning; 10% achieve significant, lasting improvement; and 30% show some improvement with intermittent relapses. Outcome is also influenced by gender, academic achievement, social skills and family support.

Gender bias in diagnosis

Loring and Powell (1988) asked 290 psychiatrists to read vignettes of patients' behaviour. 56% of patients described as 'males' were given a diagnosis of schizophrenia. Only 20% of patients labelled as 'female' were given a diagnosis of schizophrenia. Female psychiatrists showed less gender bias.

The consequences of co-morbidity

Weber *et al.* (2009) looked at six million hospital discharge records, finding that many patients with schizophrenia also had medical problems including asthma, hypertension and diabetes, but received a lower standard of care because of their primary psychiatric diagnosis. This suggests that the physical health outcomes for individuals with schizophrenia are less favourable than for non-schizophrenics.

KEY TERMS

Co-morbidity The extent that two (or more) conditions or diseases occur simultaneously in a patient, e.g. schizophrenia and depression.

Culture The rules, customs, morals, childrearing practices, etc. that bind a group of people together and define how they are likely to behave.

Gender bias The tendency to describe the behaviour of men and women in psychological theory and research in such a way that might not represent accurately the characteristics of one gender.

Reliability The consistency of measurements. We would expect any measurement to produce the same data if taken on successive occasions.

Symptom overlap Symptoms of a disorder may not be unique to that disorder but may also be found in other disorders, making accurate diagnosis difficult.

Validity Whether an observed effect is a genuine one.

Apply it

Scenario. Harrison *et al.* (1997) reported that the incidence rate for schizophrenia was eight times higher for Afro-Caribbean groups (46.7 per 100,000) than white groups (5.7 per 100,000) in the UK.

How could issues with the validity of diagnosis of schizophrenia contribute to this difference? (4 marks)

Application. There may be socio-economic or cultural differences, or even genetic differences, which make it more likely for Afro-Caribbean people to develop schizophrenia in the UK. However, it is possible that psychiatrists (mostly white, middle class) may misdiagnose people because of their cultural differences in behaviour or the way they talk. For example, hearing voices may be a more normal experience in some cultures but could be thought of as 'bizarre' by a psychiatrist. Certain cultural beliefs may seem like bizarre delusions to someone from a different culture. This leads to invalid diagnosis of schizophrenia.

KEY TERMS

Biological explanations The role of inherited factors and dysfunction of brain activity in the development of a behaviour or mental disorder.

Dopamine hypothesis An excess of the neurotransmitter dopamine in certain regions of the brain is associated with the positive symptoms of schizophrenia.

Genetic Inherited characteristics that are passed from parents to their children in the form of information carried on their chromosomes.

Neural correlates Changes in neuronal events and mechanisms that result in the characteristic symptoms of a behaviour or mental disorder.

Apply it

Scenario. When schizophrenia patients were given drugs that lowered their dopamine levels, they showed improvement in some symptoms (e.g. hallucinations) but a worsening in others (e.g. cognitive impairment). When the same patients took psychostimulants, which raised dopamine levels, the opposite pattern emerged, with increased hallucinations but reduced cognitive impairment.

Explain how this evidence supports the dopamine hypothesis of schizophrenia. (4 marks)

Application. Positive symptoms of schizophrenia (such as hallucinations) are caused by an excess of dopamine in mesolimbic pathways in the brain. Drugs that lowered dopamine levels in this study would have blocked dopamine transmission in these areas and so reduced these positive symptoms. Negative symptoms, such as cognitive impairment, are caused by a depletion of dopamine in the mesocortical pathways. Drugs that lowered dopamine levels would have mimicked this depletion and caused cognitive impairments. Reversing this by the use of psychostimulants would have increased positive symptoms and cognitive impairments, which is what was found in this study.

Biological explanations for schizophrenia

Genetic factors

Family studies: the risk of schizophrenia is higher the closer the degree of **genetic** relatedness. For example, Gottesman (1991) showed that children with two schizophrenic parents gave a concordance rate of 46%, one schizophrenic parent gave a rate of 13% and siblings gave 9%.

Twin studies: MZ twins have a concordance rate for schizophrenia of 40.4% and 7.4% for DZ twins (Joseph, 2004) – good evidence for genetic factors.

Adoption studies: separate out genetic and environmental influences. 6.7% of adoptees with a biological mother with schizophrenia also had a diagnosis, but only 2% of controls (Tienari, 2000).

The dopamine hypothesis

Excess dopamine causes positive symptoms, as neurons fire too easily or too often. Abnormally high numbers of D_2 receptors result in more dopamine binding on post-synaptic neurons.

Drugs that increase dopaminergic activity produce hallucinations and delusions, e.g. amphetamines.

Drugs that decrease dopaminergic activity eliminate hallucinations and delusions, e.g. antipsychotics (dopamine antagonists).

The revised dopamine hypothesis (Davis & Kahn, 1991)

Positive symptoms are caused by excess dopamine in subcortical areas such as the mesolimbic pathway. Negative symptoms come from a deficit of dopamine in the mesocortical pathway of the prefrontal cortex (PFC).

Evidence comes from:

Neural imaging: PET scans show less dopamine than normal in the dorsolateral PFC of schizophrenic patients (Patel *et al.*, 2010).

Neural correlates

The prefrontal cortex: the PFC is the main area of the brain involved in executive control. This suggests that the cognitive symptoms of schizophrenia are a consequence of a functional impairment in the PFC.

The hippocampus: research (e.g. Heckers, 2001) suggests that many of the symptoms of schizophrenia may be a consequence of abnormally heightened hippocampal activity.

Grey matter loss: individuals with schizophrenia have a reduced volume of grey matter in the brain, especially in the temporal and frontal lobes. The greater the tissue loss, the worse the symptoms (Hulshoff *et al.*, 2002).

White matter abnormalities: white matter is made up of nerve fibres covered in myelin sheaths, enabling efficient information processing. Research (e.g. Du *et al.*, 2013) has found white matter abnormalities among patients with schizophrenia, when compared with healthy individuals.

Evaluation

Genetics: environmental factors may explain family similarities
Schizophrenia runs in families, but this may be due to common rearing patterns or negative emotional climate in some families, leading to stress and triggering schizophrenic episodes. Also, MZ twins are treated more similarly so have fewer environmental differences than DZ twins.

Genetics: adoptees may be selectively placed
Adoptive parents are often informed of the genetic background of children, so the allocation to families is not random. Families adopting children of schizophrenic parents may have particular characteristics.

Dopamine: evidence from treatment with antipsychotic drugs
A meta-analysis (Leucht *et al.*, 2013) showed that antipsychotic drugs were significantly more effective than a placebo at treating positive and negative symptoms, supporting the involvement of dopamine.

Dopamine: challenges to the dopamine hypothesis
Noll (2009) argued that one third of people taking antipsychotics do not benefit. Psychotic symptoms can also be experienced despite normal dopamine levels, so positive symptoms must be produced via another system.

Neural correlates: support for grey matter deficit
Vita *et al.*'s (2012) meta-analysis of 19 studies showed that patients with schizophrenia, compared with healthy controls, showed a significantly higher progressive reduction in cortical grey matter volume over time.

Neural correlates: implications for treatment
Research in this area suggests that early detection and intervention might prevent development of the later stages of schizophrenia. The concept of 'treatment as prevention' uses biological assessments to predict who is likely to develop schizophrenia and to develop new treatment and prevention approaches.

Psychological explanations for schizophrenia

◎ Family dysfunction
Double bind theory: Bateson *et al.* (1956) suggested that children who frequently receive contradictory verbal and non-verbal messages from their parents develop incoherent representations of reality, and could develop schizophrenia.

Expressed emotion (EE): a family communication style in which family members talk about the patient in a hostile or critical way, or are over-concerned. High EE relatives talk more and listen less. Patients returning to high EE families are four times more likely to relapse than those with low EE families (Linszen *et al.*, 1997). People with schizophrenia may be less able to cope with a negative emotional climate, while those with supportive families can reduce their dependence on antipsychotic medication (Noll, 2009).

◎ Cognitive explanations
People with schizophrenia have **dysfunctional thought processing**.

Cognitive explanations of delusions: delusional thinking is characterised by egocentric bias, in which the individual perceives themselves as central to events. They interpret irrelevant events (such as muffled voices or flashes of light) as relating to themselves. They are unwilling to consider that they may be wrong or consider more realistic explanations – impaired insight.

Cognitive explanations of hallucinations: hypervigilance leads to excessive attention on auditory stimuli, and difficulty distinguishing between imagery and sensory-based perception. Source misattribution means patients think that self-generated auditory experiences originate externally, and do not carry out reality-testing processes normally.

◎ Evaluation
Family relationships
Adoption studies (Tienari *et al.*, 1994) show that genetic vulnerability alone was not sufficient for development of schizophrenia. Children with schizophrenic biological parents were more likely to become ill than those with non-schizophrenic parents, but only when their adopted family was also rated as disturbed.

Double bind theory
Schizophrenic patients recalled more double bind statements by their mothers than non-schizophrenics (Berger, 1965). However, patients' recall may be unreliable. Other studies find no difference in the agreement between verbal and non-verbal communication in families with or without a schizophrenic member.

Individual differences in vulnerability to EE
Some patients become stressed by EE behaviours (stressful comments by their relatives), whereas others do not, and this affects their outcome in the family. More resilient patients do not appraise their relatives' behaviour as stressful, and are less vulnerable to it.

Supporting evidence for the cognitive model of schizophrenia
Schizophrenic patients have impaired self-monitoring and tend to experience their own thoughts as voices. Negative symptoms are associated with dysfunctional thought processes such as low expectations of pleasure and success. Cognitive behavioural therapy (CBT), testing the validity of false beliefs and evaluating the content of voices or delusions, is more effective than antipsychotic medication in reducing symptom severity (NICE, 2014).

An integrated model of schizophrenia (diathesis–stress model – see p.68)
Early vulnerability factors (genes, birth complications, etc.), together with significant social stressors (e.g. adversity), sensitise the dopamine system, increasing dopamine release. Biased cognitive processing and misinterpretation of this dopamine activity then results in paranoia and hallucinations. This increases stress, leading to more dopamine release, and so on (Howes & Murray, 2014).

KEY TERMS
Cognitive explanations Propose that abnormalities in cognitive function are a key component of schizophrenia.

Dysfunctional thought processing Cognitive habits or beliefs that cause the individual to evaluate information inappropriately.

Family dysfunction The presence of problems within a family that contribute to relapse rates in recovering schizophrenics, including lack of warmth between parents and child, dysfunctional communication patterns and parental overprotection.

🐾 Apply it
Scenario. Emmanuel has been diagnosed with schizophrenia. His family are very stressed by his odd behaviour and are trying to find someone to blame. Emmanuel's father blames his mother, as he thinks she was too soft on him as a little boy. Meanwhile she blames Emmanuel's genes, as there were several relatives in his father's family who had schizophrenia. Emmanuel's sister keeps telling him his delusions and hallucinations are not real, but it doesn't seem to help.

Discuss the psychological explanations of schizophrenia, referring to Emmanuel's family's ideas. (16 marks)

Application extract… The family may have high levels of expressed emotion (EE), as they have become stressed and it is possible that the blaming could be quite emotional. Also Emmanuel's father thinks his mother was too soft on him, so Emmanuel may have received inconsistent messages from his parents, simultaneously communicating affection and animosity, which fits the double bind theory. Emmanuel's sister is attempting to take a cognitive approach, identifying his faulty cognitions. This could be effective as part of CBT (NICE, 2014), but he would need to do this himself rather than being told by his sister. An integrated approach may be a better explanation, as there is evidence of genetic links and Emmanuel's father's family had several incidences of schizophrenia. This model proposes interactions. …

KEY TERMS

Atypical antipsychotics A lower risk of extrapyramidal side effects, a beneficial effect on negative symptoms and cognitive impairment, and suitable for treatment-resistant patients.

Drug therapy Treatment of mental disorders such as schizophrenia through the use of antipsychotics to reduce the symptoms of the disorder.

Typical antipsychotics Dopamine antagonists. They bind to but do not stimulate dopamine receptors and so reduce the symptoms of schizophrenia.

Drug therapy

Before the 1950s there was no treatment for schizophrenia, other than a safe and supportive long-stay psychiatric hospital. The neurotransmitter dopamine was discovered in 1952, then drugs were developed to target dopamine pathways.

Antipsychotics

Drugs targeting psychotic disorders such as schizophrenia and bipolar disorder are known as antipsychotics. **Drug therapy** aims to enable the person to function and improve their well-being. Antipsychotics all reduce dopaminergic transmission in particular brain areas.

Typical antipsychotics (e.g. chlorpromazine) combat the positive symptoms of schizophrenia. They are dopamine antagonists; they bind to dopamine receptors without stimulating them, blocking the action of dopamine. Hallucinations and delusions diminish within a few days. 60–75% of D_2 dopamine receptors in the mesolimbic pathway must be blocked to be effective (Kapur *et al.*, 2000). However, D_2 receptors in other brain areas are also blocked, causing harmful side effects.

Atypical antipsychotics (e.g. clozapine) only temporarily occupy the D_2 receptors, then rapidly dissociate to allow dopamine transmission. This avoids side effects. They also occupy 5-HT_{2A} serotonin receptors and so are claimed to benefit the negative and cognitive symptoms of schizophrenia as well as positive symptoms.

Evaluation

Effectiveness: antipsychotics versus placebo

A meta-analysis of 65 studies including 6,000 patients (Leucht *et al.*, 2012) concluded that 64% of patients taken off antipsychotics and given a placebo relapsed within 12 months, compared to 27% of those who stayed on antipsychotics. This shows the effectiveness of antipsychotic treatment.

Extrapyramidal side effects

Typical antipsychotics produce movement problems such as Parkinsonism in 50% of patients. They affect the extrapyramidal area of the brain which helps control motor function. After an extended treatment period, tardive dyskinesia can also occur – involuntary movements of tongue, face and jaw. These distressing symptoms cause many patients to stop taking their medication, and also raise ethical issues in prescribing these drugs.

Advantages of atypical over typical antipsychotics

Newly developed atypical antipsychotics (e.g. olanzapine, quetiapine) have fewer side effects, so patients are more likely to continue taking them and experience symptom reduction, thus increasing their effectiveness.

Are atypical antipsychotics better?

A meta-analysis of 15 studies (Crossley *et al.*, 2010) found no significant differences between typical and atypical antipsychotics in their effect on symptoms. Side effects were different: patients on atypical drugs gained more weight but had fewer extrapyramidal side effects than those on typical drugs.

Motivational deficits

Ross and Read (2004) claim that prescribing medication reinforces a biological explanation of schizophrenia, so people aren't motivated to look for solutions to social or cognitive factors which may be contributing to their suffering.

Apply it

Scenario. Your cousin Jasmine has schizophrenia and has been prescribed antipsychotic medication. She has noticed her 'voices' have gone away, but she says she feels lonely without them, and is also experiencing hand tremors which embarrass her. She says she's going to stop her medication as she feels unhappy and has no energy, and is blaming this on the drugs. She doesn't want to go back to the doctor as she thinks they don't understand her.

What advice could you give Jasmine, based on your knowledge of drug therapies for schizophrenia? Include an evaluation of drug therapies in your answer. (16 marks)

Application extract... The drugs were helping with Jasmine's positive symptoms (auditory hallucinations) but not her negative symptoms (avolition, anhedonia). She may also have co-morbid depressive symptoms. The tremors could be Parkinsonism, a sign of extrapyramidal side effects. If she is currently taking typical antipsychotics, you could tell her that there are other drugs, atypical antipsychotics, which might give her fewer side effects and could also benefit her negative symptoms (although evidence for this is inconclusive). You could offer to go to the doctor with her, as she may be feeling socially isolated and the social/cognitive factors are also important in her treatment. There is a high risk of relapse if she stops taking the drugs without medical support – 64% of patients going onto a placebo relapsed within a year compared to 27% who stayed on antipsychotics, and if she stops she won't even have the placebo effect. ...

Cognitive behavioural therapy

NICE (The National Institute for Health and Care Excellence) recommends everyone with schizophrenia should be offered **cognitive behavioural therapy** to help patients deal with residual symptoms which persist despite antipsychotic drugs.

Cognitive behavioural therapy for psychosis (CBTp)

The basic assumption of CBTp is that distorted beliefs negatively influence feelings and behaviour. Delusions result from faulty interpretations of events. NICE recommends 16 sessions of CBTp, usually one-to-one but sometimes in groups.

Patients are encouraged to evaluate the content of their delusions or voices and test validity of beliefs. They are set behavioural assignments to improve functioning. Distorted thinking and maladaptive beliefs are identified with the help of the therapist, looking for alternative explanations and coping strategies.

How does it work?

Assessment: the patient expresses their thoughts, and goals are discussed, using their distress as motivation for change.

Engagement: the therapist empathises with the patient's perspective and distress. The ABC model: activating events (A), beliefs about them (B) and behavioural and emotional consequences (C) are discussed. Irrational beliefs are disputed.

Normalisation: patients are reassured that many people have hallucinations and delusions when they are stressed. This helps patients to feel less anxious about their symptoms, and to believe in the possibility of recovery.

Critical collaborative analysis: the therapist uses gentle questioning to challenge the patient's beliefs, in an atmosphere of trust and non-judgmental acceptance.

Developing alternative explanations: the patient develops their own alternative explanations for previously unhealthy assumptions, with the support of the therapist.

Evaluation

Advantages of CBTp over standard care

The NICE review (2014) found that CBTp is effective in reducing symptom severity and re-hospitalisation rates up to 18 months after the treatment ends, compared with drug treatment alone. CBTp is generally combined with drug treatment, so its independent effectiveness cannot be assessed.

Effectiveness is dependent on the stage of the disorder

CBTp is not appropriate in the initial acute phase of psychosis, but when symptoms have been stabilised with drugs, it can be more effective (Addington & Addington, 2005). Group-based CBTp can help to normalise patients' experience. Individuals with more experience and self-awareness benefit more from individual CBTp.

Lack of availability of CBTp

Only 1 in 10 patients who could benefit are able to access CBTp in the UK. Availability varies between areas of the country. Many who are offered CBTp refuse treatment or fail to attend.

Problems with meta-analysis of CBTp as a treatment for schizophrenia

Studies vary in quality: some fail to randomly allocate patients to conditions, others fail to mask conditions for assessors. This weakens the validity of conclusions of meta-analyses. Wykes *et al.* (2008) found that the more rigorous the study, the weaker the effect of CBTp.

The benefits of CBTp may have been overstated

More recent meta-analyses of CBTp as a sole treatment show only a small effect on positive symptoms. These effects disappeared when symptoms were assessed 'blind'. This has led to conflicting treatment advice in different regions of the UK: CBTp in England and Wales, and antipsychotic medications in Scotland.

KEY TERM

Cognitive behavioural therapy A combination of cognitive therapy (a way of changing maladaptive thoughts and beliefs) and behavioural therapy (a way of changing behaviour in response to these thoughts and beliefs).

Apply it

Scenario. Jon has been offered cognitive behavioural therapy as part of his treatment for schizophrenia.

Outline what Jon should expect to experience during his treatment, and how it could help him. (6 marks)

Application. Jon's psychiatrist has recommended CBTp as NICE (2014) advises. It is only part of his treatment, so he is probably taking antipsychotic drugs too. He should wait until hallucinations and delusions settle down before he starts the CBT, as it is more effective in the non-acute stage, once he is less delusional. He will then be working with a therapist, probably one-to-one, although a group may be more helpful if he feels isolated and will help to normalise his experience when he meets other people with similar symptoms. He will probably have 16 sessions, and will be encouraged to find alternative explanations for events, using the ABC model to challenge his faulty beliefs about activating circumstances, so that his emotional and behavioural consequences are improved. This should help to reduce his distress as he will have some sense of control over his cognitive symptoms. It can be effective and reduce symptom severity and re-hospitalisation.

KEY TERM

Family therapy A range of interventions aimed at the family (e.g. parents, siblings, partners) of someone with a mental disorder.

Apply it

Scenario. Kyle is 18 and was diagnosed with schizophrenia about six months ago. His family find it very stressful and worry that they are doing the wrong thing and that nothing they do helps Kyle. As a result, Kyle's psychiatrist has recommended that family therapy might be provided to help Kyle and his family deal effectively with Kyle's illness. His parents are very apprehensive about this and don't really understand what it is or why they need it, so they ask you to explain because you study Psychology.

Using your knowledge of family therapy, explain what you could tell Kyle's parents about why family therapy will help them all deal with Kyle's schizophrenia. (6 marks)

Application. Kyle's parents' anxiety is a reason why family therapy may help. It aims to reduce anxiety and stress around the illness within a family. Getting information about schizophrenia and its treatment can help them to understand what's going on with Kyle, and how they can help him. Family therapy has been shown to improve outcomes for patients by increasing compliance with medication; it will help Kyle's family to remind Kyle to take his medication if they understand how much he needs it, and how it can help him. Also Kyle will have a chance to talk to his family about what support he wants, so they know they are doing the best for him. Family therapy will help them to feel able to support him effectively, which will reduce their anxiety, guilt and stress levels, in turn improving the caring environment for Kyle. They may be worried that they are going to be told they are doing things wrong, but family therapy actually aims to help everyone improve their relationships and solve problems more effectively, so it can be a positive experience for the family as well as for Kyle himself.

Family therapy

The long-term outcome for an individual with schizophrenia depends on their relationship with those who care for them. The aim of **family therapy** is to support carers in making family life less stressful and reduce relapse.

NICE recommends that family therapy should be offered to 'all individuals diagnosed with schizophrenia who are in contact with or live with family members'. These interventions should be a priority where there are persistent symptoms or a high risk of relapse. Schizophrenic people in high EE families (critical, hostile or over-involved) have a higher risk of relapse than those in less EE families.

The nature of family therapy

At least 10 sessions over 3–12 months, aiming to reduce EE and stress in a family, provide information about schizophrenia, resolve practical problems and help families to support the patient in their treatment.

How does it work?

- Psychoeducation: helping the person and their carers better understand the illness.
- Forming an alliance with relatives who care for the patient.
- Reducing the emotional climate in the family.
- Enhancing relatives' ability to anticipate and solve problems.
- Reducing expressions of anger and guilt by family members.
- Maintaining reasonable expectations of patient performance by relatives.
- Encouraging relatives to set appropriate limits.
- Enabling the patient to explain to their family what support they find helpful, and what makes things worse for them.

Key study: Pharoah *et al.* (2010)

How? Review of 53 randomised controlled trials in Europe, Asia and North America. Compared outcomes from family therapy to treatment involving antipsychotic medication alone.

Showed? Mixed results on improvement in mental state of the patient. Increased compliance with medication. Some improvement in general functioning, but no effect on independent living or employment. Reduction in the risk of relapse and hospital admission during family therapy and for 24 months after.

Evaluation

Why is family therapy effective?

It can improve clinical outcomes and social functioning, but the main reason for its effectiveness is the increase in medication compliance (Pharoah *et al.*, 2010).

Methodological limitations of family therapy studies

In the Pharoah *et al.* meta-analysis, many of the Chinese studies may not have actually used random allocation of participants to treatment conditions. Ten studies did not 'blind' raters to the condition, and 16 did not mention whether blinding had been used.

Economic benefits of family therapy

The NICE review of family therapy studies (2009) showed that the extra cost of family therapy is offset by a reduction in costs of hospitalisation because of lower relapse rates.

Impact on family members

Family therapy improves outcomes for the individual and also has a positive impact on family members' relationships and problem-solving skills (Lobban *et al.*, 2013). However, many of the studies in this review used poor methodology, so the conclusions may not be valid.

Is family therapy worthwhile?

If a patient has a good standard of care, in a family with relatively low EE, then family therapy may give no further advantages. The difference found by Garety *et al.* (2008) was between patients with carers and those with no carer, who had a much higher rate of relapse.

Token economy and the management of schizophrenia

Negative symptoms of schizophrenia, such as apathy and social withdrawal, mean that patients can neglect self-care (washing, eating). **Token economy** systems aim to encourage more positive behaviours (self-care or positive social interactions) using the principles of operant conditioning.

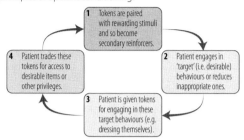

1 Tokens are paired with rewarding stimuli and so become secondary reinforcers.

2 Patient engages in 'target' (i.e. desirable) behaviours or reduces inappropriate ones.

3 Patient is given tokens for engaging in these target behaviours (e.g. dressing themselves).

4 Patient trades these tokens for access to desirable items or other privileges.

Primary reinforcers are anything that gives pleasure (e.g. food or privileges) or removes unpleasant states (e.g. boredom). Secondary reinforcers (tokens) only have value after pairing with primary reinforcers.

Ayllon and Azrin (1968) used a token economy on a ward of female schizophrenic patients who had been hospitalised for many years. They were given plastic tokens embossed with 'one gift' for behaviours such as making their bed or carrying out domestic chores. These tokens were then exchanged for privileges such as being able to watch a movie. This increased dramatically the number of desirable behaviours that the patients performed each day.

◉ Assigning value to the tokens
The token must initially be repeatedly presented alongside or immediately before the reinforcing stimulus (e.g. watching a movie). Classical conditioning creates an association between the primary and secondary reinforcers.

◉ Reinforcing target behaviours
To be most effective, tokens must be given immediately after the performance of the target behaviour, otherwise an intervening behaviour would be reinforced. A **generalised** reinforcer can be exchanged for a variety of rewards. Sran and Borrero (2010) found that participants had a higher response rate to generalised tokens than those which could only be exchanged for a single edible item.

◉ The 'trade'
During the early stages, frequent exchange periods allow rapid reinforcement of target behaviours. The effectiveness decreases if more time passes between presentation of the token and exchange for primary reinforcers (Kazdin, 1977).

◉ Evaluation
Research support
Dickerson *et al.* (2005) reviewed 13 studies of token economy systems used in treating schizophrenia. Eleven reported beneficial effects. However, methodological shortcomings in many of the studies limit the validity of these conclusions.

Difficulties assessing the success of a token economy
Comer (2013) suggests that programmes are difficult to assess as all patients on a ward are usually included in the programme. The lack of a control group means improvements are compared with past behaviours, and other factors could be confounding (e.g. increased staff attention).

Less useful for patients living in the community
Token economies only work in a hospital setting, where there is 24-hour care. Patients living in the community only receive a few hours' care a day, so staff would not be able to reward them consistently. Positive behaviours in a ward setting may not continue when a patient is discharged from hospital into a different environment.

Ethical concerns
Clinicians may control important primary reinforcers like food, privacy or social activities. However, all human beings have basic rights that should not be violated, regardless of the positive consequences that might result from their manipulation.

Does it actually work?
Very few randomised trials have been carried out. Token economy programmes have fallen out of use in most developed countries. McMonagle and Sultana (2000) suggest that randomised clinical trials (RCTs) could be carried out in developing countries where token economies are still practised.

KEY TERM
Token economy A form of therapy where desirable behaviours are encouraged by the use of selective reinforcements. Rewards (tokens) are given as *secondary reinforcers* when individuals engage in correct/socially desirable behaviours. The tokens can then be exchanged for *primary reinforcers* – food or privileges.

Apply it

Scenario. Annie is a clinical psychologist who is asked to talk to staff at a local psychiatric unit about setting up a token economy in one of the wards. It is a ward of eight female patients between the ages of 30 and 45. These women have been on antipsychotic medication for an average of 12 years and display a variety of negative symptoms including speech poverty and avolition.

Outline what advice Annie might give to staff in the unit about setting up a token economy to address these two particular symptoms. (6 marks)

Application. First, suitable rewards should be identified as primary reinforcers. A variety of rewards should be chosen which the women will be able to choose from, such as watching movies or food treats, as this is more effective than simple food rewards. Then the staff should start presenting tokens every time these rewards are given. This will create an association between the reward and the token. Then the staff should give the women tokens every time they carry out a positive behaviour, such as talking or making an effort to do something (the opposite of speech poverty and avolition). These tokens must be exchanged quite quickly for rewards in the early stages, so that the connection is made. Staff will need to be consistent in rewarding positive behaviour very promptly so that the tokens reinforce the desired behaviour, not an intervening one.

KEY TERM

Diathesis–stress model Explains mental disorders as the result of an interaction between biological (the diathesis) and environmental (stress) influences.

Apply it

Scenario. Carla has a history of schizophrenia, which began when she smoked cannabis as a teenager, to deal with the stress of her alcoholic father who was subsequently imprisoned for violence against her mother and her younger sister. Carla's mental health has been more stable for the last few years, and she has stopped taking her medication because she wants to have a baby. She manages her symptoms with the help of skills she learnt in CBT. She is worried that her baby might inherit her vulnerability to schizophrenia.

Discuss the diathesis–stress model of schizophrenia, and suggest how Carla could reduce her baby's chances of developing the disorder. (16 marks)

Application extract… Carla's schizophrenia was probably caused by an interaction between biological factors (genetic susceptibility) and environmental stress (the stress of having an alcoholic father, the violence in the family, and the court case against her father). The cannabis may also have made changes in her brain which made her more vulnerable. These biological factors (the diathesis) interacted with the stress to cause the onset of her schizophrenia. Her baby could indeed have the same faulty gene, but if she cares for the baby well there is no reason the schizophrenia will necessarily develop, as even identical twins of someone with schizophrenia only have 50% chance of developing it, although they have 100% the same genes. It is important for Carla to be consistent in her parenting to avoid the double bind situation or the critical or hostile style, or the over-involvement associated with high expressed emotion (EE) families. Her CBT skills should help. …

An interactionist approach

◉ The diathesis–stress model

The **diathesis–stress model** proposes that schizophrenia is a result of an interaction between genetic and environmental influences. A biological vulnerability (diathesis) increases the chances that significant stressors will trigger symptoms of schizophrenia.

Diathesis: schizophrenia has a genetic component. Identical (MZ) twins of schizophrenic parents are at greater risk of developing it than siblings or dizygotic (DZ) twins. However, the concordance rate for identical twins is only 50%, showing that environmental factors must also play a role.

Stress: experiences such as childhood trauma or the stress of living in big cities can increase the risk of developing psychotic symptoms. Varese *et al.* (2012) found that children who experienced severe trauma were three times more likely to develop schizophrenia as adults than the general population. Those who were severely traumatised were at even greater risk. A meta-analysis by Vassos *et al.* (2012) found that the risk of schizophrenia in densely populated urban environments was 2.37 times higher than in rural environments.

The additive nature of diathesis and stress: minor stresses could lead to the onset of the disorder for highly vulnerable individuals, or a major stressful event could be required to trigger it in a less vulnerable person. This suggests an additive interaction between diathesis and stress.

◉ Key study: Tienari *et al.* (2004)

How? Hospital records for 20,000 women admitted with schizophrenic or paranoid psychoses to Finnish psychiatric hospitals between 1960 and 1979. 145 women had children adopted away; these children were compared with matched adoptees without the genetic risk. They were assessed after 12 and 21 years, and family functioning was blind tested.

Showed? 14 adoptees developed schizophrenia, 11 of which were from the high-risk group. Being reared in a 'healthy' adoptive family had a protective effect even for high-risk children, and adoptive-family stress was a significant predictor of schizophrenia in high-genetic-risk children.

◉ Evaluation

Diatheses may not be exclusively genetic

Most diathesis–stress models assume that genetic influences cause neurochemical abnormalities, which result in increased risk of schizophrenia. However, brain damage, caused by oxygen deprivation during birth, increases the risk of schizophrenia by four times: a non-genetic biological influence (Verdoux *et al.*, 1998).

Urban environments are not necessarily more stressful

Romans-Clarkson *et al.* (1990) found no urban–rural differences in mental health in women in New Zealand. Other studies found differences, but these were accounted for by socioeconomic factors. Social adversity may be more important than urbanisation as a trigger.

Difficulties in determining causal stress

Diathesis–stress models often refer to stressful events shortly before the onset of symptoms. However, maladaptive methods of coping with stress in childhood compromise resilience. This may increase vulnerability to mental illness.

Limitations of the Tienari *et al.* study

The researchers identified limitations in the assessment of family functioning, which was only assessed once, failing to reflect changes over time. Observing reciprocal interactions between family and adoptee makes it impossible to determine whether the stress originates with the family or the child.

Implications for treatment

Genes cannot be altered, but factors interacting with genetic vulnerability can be addressed. For example, women infected with cytomegalovirus during pregnancy are more likely to have a child who later develops schizophrenia, but only if the mother and child carry a particular gene defect (Borglum *et al.*, 2014). Anti-viral medication during pregnancy could protect children of women known to have this gene.

Chapter 7

Eating behaviour

Paper 3, Section C, option 2. 4.3.6 Eating behaviour

- Explanations for food preference: the evolutionary explanation, including reference to neophobia and taste aversion; the role of learning in food preference, including social and cultural influences.
- Neural and hormonal mechanisms involved in the control of eating behaviour, including the role of the hypothalamus, ghrelin and leptin.
- Biological explanations for anorexia nervosa, including the genetic and neural explanations.
- Psychological explanations for anorexia nervosa: family systems theory, including enmeshment, autonomy and control; social learning theory; cognitive theory, including distortions and irrational beliefs.
- Biological explanations for obesity, including genetic and neural explanations.
- Psychological explanations for obesity, including restraint theory, disinhibition and the boundary model. Explanations for the success and failure of dieting.

Key terms (highlight each cell when you can define the term confidently)

Explanations for food preference	Neural and hormonal mechanism	Biological explanations for anorexia nervosa	Psychological explanations for anorexia nervosa	Biological explanations for obesity	Psychological explanations for obesity
Neophobia	Hypothalamus	Genetic explanations	Family systems theory	Genetic explanations	Restraint theory
Taste aversion	Ghrelin	Neural explanations	Autonomy, enmeshment and control	Neural explanations	Disinhibition
Social influences	Leptin	Serotonin	Social learning theory	Hypothalamus	Boundary model
Cultural influences		Dopamine	Modelling and reinforcement	Leptin	Dieting
		Limbic system dysfunction	Media	Thrifty gene hypothesis	Hedonic eating
			Cognitive theory		Denial and ironic process
			Distortions and irrational beliefs		Detail

Content checklist

1. In each 'describe', 'apply' and 'evaluate' cell tick when you have produced brief notes.
2. Once you feel you have a good grasp of the topic add a second tick to the cell.
3. When you feel you have complete mastery of the topic and would be able to answer an exam question without the aid of notes highlight the cell.

I am able to ...	Describe	Apply	Evaluate
Explanations for food preference: the evolutionary explanation, including reference to neophobia and taste aversion			
Explanations for food preference: the role of learning, including social and cultural influences			
Neural and hormonal mechanisms involved in the control of eating behaviour, including the role of the hypothalamus, ghrelin and leptin			
Biological explanations for anorexia nervosa, including genetic and neural explanations			
Psychological explanations for anorexia nervosa: family systems theory, including enmeshment, autonomy and control			
Psychological explanations for anorexia nervosa: social learning theory, including modelling, reinforcement and media			
Psychological explanations for anorexia nervosa: cognitive theory, including distortions and irrational beliefs			
Biological explanations for obesity, including genetic and neural explanations			
Psychological explanations for obesity, including restraint theory, disinhibition and the boundary model			
Explanations for the success and failure of diets			

KEY TERMS

Evolutionary explanations Focus on the adaptive nature of behaviour, i.e. modern behaviours are believed to have evolved because they solved challenges faced by our distant ancestors and so became more widespread in the gene pool.

Food preference Refers to the way in which people choose from among available foods on the basis of biological and learned perceptions such as taste, health characteristics, value, habit, etc.

Neophobia An extreme dislike and avoidance of anything that is new or unfamiliar. Neophobia is a natural reaction to protect against consuming potentially harmful substances – an important survival strategy when faced with 'a world of potential foods whose safety is uncertain' (Prescott, 2013).

Taste aversion A learned response to eating toxic, spoiled or poisonous food, which results in the animal avoiding eating the food that made it ill in the future.

Apply it

Scenario. Sonia will happily eat mashed potato, carrots and peas. But when her mum tries to introduce her to Brussels sprouts she refuses to take even a tiny bite. She tells her mum she is not eating them as they look and smell funny.

With reference to Sonia's behaviour, briefly outline neophobia as an explanation for food preferences. (3 marks)

Explanation. Sonia is reluctant to consume the Brussels sprouts as they are a new and unusual food that looks and smells different to the foods she considers to be 'acceptable'. This neophobic response is a naturally occurring reaction that has evolved to protect a species from the risk of consuming potentially harmful substances. Humans as a species have a varied diet and so are more likely to display neophobia than animals with a more restricted diet, such as koalas who mostly eat eucalyptus leaves. This suggests Sonia's mum will have difficulty introducing a range of new foods to Sonia.

The evolution of food preferences

◎ Early diets

Early humans were hunter-gatherers who ate the animals and plants in their natural environment. Preference for fatty food would have been adaptive because conditions in the EEA meant energy resources were vital for finding the next meal.

Preference for meat

Fossil evidence suggests the daily diet of early hunter-gatherers was primarily animal-based foods which provided the catalyst for brain growth. Milton (2008) claims it is unlikely a vegetarian diet would have provided enough nutrition for early humans to evolve into the active, intelligent creatures they became.

Preference for sweet foods

In the EEA (Environment of Evolutionary Adaptedness), ripe fruit was a source of sugar and calories as well as vitamins and minerals. Mennella (2014) found that children who preferred sweet over salty solutions tended to be tall for their age. An innate preference for sweetness is adaptive as growth and survival in the EEA is more likely in children who sought out high calorie foods.

◎ Taste aversion

Farmers trying to rid themselves of vermin found that rats took small bites of new foods and quickly learned to avoid poisoned bait that had previously made them ill. Garcia *et al.* (1955) showed how rats made ill through radiation shortly after eating saccharin developed an aversion: they had associated the taste with illness.

The adaptive advantage of taste aversion

Food odour can also be linked to illness, resulting in aversion to specific foods. **Taste aversions** would have helped our ancestors to survive because, should they recover from eating poisonous food, they would not make the same mistake again. Learned aversions are very hard to overcome – ensuring prolonged safety.

◎ Neophobia

Species with a varied diet (e.g. rats) display neophobia. Rozin (1997) found that rats who became ill after eating both familiar and unfamiliar food avoid the unfamiliar food in the future. Humans express a reluctance to consume foods alien to their culture and current diet. Unfamiliar foods that fall outside of the definition of 'acceptable foods' in terms of look and smell are rejected. This is more likely for animal products than non-animal products, probably because of the greater illness risk posed by rotting meat (Fessler, 2002).

◎ Evaluation

Are all food preferences a product of evolution?

Traits beneficial for health today (e.g. low cholesterol foods) wouldn't have evolved because it would not have been beneficial in the EEA. Many of the preferences important for our ancestors (e.g. saturated animal fats) are more likely to be avoided today due to their harmful effect on health. Krebs (2009) suggests many of the major global health epidemics in modern societies (diabetes type 2, obesity) result from a mismatch between evolved preferences and modern environments.

Support for evolved preferences for sweet foods

Newborn infants show a slight smile and lick their upper lip the first time they taste something sweet; this innate response means whatever substance eliciting this response will be ingested (Gill & Norgren, 1978). Early exposure to sweetness is not necessary to develop a preference for sweet foods. Bell *et al.* (1973) report cases of cultures with no sweet foods and drinks regularly consuming the sugary goods of new cultures they come into contact with.

Real-world application: taste aversion and chemotherapy

Some radiation and chemotherapy cancer treatments can cause gastrointestinal illness. Bernstein and Webster (1980) gave chemotherapy patients novel-tasting ice cream prior to treatment. The finding that patients developed an aversion to the ice cream led to the 'scapegoat technique' – the patient is given a novel food along with a familiar food just before chemotherapy, so an aversion develops towards the unfamiliar food and not the familiar food.

Support for the heritability of neophobia

If neophobia evolved because of its adaptive advantages, then the trait should show a strong genetic component. 468 adult female twins (211 MZ, 257 DZ) completed the Food Neophobia Scale questionnaire. Knaapila *et al.* (2007) found the heritability estimate for food neophobia in the sample was around 67%, suggesting that about two-thirds of the variation is genetically determined.

Neophobia can also be maladaptive

Neophobia may lead individuals to restrict their diet to nutritionally poor foods, or lose potential health advantages of new foods. Perry *et al.* (2015) found neophobia is associated with poorer dietary quality among Australian children. However, repeated taste exposure without visual and olfactory cues can increase the preference for initially unfamiliar foods (Birch *et al.*, 1987). Although these modified food preferences tend to be short-lived, the underlying neophobic tendency often persists.

The role of learning in food preferences

Social influences
Parental influences
Brown and Ogden (2004) reported consistent correlations between children and parents for intake of snack foods, eating motivations and body dissatisfaction. Parents can also manipulate food availability, e.g. foods as a reward (sweets) or for health benefits (low sugar/salt). One food may be offered as a reward for eating another, i.e. 'If you eat the broccoli you have can have ice cream for dessert.' This approach is not very effective as the preference for the reward food increases, but preference for the distasteful food decreases (Birch et al., 1984).

Peers
Social learning theory suggests observation of role models (e.g. same-age peers) has an impact on our own attitudes and behaviour. For example, Greenhalgh et al. (2009) found that children who observed peers eating novel foods were more likely to try the food themselves, while children who saw a peer refuse a novel food also avoided the food. Birch (1980) arranged for children to sit next to other children who preferred a different vegetable to them. After four consecutive lunchtimes the children showed a change in their vegetable preference that was still evident several weeks later.

Cultural influences
Media effects
The media can have a major impact on eating patterns, but many of these behaviours are limited by personal circumstances such as age, income and family circumstances (MacIntyre et al., 1998). The information about healthy eating learnt from the media needs to be placed within a broader context (i.e. what people can afford/what is freely available). In response to this problem TV chef Jamie Oliver devised his BBC 'Sugar rush' campaign in 2015 to inform the public of the dangers of a high-sugar diet.

The context of meals
'Grazing' and a reliance on convenience foods has become increasingly common in the UK and US. Maguire et al. (2015) found that the number of takeaway restaurants has risen by 45% in the last 18 years – this is most common in areas of the highest deprivation. Gillman et al. (2000) claims young people are choosing to eat in front of the television, a behaviour that has been linked to greater consumption of pizza and salty snacks with less consumption of fruit and vegetables. This 'informal' eating leads to a learned preference for convenience food over balanced meals. Parents whose children watched more television tended to choose foods that are easily prepared as children usually ate them without complaint.

Evaluation of social influences
Limitations of the parental influence view
Typically, studies in this area have been small scale or used a highly selective sample of white Americans. Therefore, it is unclear as to whether findings can be generalised to other populations. For example, Robinson et al. (2001) studied nearly 800 eight- to nine-year-olds from different backgrounds. A complex association between parental behaviour and children's food preferences was found, with girls being more influenced by parental modelling than boys.

Not all parental influences are effective
Interviews with parents of two- to five-year-old children found that not all methods were effective in influencing children's food preferences (Russell et al., 2015). Parental modelling and food exposure was found to successfully promote healthy eating, but forcing consumption and restricting access to food were not. Children who showed health food preferences were more likely to have parents who used the effective feeding strategies, supporting the claim that children do learn food preferences from their parents – but some attempts to influence preference are more effective than others.

Research support for the role of peers
Wardle et al. (2005) found parental consumption of fruit and vegetables was a strong predictor of children's fruit and vegetable consumption. In an experimental study conducted in the Netherlands, primary-age children developed a preference for 'light' (sugar-free) products after observing significant others modelling consumption of these products (Jansen & Tenney, 2001). Social facilitation (an increase in behaviour in the presence of others displaying the same behaviour) allows consumption of foods that others have demonstrated to be safe.

KEY TERMS
Food preference Refers to the way in which people choose from among available foods on the basis of biological and learned perceptions such as taste, health characteristics, value, habit, etc.

Learning The acquisition of knowledge, skills or habits through experience, observation or teaching.

⊙ Evaluation of cultural influences

Research support for media influences on food preferences

Boyland and Halford (2013) found exposure to TV food advertising influences children's food preferences and actual food intake. This influence was dependent on weight status: adverts for high-fat, high-sugar and high-salt foods were particularly influential for overweight and obese children. Furthermore, children who watched the most TV showed the greatest preference for high-carbohydrate and high-fat foods.

Implications of media influences on food preferences

TV appears to be the dominant medium for children's exposure to food marketing, with most adverts being for unhealthy foods (Cairns et al., 2013). A number of countries have regulated TV advertising of unhealthy foods, typically limiting quantity or reducing the effectiveness of adverts. For example, the use of promotional characters and offers or making nutritional claims to promote food to children on TV is restricted by some governments.

Food preferences and the food environment

Chen and Yang (2014) studied Twitter 'tweets' posted over five weekdays in Columbus, Ohio. Food activities such as shopping in high-quality grocery stores or fast-food dining, as well as quality of food choices, were recorded. Analysis showed a significant association between healthy choices and the availability of grocery stores. However, no associations were found between the number of fast-food outlets and healthy or unhealthy food choices. This suggests people are able to resist the development of unhealthy habits if a healthy alternative is available.

Apply it

Scenario. Andre is not a healthy eater. His parents give him money to spend in the school canteen but he often skips lunch and visits the local chip shop with his friends on the way home. He always pesters his parents for chocolate bars and will only drink fizzy pop. His parents have tried to improve his eating habits by restricting the amount of treats in the house and refusing to let him leave the table until he has eaten some of the vegetables on his plate.

Outline and evaluate the role of learning in food preference, making reference to Andre in your answer. (16 marks)

Explanation extract... Andre may have learned his unhealthy habits from his peers who would be influential role models. Greenhalgh et al. (2009) found negative modelling (the model refusing to eat novel food) had an effect on eating behaviour (the observer also refused). In this case Andre is avoiding a healthy school lunch to eat chips (high fat and salt) with his friends. His parents' attempts to improve his diet may be unsuccessful – Russell et al. (2015) found that forcing consumption and restricting access are not effective. Andre's parents would be better advised to model consumption of vegetables themselves. ...

Neural and hormonal mechanisms

◉ Neural mechanisms in the control of eating

Homeostasis

To ensure the body has enough nutrients two separate systems have evolved, one for turning eating 'on', the other for turning eating 'off'. A decline in blood glucose levels activates the lateral hypothesis, producing hunger. Food is consumed and blood glucose levels rise, activating the ventromedial **hypothalamus**, leading to satiation which inhibits feeding.

The lateral hypothalamus (LH) – the ON switch

In the 1950s researchers discovered that damage to the LH in rats caused aphagia (an absence of eating) while stimulating the LH elicited feeding. When the neurotransmitter neuropeptide Y (NPY) was injected into the LH, rats immediately began to eat even when satiated (Reynolds & Wickens, 2000). Repeated NPY injections led to obesity in the rats in just a few days (Stanley et al., 1986).

The ventromedial hypothalamus (VMH) – the OFF switch

Damage to the VMH of rats led to hyperphagia (overeating), while stimulation of the VMH inhibited feeding. The VMH signals 'stop eating' as a result of the many glucose receptors in this area. Gold (1973) argues damage to the nerve fibres passing through the VMH also causes damage to the paraventricular nucleus (PVN), and it is this damage that causes hyperphagia. The PVN also detects the specific foods our body needs and so seems to be responsible for 'cravings'.

◉ Hormonal mechanisms in the control of eating

Ghrelin

Released in the stomach, this hormone stimulates the hypothalamus to increase appetite in response to low bodily resources or undereating. **Ghrelin** levels increase dramatically before we eat and then decrease for about three hours after a meal. Ghrelin is thought to be important in the development of obesity. When injected into the bloodstream of rats food intake increased, while mice lacking either ghrelin or its receptor in the hypothalamus are protected from diet-induced obesity.

Leptin

Produced by fat tissue and secreted into the bloodstream, this hormone travels to the brain, causing a decrease in appetite. Circulating **leptin** levels act as a long-term signal of the amount of fat stored in adipose tissue, while short-term fluctuations provide information regarding changes in calorific intake. By binding to receptors in the hypothalamus, leptin counteracts the effects of NPY (a feeding stimulant secreted by the gut and hypothalamus). Leptin also increases activity of the sympathetic nervous system, which stimulates fatty tissue to burn energy.

◉ Evaluation

Homeostatic mechanisms offer a limited perspective on eating behaviour

The theory that hunger and eating are only triggered by low energy levels is incompatible with the demands of the EEA. For a feeding mechanism to be truly adaptive, it must promote increased consumption (above the body's optimal level) when food is plentiful to protect against food scarcity in the future.

Problems with the role of the lateral hypothalamus

Damage to the LH causes deficits in other behaviours such as thirst and sex. Recent research shows eating is controlled by neural circuits running through the brain rather than control just being located in the hypothalamus. This means the LH plays an important role in controlling eating behaviour but it is not the brain's 'eating centre' (Sakurai et al., 1998).

Support for the role of the ventromedial hypothalamus

The findings that lesions to the VMH resulted in hyerphagia and obesity in animals and humans led to the VMH being named as the 'satiety centre', with the PVN having an important role in this process. Compared to lesions in other brain areas, damage to the VMH caused a substantial increase in eating and weight gain in animals.

Research support for the role of ghrelin in appetite control

In Wren et al.'s (2001) double-blind study, nine healthy volunteers received either ghrelin or saline intravenously. A week later the same participants took part in the other condition. Results showed an increase in food consumption at a free-choice buffet (taken as an indication of appetite) in the ghrelin condition compared to the saline condition – a mean difference of 28% was recorded.

Leptin resistance

Some individuals develop a resistance to leptin, resulting in a failure to control appetite and weight gain. This may be because leptin receptors stop functioning properly and so cells fail to respond to the hormone. Resistance is common in overweight and obese people, making weight loss even harder. Heymsfield et al. (1999) found obese adults needed doses of leptin 20 to 30 times that of normal concentrations to produce significant weight loss. This suggests the problem cannot be linked to leptin deficiency.

KEY TERMS

Ghrelin A hormone that is released in the stomach and which stimulates the hypothalamus to increase appetite. Ghrelin levels increase when a person's bodily resources are low.

Homeostasis The mechanism by which an organism maintains a steady internal environment.

Hypothalamus An area of the brain which has a number of important functions, including the regulation of body temperature, hunger and thirst.

Leptin A hormone that plays a crucial role in appetite and weight control. It is normally produced by fat tissue and secreted into the bloodstream, where it travels to the brain and decreases appetite.

Apply it

Scenario. Researchers interested in the neural control of eating caused damage to the LH in a group of rats. In a separate study, the VMH in a second group of rats was damaged. Finally, either the LH or the VMH was stimulated in a third group of rats.

What changes to eating behaviour would you expect researchers to observe as a result of their interventions? (4 marks)

Explanation. The rats with damage to their LH are likely to show an absence of eating (aphagia) while those whose LH was stimulated will show increased feeding. This is because the LH is thought to be the 'on' switch for eating, causing feelings of hunger to encourage food consumption. VMH damage would lead to hyperphagia (increased eating), but rats whose VMH was stimulated would stop eating. This is because the VMH creates satiety to discourage further eating.

KEY TERMS

Anorexia nervosa (AN) A type of eating disorder in which an individual, despite being seriously underweight, fears that she or he might become obese and therefore engages in self-starvation to prevent this happening. There are two main sub-types: restricting type and binge eating or purging type.

Biological explanations A belief that a full understanding of thoughts, emotions and behaviour must include an understanding of their biological basis, i.e. the role of genetics, neural correlates and hormones.

Genetic explanations The likelihood of behaving in a particular way is determined by a person's genetic makeup, i.e. it is inherited from parents.

Neural explanations Involve the areas of the brain and nervous system and the action of chemical messengers (neurotransmitters) in controlling behaviour.

Biological explanations for anorexia nervosa (AN)

◎ Genetic explanations

Family studies
Strober et al. (2000) found that the first-degree relatives (i.e. parent, sibling, child) of anorexic individuals have a ten times greater lifetime risk of having the disorder. People may inherit a genetic vulnerability to eating disorders rather than **anorexia nervosa (AN)** specifically, a claim supported by the finding that relatives of AN sufferers have an increased risk of developing other eating disorders (Tozzi et al., 2005).

Twin studies
Research generally suggests a moderate to high heritability of AN, with estimates varying between 28% and 75% (Thornton et al., 2010). Wade et al. (2000) interviewed over 2,000 female identical (MZ) twins (100% shared genes) and non-identical (DZ) twins (50% shared genes), evaluating them using the DSM criteria for AN. A heritability rate of 58% was reported.

Adoption studies
Adoption studies overcome the problem of shared environments faced by twin studies. Klump et al. (2009) studied 123 adopted sibling pairs (adopted females and their sisters from their adoptive family) and 56 biological sibling pairs (adopted females and their biological sisters raised separately). Heritability estimates ranged from 59% to 82% for different aspects of disordered eating, e.g. body dissatisfaction, weight preoccupation. Non-shared environmental factors accounted for the remaining variance.

◎ Neural explanations

Serotonin
Bailer et al. (2007) measured serotonin activity in women recovering from restricting-type AN or binge-eating/purging-type AN. Compared to healthy controls and the restricting AN recovery group, significantly higher serotonin activity was recorded in those recovered from binge-eating/purging AN. Furthermore, those who showed the most anxiety had the highest levels of serotonin activity, suggesting persistent disruption of serotonin levels may lead to anxiety, which triggers AN.

Dopamine
PET scans of 10 women recovering from AN were compared to the scans of 12 healthy women. Overactivity in dopamine receptors in the basal ganglia (an area where dopamine plays a part in the interpretation of harm and pleasure) was seen in the AN group. It seems increased dopamine activity in this area alters the way rewards are interpreted. This is in line with the finding that AN sufferers find it hard to associate positive feelings with things others find pleasurable (e.g. food).

Limbic system dysfunction
The neural roots of AN appear to be related to dysfunction of the subcallosal cingulate and insular cortex located in the limbic system. Lipsman et al. (2015) claim that, as these areas regulate emotion, dysfunction can lead to deficits in emotional processing which may then lead to the pathological thoughts and behaviours associated with AN.

◎ Evaluation of genetic explanations

The actual heritability of AN is still unknown
Fairburn et al. (1999) point out the inconsistency in heritability estimates from various studies. In addition, twin research often assumes MZ and DZ twins raised together experience equally similar environments. However, MZ twins are often treated more similarly than DZ twins, which invalidates the claim that the greater concordance seen for MZ twins is due to greater genetic similarity.

Genetic explanations ignore the role of the media in AN
The media's promotion of the ultra-thin female body shape has been viewed as an important risk factor. However, genetically vulnerable individuals might seek out such pictures to reinforce their body image (Bulik, 2004). This is supported by findings that adolescent girls whose AN symptom severity increased over a 16-month period also reported a significantly greater reading of fashion magazines over the same period (Vaughn & Fouts, 2003).

Real-life implications of a biological basis of AN
In many US states AN treatment is restricted under many health insurance plans because AN is not considered to be 'biologically based'. In 2014, the Eating Disorders Coalition was unsuccessful in its bid to get eating disorders included in the 'essential health benefits' that US law requires insurers provide. Research supporting a biological basis creates a case for insurance companies to consider AN in the same way as other psychiatric conditions (e.g. schizophrenia) that are deemed to be biological in origin.

○ Evaluation of neural explanations
Problems with the serotonin explanation

SSRIs which alter serotonin levels are ineffective when used with AN patients. Ferguson *et al.* (1999) found no difference in symptom outcomes between patients taking an SSRI and patients of a similar age, body weight and symptoms not taking the drug. However, SSRIs have been found to be effective in preventing relapse in recovering AN patients (Kate *et al.*, 2001). This suggests malnutrition-related changes in serotonin function might negate SSRI action; only when weight returns to a more normal level do they become effective.

Support for the dopamine–AN relationship

Increased activity in dopamine pathways has been related to food aversion, weight loss, menstrual dysfunction and distorted body image (Kaye, 2008). Increased eye blink is indicative of higher levels of dopamine activity. Barbato *et al.* (2006) found a significant correlation between blink rate and the duration of AN, suggesting the relationship between dopamine activity and AN symptoms develops over time.

Advantages of biological explanations of AN

Biological explanations reduce the stigma patients experience as they challenge the belief that AN is somehow 'their fault'. They also offer the possibility of treating AN through regulation of brain areas associated with the disorder. For example, Lipsman *et al.* (2013) used deep brain stimulation (DBS) to change activity levels of the subcallosal cingulate in those with chronic, severe and treatment-resistant AN. DBS led to an improvement in mood, emotional regulation and quality of life in most of the patients.

Apply it

Scenario. Tanya and her friends are discussing what they believe to be the cause of anorexia nervosa. Some of her friends suggest the media's promotion of ultra-thin models as the ideal female form is to blame. Tanya disagrees, suggesting anorexia nervosa has an internal rather than an external cause. She mentions she has read the disorder seems to run in families and thinks the brain functions differently in individuals with the disorder.

With reference to Tanya's claims, discuss the biological explanations for anorexia nervosa. (16 marks)

Explanation extract… By claiming AN runs in families Tanya is referring to research into genetic explanations which have suggested heritability rates between 28% and 74%. Adoption studies further support the involvement of genes in the disorder, as Klump *et al.* (2009) reported heritability estimates ranging from 59% to 82% for various aspects of disordered eating. However, Tanya should not discount the effect of environmental influences as the actual heritability of the disorder is still unknown. MZ twins are often treated more similarly than DZ twins, which might explain the greater concordance seen in MZ twins compared to DZ twins. …

Autonomy The freedom to make decisions and determine actions without the constraints imposed by others.

Control To direct or to exercise authoritative influence over events or behaviours.

Enmeshment Describes a family where parents are over-emotionally involved with their children but may be dismissive of their emotional needs. This can make it difficult for the child to develop an independent self-concept. The concept is used in family systems explanations of disorders such as anorexia.

Family systems theory Claims that individuals cannot be understood in isolation from one another, but rather as a part of their family.

Apply it

Scenario. When analysing transcripts of AN patients discussing their home life, Morgan noticed that a number of individuals mentioned intense family interactions, a lack of freedom and overprotective parents. *How might family systems theory interpret these findings? (6 marks)*

Explanation. The AN patients' comments could be seen as evidence of the psychosomatic family. One characteristic of this family type is enmeshment. As mentioned in the transcripts Morgan is analysing, enmeshed families show an extreme form of proximity and intense family interactions. This over-involvement stifles children's development in terms of their ability to deal with common stressors. The AN patients also report a lack of freedom, which further suggests they are living in a psychosomatic family as the family is resisting making the necessary changes to allow the adolescent a sense of autonomy. Finally, the overprotectiveness of the parents would reduce the individual's sense of control over their own life, which may lead them to rebel by refusing to eat.

Family systems theory

◉ The psychosomatic family (Minuchin *et al.*, 1978)
A dysfunctional family alongside a physiological vulnerability leads to AN. Therefore, treatment focuses on changing the way the family functions.

Enmeshment
The extreme proximity and intense family interactions cause members to become over-involved, resulting in a lack of boundaries. The individual becomes 'lost in the system' (Minuchin *et al.*, 1978). **Enmeshment** stifles the child's development of the skills needed to deal with common stressors, making development of AN more likely (Barber & Buehler, 1996).

Autonomy
Non-enmeshed families change their transactional patterns when family member(s) reach adolescence to allow for age-appropriate **autonomy**. Enmeshed families insist on retaining usual patterns of transaction, denying the need for change. Family members are not allowed to become independent and so the adolescent struggles to develop autonomy.

Control
Overprotectiveness – having a high degree of concern for each other's welfare – can limit individuals' beliefs regarding the extent to which they are in **control** of their own life. An adolescent may rebel against this control by refusing to eat.

Other characteristics of the psychosomatic family
Rigidity – in the face of stress, rigid families show a lack of flexibility, instead increasing the rigidity of their patterns of behaviour so alternatives go unexplored.
Lack of conflict resolution – AN families have a low tolerance for conflict and find it difficult to acknowledge and resolve problems. AN families are in a constant state of unresolved conflict: intense conflicts are abandoned without resolution. Latzer and Gaber (1998) describe AN families as presenting a façade of togetherness.

Three patterns of conflict-related behaviour identified by Minuchin *et al.* (2009)
1. *Triangulation* – a pair of family members either incorporate or reject a third member, e.g. the child sides with one parent in the rejection of the other parent; the child feels unable to express themselves without appearing to side with one parent against the other.
2. *Parent–child coalition* – the parent the child has sided with responds with excessive concern (enmeshment) to the child's needs; the other parent withdraws.
3. *Detouring* – parents cannot resolve problems so concern is directed onto the child: the child becomes the problem in order to avoid marital conflict.

◉ Evaluation
Support for the concept of enmeshment
Family cohesion is indicative of supportive family interactions, which is linked to positive outcomes and psychological well-being in adolescents. In comparison, enmeshment is rooted in manipulation and control which have a negative impact on adolescents' well-being (Manzi *et al.*, 2006). These findings apply across different cultural groups, supporting Minuchin *et al.*'s predictions.

Research is generally disappointing and inconsistent
Kog and Vandereycken (1989) reported families with an AN member did not show characteristics of the psychosomatic family. Mounting evidence suggests families with an AN member are diverse in terms of family relationships, emotional climate and patterns of interaction.

Inconclusive support from family-based therapy
Carr (2009) argues there is compelling evidence for the effectiveness of family interventions for adolescent AN. However, while there is some evidence that family-focused therapy leads to changes in family functioning, these changes are not necessarily those predicted by the psychosomatic family model and may not happen in all families (le Grange & Eisler, 2009).

Gender bias in family systems theory
Although enmeshment can occur between any family member, **family systems theory** predominantly focuses on reforming 'dysfunctional mothers' and ignores the role fathers play even though fathers also contribute to the enmeshment process. The father's tendency to be overly controlling, demanding action and change from the AN patient, is often overlooked (Gremillion, 2003).

Research support for lack of conflict resolution
Latzer and Gaber (1998) observed parents and their daughters discussing two areas of disagreement unrelated to food and eating. Forty families of adolescent daughters with AN were matched to 40 families without an AN member. The AN families found it more difficult to choose a topic, remain focused on the topic and move forward with a resolution. This supports claims that the psychosomatic family seeks to avoid conflict with family members.

The influence of social learning

Modelling and reinforcement

Modelling – Models may be parents, peers or 'symbolic' models such as celebrities in the **media**. The particular attitude to food or dieting behaviour modelled is observed by the individual and imitated.

Reinforcement – Imitation of modelled behaviour receives positive reinforcement from others, e.g. 'You've lost weight; you look great', making the individual feel better about themselves and continue dieting. Observing positive feedback received for dieting makes the individual also diet as they expect the same reaction from others (vicarious reinforcement).

Maternal role models

Research has suggested mothers 'model' weight concerns for their daughters. Hill *et al.* (1990) found similarities between mothers' and daughters' restraint and dieting behaviour among children as young as 10. Smolak *et al.* (1999) showed that mothers who complained about their own weight tended to have children with weight concerns. These influences tended to be greater for daughters than for sons, and mothers are more influential than fathers.

Peer influences

Eisenberg *et al.*'s (2005) US study found dieting among friends was significantly related to behaviours such as diet pills or purging. Teasing relates to gender-based ideals in that overweight girls and underweight boys were most likely to be teased (Jones & Crawford, 2006). A study of over 2,000 men and women found significant associations between perceived peer dieting and a drive for thinness in both genders. For women, this drive was strongest in late adolescence and for same-sex peers. For men, the strength of association did not differ by age or sex of dieting peers (Gravener *et al.*, 2008).

Media influences

Portrayal of thin models is a significant contributory factor in body image concerns among Western adolescent girls. Those with low self-esteem are more likely to compare themselves to these idealised media images (Jones & Buckingham, 2005). Button *et al.* (1996) found that girls with low self-esteem aged 11–12 were at significant risk of developing an eating disorder at 15–17. The BMA (2000) expressed concern about the use of very thin models in advertising and the fashion industry, stating the degree of thinness promoted is unachievable and biologically inappropriate. *Health* magazine's 2002 study found 32% of female characters on US TV are underweight compared to just 5% of the female audience.

Evaluation

Maternal influence is more complex than social learning

Pike and Rodin (1991) found no evidence for daughters imitating their parents' weight concerns. Ogden and Stewart (2000) found that even though mothers and daughters were similar in weight and BMI there were no associations for their restrained eating or body dissatisfaction. Rather, Ogden and Stewart suggest, the nature of the mother–daughter relationship is important, particularly the degree of enmeshment.

Research support for peer influences

Costa-Font and Jofre-Bonet (2013) found that individuals (especially young women) who had peers with a larger BMI had a lower likelihood of subsequently developing an eating disorder. This suggests that having peers with an average or higher than average BMI offers some protection against AN, whereas when peers have a lower than average BMI the development of AN is more likely.

Another look at peer influences

While Shroff and Thompson (2006) found no correlation among adolescent friends on measures of disordered eating, Jones and Crawford (2006) found overweight girls and underweight boys were more likely to be teased during adolescence. In addition, Cash's (1995) interviews of young adult women found it was the perceived severity of the teasing experienced during adolescence that was linked to future body image rather than the presence or absence of teasing.

Research support for media influences

Becker *et al.*'s (2002) research of adolescent Fijian girls supports the claim the media can be a powerful influence in the development of eating disorders. In 1995 TV was introduced to Fiji; the resulting exposure to Western TV characters led Fijian girls to report a desire to lose weight to become more like the TV characters observed. However, Yamamiya *et al.* (2005) found instructional intervention prior to exposure to idealised female images prevents the adverse effects of the media.

Not all forms of media have the same effects

Harrison and Cantor (1997) found no association between TV exposure and eating disorders but did report a significant association between reading fitness magazines and attitudes to food and dieting. Fashion magazines have also been associated with a preference for lower weight and lower confidence about body image, and feeling frustrated because of this (Turner *et al.*, 1997).

KEY TERMS

Media The various means of communication, such as radio, television, newspapers and the internet, that reach or influence people widely.

Modelling A form of learning where individuals learn a particular behaviour by observing another individual performing that behaviour.

Reinforcement A term used in psychology to refer to anything that strengthens a response and increases the likelihood that it will occur again in the future.

Social learning Learning through observing others and imitating behaviours that are rewarded.

Apply it

Scenario. Anouchka's mother is very careful about the media her daughter is exposed to. Even though Anouchka is 14 years old, her mother does not let her read fashion magazines and discourages her from watching TV shows with very slim actresses. Although her mother follows a strict diet, she tries not to discuss her eating habits or share her body dissatisfaction with Anouchka.

Outline and evaluate the social learning theory explanation of anorexia nervosa. Make reference to Anouchka's mother in your answer. (16 marks)

Explanation extract... Anouchka's mother believes the celebrities and fashion models presented in the media may act as a role model to encourage Anouchka to try to lose weight to receive the same praise and status associated with thinness. Research by Harrison and Cantor found no association between TV exposure and eating disorders but did find reading of fashion magazines was linked to a preference for lower weight. This suggests Anouchka's mother should continue to limit her daughter's exposure to such magazines. Her mother also realises she can be a role model for her daughter and so tries to avoid expressing her own weight concerns and eating patterns. However, she may not need to worry as much as she does as Ogden and Stewart found it was the degree of enmeshment that was influential rather than the presence of the mother as a role model in the development of eating disorders such as AN. ...

KEY TERMS

Cognitive theory When applied to disorders, this is any explanation about the way in which a person processes information that affects their feelings and their behaviour. Cognitive theories emphasise how individuals with AN think differently about themselves and their social world, compared to individuals without the disorder.

Distortions Thinking that has a bias such that what is perceived by a person does not match reality.

Irrational beliefs Beliefs that are unhelpful, illogical and inconsistent with our social reality. Rational beliefs, on the other hand, are helpful, logical and consistent with our social reality.

Apply it

Scenario. Fran has been diagnosed as suffering from anorexia nervosa. Even when looking at recent photos of her thin frame, Fran continues to see herself as overweight and constantly compares herself to catwalk models. Despite friends trying to keep in contact, she claims they organise social activities without her because they find her huge body embarrassing to be around.

Distinguish between the distortions and irrational beliefs Fran is experiencing. (4 marks)

Explanation. Fran holds irrational beliefs about herself and the world around her in that she feels her peers are leaving her out because of her appearance. These beliefs are not based on fact and are unrealistic, e.g. her friends are trying to keep in contact with her. Fran is also showing distorted thinking, leading her to develop a negative body image. By comparing herself to fashion models she is experiencing self-disgust which drives her desire to lose weight.

Cognitive explanations of anorexia nervosa

Distortions and irrational beliefs

Distortions may result from comparisons with others, such as exposure to thin models in the media, in terms of how they look or what they eat. This causes the individual to mistakenly believe they are overweight, leading to self-disgust and attempts to lose weight.

Irrational beliefs – faulty beliefs about the self and the world lead to self-defeating (i.e. harmful) habits. For example, an AN sufferer may believe they have to be thin to be liked by others or blame any social exclusion on their weight.

A cognitive behavioural model of AN (Garner & Bemis, 1982)

AN patients tend to be high-achieving perfectionists, introverted and full of self-doubt. These characteristics, combined with exposure to cultural ideals of thinness, lead to the formation of ideas about the importance of body weight and shape. The irrational belief that losing weight will reduce their distress and make them more attractive to others develops.

The sense of achievement and positive comments from others reinforces weight loss. Anxiety about eating increases, gradually developing into a fear of food and weight gain. Food avoidance becomes the norm and social isolation increases, reducing the chance of realising their beliefs are abnormal. Self-worth is judged by thinness, and complete control over weight becomes desirable.

The transdiagnostic model (Fairburn et al., 2003)

All eating disorders have the same set of underlying cognitive distortions referred to as 'core psychopathology'. Overestimation of body weight, appearance and emphasis on self-control are central factors in AN. Self-esteem is determined by weight and appearance, and control of these. Control of eating is of particular importance when other areas of life seem uncontrollable. Three mechanisms maintain the restriction of food shown in AN:

1. Restriction provides positive reinforcement in the form of enhanced self-esteem.
2. The physiological and psychological changes resulting from starvation are seen as failures in self-control, leading to an intensified reliance on restriction.
3. Focusing on appearance involves regular weight checking and interpreting discomfort as a 'sense of being fat'. Any weight gain or slow weight loss leads to increased restriction to regain self-control and improve self-esteem.

Evaluation

Research support for the role of cognitive factors in AN

Lang et al. (2015) compared 41 children and adolescents diagnosed with AN with 43 health control participants. Compared to controls, AN individuals displayed a more inflexible cognitive processing style: they were less able to overcome existing beliefs in the face of new information. Individuals also showed ineffective processing independent of clinical (e.g. length of illness) and demographic (e.g. education) factors.

Support from Stroop test studies

The Stroop test requires participants to state the colour the word is written in rather than reading the word. This is difficult because processing the word interferes with naming the ink colour. Ben-Tovim et al. (1989) used a version of the Stroop test where words related to weight concerns. Compared to normal controls, AN individuals found it harder to name the colour. This suggests attention is biased towards stimuli relating to weight and fattening food as if there was a preoccupation with these stimuli.

Success of CBT-E therapies support a cognitive explanation for AN

Fairburn et al. (2015) compared CBT-E (CBT addressing the cognitive problems underlying eating disorders) with IPT (interpersonal psychotherapy – which has no cognitive element). 130 patients with eating disorders were randomly assigned to one of the two therapies. After 20 weeks, two-thirds of those receiving CBT-E met the criteria for remission compared to just one-third of the IPT group.

Methodological limitations of cognitive theories of AN

Limited understanding of cognitive distortions may be because of the reliance on self-reports of cognitive processing (Viken et al., 2002). For example, it is assumed irrational thoughts and distortions can be accessed through verbal self-report. Furthermore, self-reported cognitions relating to weight and thinness tend to be assessed retrospectively with the assumption that individuals can accurately represent previous cognitions. Most cognitive scientists now reject self-reports in favour of performance-based measures that directly sample cognitive processing.

Limitations of the cognitive approach

Cooper (1997) argues cognitive models of AN are largely based on clinical observations rather than empirical evidence. There has been comparatively little research to test hypotheses derived from cognitive models and many studies suffer from methodological problems such as over-reliance on self-reports. As such, the development of a cognitive approach to AN has fallen behind the development of cognitive theories for other disorders such as depression and anxiety disorders.

Biological explanations for obesity

Genetic explanations

Twin studies
The average heritability reported is between approximately 40% and 75%. For example, Maes et al.'s (1990) meta-analysis involving over 75,000 individuals recorded heritability estimates for BMI of 74% (MZ) and 32% (DZ). Stunkard et al. (1990) found that, even when raised apart (different environmental influences), MZ twins' BMI is more alike than the BMI of DZ twins (shared environment).

Adoption studies
Stunkard et al. (1986) studied 540 Danish adult adoptees, their adoptive parents (shared environment) and their biological parents (genetics). A strong relationship was seen between the weight category (i.e. underweight, overweight or obese) of adopted individuals and their biological parents. No significant relationship was found between the adults and their adoptive parents' weight category.

Neural explanations

The arcuate nucleus in the hypothalamus
This collection of neurons monitors circulating blood sugar levels. When energy is low, the arcuate nucleus sends messages to other parts of the body, producing a desire to eat, and coordinates this with energy utilisation: carefully adjusting food intake with physical activity. Any malfunction can result in overeating and obesity.

Leptin
Secreted by fat cells, this hormone is a crucial signal of stored bodily energy. Leptin acts on receptors in the control centres of the brain to inhibit food intake, e.g. leptin inhibits neuropeptide Y (an appetite-stimulating hormone found in the arcuate nucleus). Disruption of leptin signalling in the hypothalamus results in obesity (Bates & Myers, 2003).

An evolutionary model of obesity: the 'thrifty gene' hypothesis
Neel (1962) argues that the history of the human species is largely 'food or famine'. Those who gorged themselves during periods of food abundance would have greater fat reserves to survive when food was scarce. In modern society, thrifty genes are disadvantageous because they promote fat storage in an environment where famine is unlikely, resulting in widespread obesity and diabetes.

Evaluation

Genetic contribution to BMI is not stable across age
A meta-analysis of 88 studies found heritability estimates varied according to age. The heritability figure was highest during childhood and decreased during adulthood, probably because adults adopt dietary and exercise habits which reduce the genetic contribution to their BMI and increase the environmental contribution.

Genetic explanations cannot explain sudden increases in obesity rates
A 2015 government report described a sharp increase in UK obesity rates over the last 20 years, e.g. in 1993, 13% of males were classified obese, rising to 26% by 2013, suggesting obesity is not solely linked to genes. Obesity rates also vary geographically, e.g. in rural China overall obesity rates are below 5% but in some cities rates are over 20%. This is likely to be due to the availability of fast food in urban areas.

Research support for the leptin–obesity relationship in humans
Although most evidence is derived from studies on non-human animals, Montague et al. (1997) reported the case of two severely obese cousins, who both had very low leptin levels despite their high level of body fat. Gibson et al. (2004) also reported on a child from the same Pakistani region as the two cousins who also suffered from severe obesity. After four years of leptin injections beneficial effects were seen on the child's appetite, metabolism and weight.

Advantages of biological explanations
Focusing on genetic explanations and neural explanations can be less stigmatising as it implies the condition is beyond personal control. This is a contrast to psychological explanations that highlight personal failures (e.g. lack of exercise, overeating). Biological explanations are often more attractive than complex psychological theories which focus on numerous contributing factors. The scientific nature of biological explanations has led to the development of remedial leptin injections that offer some hope of dealing with the disorder.

Obesity may be better explained by cultural factors
If the hypothesis is correct then the majority of people should have inherited thrifty genes and so most people should be obese (Speakman, 2008). However, the disorder is both fairly recent and restricted to only a few cultures where cultural habits encourage consumption of high quantities of fat and sugar. Ng et al. (2014) found that more than half the world's 671 million obese people live in just 10 countries, suggesting obesity is better explained by cultural factors.

KEY TERMS

Biological explanations A belief that a full understanding of thoughts, emotions and behaviour must include an understanding of their biological basis, i.e. the role of genetics, neural correlates and hormones.

Genetic explanations The likelihood of behaving in a particular way is determined by a person's genetic make-up, i.e. it is inherited from parents.

Neural explanations Involve areas of the brain and nervous system and the action of chemical messengers in the brain known as neurotransmitters in controlling behaviour.

Obesity In adults a BMI of 20–24.9 is considered normal, 25–29.9 overweight and 30–39.9 clinically obese. A BMI over 40 is seen as severely obese. Waist circumference is a second measurement of obesity with weight reduction recommended when the waist is over 40 inches in men and 35 inches in women.

Apply it

Scenario. Collette and her friends are talking about a recent news story where a family of obese people had been interviewed about the impact their weight had on their physical and mental health. Collette's friends said the parents were responsible as they had developed poor eating habits over a period of time and passed these onto their children. Collette disagreed, suggesting the weight gain was beyond the control of the family members.

Discuss the biological explanations for obesity. (16 marks)

Explanation extract... By saying the weight gain was 'beyond the family's control', Collette may have been referring to genetic and neural causes of obesity. As a number of family members were obese, their situation may be a result of genetic inheritance predisposing the family to a higher BMI. For example, twin studies have reported heritability rates ranging from 40% to 74%. However, research also suggests genetic influence varies with age. Elks et al. (2012) found heritability figures were highest during childhood, with the decrease in adulthood being linked to diet and exercise. This means Collette's friends may have identified a contributing factor in the development of obesity when they mention the adults of the family may have poor eating habits. ...

KEY TERMS

Boundary model Considers the biological (feeling hunger, feeling satiation) and cognitive (self-imposed view of what/when to eat) boundaries influencing eating behaviour. Explains overeating as resulting, in part, from the 'what the hell effect'.

Disinhibition In relation to eating behaviour, this is the removal of the normal inhibitions to overeating (e.g. salivation), resulting in the tendency to overeat in response to a range of different stimuli.

Restraint theory Restraint is the conscious restriction of food intake to prevent weight gain or promote weight loss. This theory proposes that attempting to restrain eating actually increases the probability of overeating.

Hunger boundary   Satiation boundary
| Zone of biological indifference |
Normal (unrestrained) eater

Hunger boundary Diet boundary Satiation boundary
Dieting (restrained) eater

Apply it

Scenario. Chad and his GP are discussing a weight loss plan to help Chad reduce his waist circumference and BMI as his current measurements suggest he is obese. Chad explains he finds it difficult to follow a strict diet plan as in times of stress or when he is feeling down he turns to food for comfort. He says as soon as he eats one 'banned food' he just thinks 'what the hell' and eats more, telling himself he will restart the diet tomorrow.

Briefly outline two psychological explanations for obesity. Make reference to Chad's experience in your answer. (6 marks)

Explanation. Chad is finding the diet hard to maintain as restraint theory suggests denial of food can actually lead to overeating. A number of studies have found that following all-or-nothing (strict diet plans) regimes is positively associated with increased waist circumference and BMI. Placing a cognitive boundary (Chad talks about 'banned foods') can lead to the 'what the hell effect' as once Chad has broken his self-imposed boundary he overeats to the point of satiation, which is often higher than unrestrained eaters as dieters have a higher threshold for fullness. Chad also seems to be engaging in emotional disinhibition as he mentions he eats in times of stress or when he is feeling down. In these circumstances, Chad is less responsive to feelings of satiation and so is likely to overeat.

Psychological explanations for obesity

Restraint theory – Herman and Mack (1975)
Rigid restraint is an all-or-nothing approach to dieting, whereas *flexible restraint* is a less strict method where small amounts of fattening foods can be eaten without guilt. Rigid restraint tends to be positively associated with body fat, waist circumference and BMI. In contrast, flexible restraint is negatively associated with these measures (Provencher *et al.*, 2003). Westenhoefer *et al.* (1994) found women who engaged in flexible restraint reduced their intake of ice cream following a preload milkshake but women who used rigid restraint did not reduce their ice cream intake.

The boundary model – Herman and Polivy (1984)
Food intake is regulated along a continuum ranging from hunger to fullness – two extremes driven by biological processes: low energy levels promote eating (hunger), sufficient energy discourages eating (fullness). Between these two points, the 'zone of biological indifference', food intake is determined more by cultural and social factors.

Restrained eaters have a larger zone of biological indifference (lower hunger threshold/higher fullness threshold). Additionally, dieters set a self-imposed diet boundary – a cognitive boundary representing how they feel they should eat. If the dieter breaks this limit the 'what the hell effect' is experienced, prompting the individual to eat until they reach satiation or even beyond.

Disinhibition
In situations where the individual faces lots of palatable food or is under emotional stress the normal inhibitions preventing overeating are removed. Disinhibition has been shown to be strongly associated with adult weight gain and BMI (Bellisle *et al.*, 2004). Bond *et al.* (2001) identified different types of disinhibition:

Habitual – overeating in response to daily life circumstances.

Emotional – overeating in response to emotional states, e.g. anxiety.

Situational – overeating in response to specific environmental cue, e.g. party.

Due to the food-saturated environment of Western societies, habitual disinhibition has been shown to be the most important correlate of weight gain and obesity (Hays & Roberts, 2008). Bryant *et al.* (2008) suggest this form of eating is better explained as 'opportunistic eating'.

Evaluation
Support for restraint theory
Wardle and Beales (1988) randomly assigned 27 obese women to either a diet group, an exercise group or a no-treatment group. In the fourth week, food intake and appetite was assessed before and after a preload snack. In the sixth week, food intake under stressful conditions was measured. In both laboratory assessments, the diet group ate more than the other two groups.

Research is often laboratory based
Laboratory studies of restraint theory typically show violating a diet leads to overeating. However, Tomiyama *et al.* (2009) argue that outside of this artificial setting, restrained eaters would be able to control their eating. They showed dieters who tracked their food intake over a period of days did not overeat after consuming a milkshake. This finding dispels the belief that diet violations led to overeating.

The 'what the hell effect': motivational collapse or rebellious reaction?
The 'what the hell effect' is seen as a breakdown of the dieter's self-control. Ogden and Wardle (1992) suggest that rather than passively giving in, the dieter actively rebels against their self-imposed boundary. This explanation is supported by Loro and Orleans (1981) who found that obese binge eaters frequently reported bingeing as a way of 'unleashing resentment' against their diet.

Disinhibition may not be important in all groups
As most research has focused on white women, conclusions drawn cannot be applied to men or other racial groups. Atlas *et al.* (2002) reported restraint and disinhibition scores were significantly lower for African American students than for white students. Several studies report restraint and disinhibition scores are lower in men, suggesting disinhibition may be a more influential factor in adult weight gain for women.

Disinhibited eating may be linked to insecure avoidant attachment style
Wilkinson *et al.* (2010) found 'attachment anxiety' was significantly linked to disinhibited eating and BMI in their sample of 200 adults whose BMI ranged from 17 to 41. They suggest that a tendency to deal with anxiety by overeating leads, over time, to an increased BMI. Significant life events (e.g. leaving home, entering prison) can lead to BMI changes. Anxiously attached individuals may be more sensitive to these events and so more likely to use disinhibited eating as a way of coping.

Explanations for the success and failure of dieting

◉ A theory of hedonic eating – Strobe (2008)
Increased sensitivity to the hedonic (pleasurable) properties of food consumption makes it difficult for restrained eaters to maintain their diet. The cognitive processes of restrained eaters are geared towards pursuing consumption and any conflicting goal (i.e. **dieting**) is inhibited. Eating enjoyment and eating control are incompatible goals, so thoughts of pleasure inhibit thoughts of control.

◉ Attention allocation – Mischel and Ayduk (2004)
Exposure to attractive food triggers hedonic thoughts; this results in selective attention to these food items. The inhibition of dieting goals makes it difficult to withdraw attention from food and resist the temptation to eat.

◉ The role of denial and the theory of ironic process of mental control
Wegner (1994) found that participants instructed not to think about a white bear rang a bell more often (to indicate they had thought of the bear) than those not asked to suppress this thought. In terms of dieting, those trying to suppress thoughts of 'forbidden foods' may actually think about these foods more. As soon as a food is denied it is desired.

◉ Detail – the key to a successful diet
Redden (2008) claims people's enjoyment of experiences decreases with repetition, making it difficult to stick to a diet. The solution is to not focus on the details of the meal, e.g. tomatoes, apple, celery, to reduce boredom. Redden tested this idea using jelly beans.

How? 135 people were given 22 jelly beans one at a time. Each bean was accompanied with either general information (e.g. bean number 7) or specific flavour details (e.g. cherry flavour).

Showed? The group exposed to the general information became bored with eating jelly beans faster than the group who saw the flavour information. This suggests focusing on the details when consuming food reduces the repetitive feeling and boosts enjoyment, in turn making sticking to a diet more likely.

◉ Evaluation
Soetens et al.'s (2006) support for the ironic process of mental control
Participants were divided into restrained and unrestrained eaters, with the restrained group further divided into high or low disinhibition. The disinhibited restrained group (those trying to eat less but often overeat) used more thought suppression than the other groups and thought more about food they had recently eaten (a rebound effect). Although Wegner (1994) admits the ironic effects observed in studies are not particularly huge, such effects may underlie more serious pathological forms of eating behaviour.

Support for the hedonic theory
Studies have found the presence or even smell of attractive food induces more salivation in restrained than unrestrained eaters. Brunstrom et al. (2004) placed hot pizza in close proximity to 40 females. Restrained eaters showed a greater salivary response than those not dieting, supporting the claim that restrained eaters experience heightened sensitivity to the pleasurable aspects of food.

Real-world application: anti-dieting programmes
These programmes emphasise regulation of eating in response to hunger and satiety and the prevention of inappropriate attitudes to food (e.g. comfort eating, food avoidance). Higgins and Gray's (1999) meta-analysis of programmes' effectiveness found an association with improvements in eating behaviour, psychological well-being and weight stability. This suggests only eating when hungry and stopping when satiated is more effective than trying to restrict or restrain food intake.

Limitations of anecdotal evidence
Memory is not 100% accurate and assessments of the success or failure of the diet is not entirely objective. This creates problems for the reliability of anecdotal evidence of diet strategies. In addition, causal connections between a particular diet plan and weight loss are made too easily without the control over extraneous variables that is possible with randomised trials.

Free will or determinism: the role of genes
One gene codes for lipoprotein lipase (LPL), an enzyme produced by fat cells to help store calories as fat. Too much LPL increases the body's ability to store calories and makes it easier to regain lost weight. Kern et al. (1990) measured LPL levels in nine people who had lost an average of 90 pounds. Compared to before dieting, LPL levels were higher after weight loss, and the fatter the person was at the start of the diet the higher the LPL levels – as if the body was fighting to regain the lost weight. Researchers suggest weight loss activated the gene producing the enzyme. This might be why obese people often easily regain lost weight.

KEY TERM
Dieting A deliberate reduction of food intake in an attempt to lose weight. There are three basic forms: restricting total food intake, refraining from eating certain foods, avoiding eating for long periods of time.

Apply it
Scenario. Demi always seems to be on a diet but never seems to lose much weight. At the start of each diet she makes a list of 'forbidden foods' and tries her best to avoid temptation. However, it's not long before she gets bored and finds herself longing for sweet, sticky cakes and the rich, cheesy taste of hot pizza.

Outline and evaluate one or more explanations for the success and/or failure of dieting. (16 marks)

Explanation extract... Demi may be more sensitive to the pleasurable properties of food like pizza and cake which trigger her desire to eat these foods. The theory of hedonistic eating suggests that eating enjoyment is incompatible with eating control, meaning Demi's increasing thoughts of the pleasure of eating will reduce the likelihood of maintaining her diet. Brunstrom et al. (2004) support this explanation of diet failure as they found that, when presented with a hot pizza, female restrained eaters showed a greater salivary response than unrestrained eaters.

Creating a list of 'forbidden foods' may result in Demi thinking more about these foods, which may increase the likelihood of consuming them. Soetens et al. (2006) found that dieters who often overate (disinhibition restrained eaters) used more thought suppression than restrained eaters who showed low levels of disinhibition and unrestrained eaters. ...

Chapter 8

Stress

Paper 3, Section C, option 3. 4.3.7 Stress

- The physiology of stress, including general adaptation syndrome, the hypothalamic pituitary-adrenal system, the sympathomedullary pathway and the role of cortisol.
- The role of stress in illness, including reference to immunosuppression and cardiovascular disorders.
- Sources of stress: life changes and daily hassles. Workplace stress, including the effects of workload and control.
- Measuring stress: self-report scales (Social Readjustment Rating Scale, and Hassles and Uplifts Scale) and physiological measures, including skin conductance response.
- Individual differences in stress: personality types A, B and C and associated behaviours; hardiness, including commitment, challenge and control.
- Managing and coping with stress: drug therapy (benzodiazepines, beta blockers), stress inoculation therapy and biofeedback. Gender differences in coping with stress. The role of social support in coping with stress; types of social support, including instrumental, emotional and esteem support.

Key terms (highlight each cell when you can confidently explain each term)

The physiology of stress and the role of stress in illness	Sources of stress (Holmes & Rahe, Lazarus)	Measuring stress	Individual differences in stress (Friedman & Rosenman, Kobasa & Maddi)	Managing and coping with stress	Factors in coping with stress: gender differences, social support
Adrenaline and noradrenaline	Life changes	Hassles and Uplifts Scale (HSUP)	Type A personality	Benzodiazepines	Emotion-focused coping
Cortisol	Life change units (LCUs)	Physiological measures of stress	Type B personality	Beta blockers	Problem-focused coping
General adaptation syndrome	Daily hassles	Skin conductance response	Type C personality	Stress inoculation therapy	Tend-and-befriend response
Hypothalamic pituitary-adrenal system	Daily uplifts	Social Readjustment Rating Scale (SRRS)	Hardiness	Biofeedback	Emotional support
Sympathomedullary pathway	Job control				Esteem support
Cardiovascular disorder	Workload				Instrumental support
Immunosuppression	Workplace stress				

Content checklist

1. In each 'describe', 'apply' and 'evaluate' cell tick when you have produced brief notes.
2. Once you feel you have a good grasp of the topic add a second tick to the cell.
3. When you feel you have complete mastery of the topic and would be able to answer an exam question without the aid of notes highlight the cell.

I am able to ...	Describe	Apply	Evaluate
The physiology of stress, including general adaptation syndrome			
The hypothalamic pituitary-adrenal system			
The sympathomedullary pathway			
The role of cortisol			
The role of stress in illness, including reference to immunosuppression			
Stress and cardiovascular disorders			
Sources of stress: life changes			
Sources of stress: daily hassles			
Workplace stress, including the effects of workload and control			
Measuring stress: self-report scales (Social Readjustment Rating Scale, and Hassles and Uplifts Scale)			
Physiological measures, including skin conductance response			
Individual differences in stress: personality types A, B and C and associated behaviours			
Hardiness, including commitment, challenge and control			
Managing and coping with stress: drug therapy (benzodiazepines, beta blockers)			
Managing stress: stress inoculation therapy			
Managing stress: biofeedback			
Gender differences in coping with stress			
The role of social support in coping with stress; types of social support, including instrumental, emotional and esteem support			

The physiology of stress

Stress is an emotional response to physical or psychological threats.

◉ Short-term stress response

The immediate fight-or-flight response is the **sympathomedullary pathway**, or SAM system.

S – sympathetic nervous system – a branch of the autonomic nervous system (ANS), alerted as soon as a stressor is perceived

AM – adrenal medulla – responds by releasing **adrenaline** and **noradrenaline** into the bloodstream

When the threat has passed, the parasympathetic branch of the ANS returns the body to its normal resting state (rest and digest).

◉ Long-term stress response

The **hypothalamic pituitary-adrenal system** (HPA axis) is also activated by the stress, but is slower.

H – hypothalamus – releases corticotrophin-releasing hormone into the bloodstream

P – pituitary gland – CRH causes the pituitary to release adrenocorticotrophic hormone (ACTH)

A – adrenal cortex – stimulated by ACTH, releases **cortisol**. This lowers sensitivity to pain and gives a quick burst of energy via release of glucose from stores, but also impairs cognitive performance and immune response.

◉ General adaptation syndrome (GAS)

Selye (1930s) described how animals have a universal, adaptive response to all stressors. The **general adaptation syndrome** has three stages:

Stage 1 – Alarm reaction: the threat is identified. The hypothalamus triggers the SAM pathway, preparing the body for fight-or-flight.

Stage 2 – Resistance: the body adapts to the demands of the environment. Resources (sugars, proteins, neurotransmitters) are being depleted, leading to deterioration of the immune system.

Stage 3 – Exhaustion: systems cannot maintain normal functioning. This results in stress-related illnesses: ulcers, depression, cardiovascular problems, etc.

◉ Evaluation

Gender differences

Biological research uses male animals to avoid cyclical fluctuations in female hormones, and is therefore gender biased. Taylor *et al.* (2000) suggest that female stress responses, the 'tend and befriend' response, were developed during our evolutionary past (the environment of evolutionary adaptiveness, EEA) to protect children. Women form alliances and the fight/flight response is inhibited by oxytocin.

Negative consequences of the fight-or-flight response

The physiological responses would be adaptive for threats requiring energetic behaviour. Many modern stressors do not, and increased blood pressure results in physical damage to blood vessels and heart disease. Long-term raised cortisol causes immunosuppression, increasing the risk of infection.

The transactional model of stress

Lazarus and Folkman (1984) argued that **cognitive appraisal** – perceived demands and perceived ability to cope – determines an individual's stress response. Evidence comes from participants who watched a gruesome film, having been told it showed 'exciting' or 'painful' events. The 'exciting' group had less ANS arousal than the 'painful' group.

Research support for GAS

Selye observed that human patients exposed to stress all had similar symptoms (pains, loss of appetite), and that rats produce similar responses to many stressful experiences, such as surgical injury, excessive exercise and sublethal doses of drugs.

Stress-related illness may not be due to depletion of resources

Recent research shows that many 'resources' are not depleted, even under extreme stress. The exhaustion phase is probably due to increased cortisol activity, which leads to stress-related illness.

KEY TERMS

Adrenaline and noradrenaline Hormones associated with arousal of the sympathetic nervous system, causing the physiological sensations related to the stress response (raised heart rate, sweating, etc.). Also function as neurotransmitters.

Cortisol Hormone produced as a result of chronic stress, with both positive and negative effects (e.g. burst of energy and reduced immune response).

General adaptation syndrome How all animals cope with stress in an initially adaptive way, but ultimately leading to illness. The three stages are alarm, resistance and exhaustion.

Hypothalamic pituitary-adrenal system Physiological pathway involved in the long-term (chronic) stress response, involving cortisol.

Sympathomedullary pathway System involved in the immediate (acute) response to stress (fight-or-flight), involving adrenaline.

Apply it

Scenario. Sophie has started a new job working as a PA for the boss of a chain of restaurants. She soon finds that her workaholic boss expects her to work long hours and take on a great deal more responsibility than she had anticipated. She appeared to be coping with this stressful job for the first few weeks. However, after four weeks she is completely exhausted and feels unable to cope.

Using your knowledge of the general adaptation syndrome, explain why Sophie feels the way she does. (4 marks)

Application. Sophie's stress response is activated to enable her to work hard and meet her boss's expectations – this is the alarm reaction stage. Next her body adapts to the needs of ongoing stress of long hours and responsibility, and uses up resources in maintaining the stress response, like sugars, proteins, neurotransmitters, etc. – the resistance stage. Finally, she becomes exhausted as she has depleted resources, and this will lead to health problems.

KEY TERMS

Cardiovascular disorder Any disorder of the heart (such as coronary heart disease, CHD) and circulatory system (such as hypertension, commonly known as high blood pressure) as well as strokes (restricted blood flow to parts of the brain).

Immunosuppression Suppression of the immune system – a system of cells within the body that is concerned with fighting intruders such as viruses and bacteria so they cannot infect the body. For example, white blood cells (leucocytes) identify and eliminate foreign bodies (antigens).

The physiology of stress

Immediate stress: Adrenaline and cardiovascular disorders

Stress activates the SAM pathway, leading to production of adrenaline and noradrenaline. These cause **cardiovascular disorders**:

- increased heart rate makes the heart work harder, wearing it out over time
- constriction of blood vessels to increase blood pressure causes wear on blood vessels
- increased blood pressure dislodges plaques on blood vessel walls, which can block arteries (atherosclerosis). This can cause a heart attack or stroke.

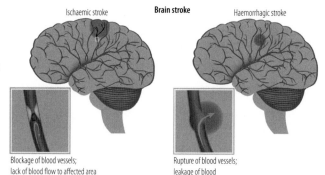

Ischaemic stroke | **Brain stroke** | Haemorrhagic stroke

Blockage of blood vessels; lack of blood flow to affected area

Rupture of blood vessels; leakage of blood

Key study: Cardiovascular disorders – Williams *et al.* (2000)

How? 13,000 people completed a self-report anger scale. None had CHD.

Showed? Six years later, 256 had experienced heart attacks. High scorers on the anger scale were two and a half times more likely to have a heart attack, and moderate scorers were 35% more likely than low scorers.

Ongoing stress: Cortisol and immunosuppression

Ongoing stress activates the HPA system, resulting in the production of several hormones including cortisol. One effect of cortisol is **immunosuppression**.

Key study: Immunosuppression – Kiecolt-Glaser *et al.* (1984)

How? Blood samples taken from 75 medical students one month before exams (low stress) and during the exam period (high ongoing stress). Immune system functioning was measured by counting natural killer (NK) cells in the blood. Participants completed the SRRS and a loneliness scale to assess social support.

Showed? NK activity was reduced in the second blood samples compared to the first. Those with high SRRS scores and those with the least friends had the lowest NK counts. This shows that ongoing stress reduces immune function, and loneliness contributes to the effect.

Evaluation
Self-report
Stress and cardiovascular outcomes are often based on self-report questionnaires. These may be biased by negative perceptions, which would cause people to score high on both measures, leading to a spurious correlation.

Supporting research for the effect of stress on cardiovascular disorders
A large body of research links stress with cardiovascular disease. Sheps *et al.* (2002) tested 173 volunteers with ischaemia (reduced blood flow to the heart). Their blood pressure soared during a public speaking test. 50% had erratic heartbeats; 44% of these died within four years, compared to 18% who did not.

Individual differences in cardiovascular effects
Women show more adverse hormonal and immunological reactions to marital conflict (Kiecolt-Glaser *et al.*, 2005). Stress has a greater effect on older people's immune systems (Segerstrom & Miller, 2004). Some hyperresponsive individuals respond to stress with greater increases in blood pressure and heart rate, leading to more cardiovascular damage (Rozanski *et al.*, 1999).

Stress does not always have a negative effect on the immune system
Stress can enhance immune activity: up-regulation for acute stress, down-regulation for chronic stress. A meta-analysis (Segerstrom & Miller, 2004) reviewed 300 studies, finding that the longer the stress, the more the immune system shifted from adaptive to detrimental changes.

Stress and illness is not a simple relationship
Health is affected by genetics, lifestyle and many other factors. Health changes slowly, so it is difficult to link to particular stressors. Continuous monitoring over long periods is impractical, so it is difficult to establish a relationship between long-term stress and illness (Lazarus, 1992).

Apply it

Scenario. A group of students studied the role of stress in illness over two months. Every week they asked their friends to rate how stressed they felt and whether they had been ill in the previous week. They calculated a stress score and an illness score for each participant. The students found a positive correlation between stress and illness scores.

Discuss what these findings indicate about the relationship between stress and illness, evaluating the research methods used. (4 marks)

Application extract. The students tested their friends, who may not be a representative sample of a wider student population ... The correlation does not imply causation; it is possible that being ill made their friends more stressed as they had work to catch up ... The self-report measures may be biased by negative perceptions of the degree of both stress and illness experienced... As a result, people would consistently score high on both measures, artificially strengthening the correlation.

Sources of stress: life changes

Life changes are events that necessitate a major transition in some aspects of life. They can be positive or negative events, and require 'psychic energy' (mental and emotional effort).

◎ Measuring life change

Holmes and Rahe (1967) developed the Social Readjustment Rating Scale (SRRS). Individuals identify which of 43 life events have occurred during a set time period (three months, six months or a year). Each has a score in **life change units (LCUs)**, e.g. death of a spouse is 100 LCU, pregnancy is 40 LCU.

◎ Key study: Rahe *et al.* (1970)

How? 2,664 male naval and marine personnel on three US Navy cruisers completed the Schedule of Recent Experiences (SRE) for events in the last two years. SRE was a form of SRRS adapted to include events relevant for this sample. Illness records were kept over six to eight months on the ships.

Showed? A significant positive correlation of +.118 between LCU and illness score. Lower SRE was associated with lower levels of illness while at sea.

◎ Other research on life changes

Cohen *et al.* (1993) gave participants the cold virus and assessed life changes and stress using the SRE and a perceived stress scale. Those with higher LCUs were more likely to develop colds. There was no link between perceived stress and illness – it was the actual stress that mattered, not the perception. This suggests life changes result in immunosuppression.

◎ Evaluation

A valuable approach

The SRRS has been used extensively in further research. For example, Heikkinen and Lonnqvist (1995) found that people in Finland who died by suicide had significant life changes in the preceding three months, such as bereavement, financial troubles and unemployment.

Reliability of recall

The SRRS relies on people's recall of past events, which may be unreliable. Rahe (1974) found test–retest reliability varies depending on the time interval between testing. However, Hardt *et al.* (2006) found good reliability of recall of childhood events in 100 patients.

Individual differences

The life change approach ignores the different impact of events on individuals. The death of a spouse may be less stressful if they are elderly and have been ill for a long time, for example. Christmas may be peaceful for some people but very stressful for others.

Daily hassles may be a better predictor of stress

Major life changes are rare. For most people, minor daily hassles contribute more to stress. DeLongis *et al.* (1988) found no relationship between LCU and health, but a significant +.59 correlation between hassles and next-day health problems such as flu, headaches and backaches, in 75 married couples.

Spurious relationship

Correlational data does not imply causation. Anxiety could be an intervening variable: Brown (1974) suggests that anxious people report more negative life events and would be prone to more illness. Also, ill people look for causes, and may report more stressful events.

Apply it

Scenario. In the past, mothers of children with Down's syndrome reported far more traumatic events in their pregnancy than did mothers of non-Down's children – at that time they didn't know that Down's was a chromosomal abnormality.

Discuss how the SRRS could be used to analyse a relationship between stressful life events and a birth disorder. Refer to issues of reliability and validity in your answer. (16 marks)

Application extract… Mothers of babies with a birth disorder could complete the SRRS and compare with a control group of mothers without a birth disorder. An association could show a causal link. However, the reliability of SRRS depends on the time interval, so it should be completed as soon as possible after the pregnancy. Also, mothers of babies with a birth disorder may look for a cause and recall more stressful events, so this could be a confounding factor, reducing the validity of the findings. Birth disorders could be caused by chromosome abnormalities, or by the mother's behaviour during pregnancy, e.g. using drugs or alcohol – these behaviours may be affected by anxiety so a link between LCU scores and birth disorders could be due to anxiety and alchohol use rather than the events themselves. …

KEY TERMS

Life changes Events (such as divorce or bereavement) that require an adjustment in various aspects of a person's life. As such, they are significant sources of stress.

Life change units (LCUs) A number assigned to each life event to represent how much stress is created. The higher the number, the more stressful.

The Social Readjustment Rating Scale (SRRS)	
Example items	
Rank	Life event (number in brackets represents LCU)
1	Death of a spouse (100)
2	Divorce (73)
4	Jail term (63)
6	Personal injury or illness (53)
7	Marriage (50)
8	Fired at work (47)
10	Retirement (45)
12	Pregnancy (40)
17	Death of a close friend (37)
22	Change in responsibilities at work (29)
23	Son or daughter leaving home (29)
25	Outstanding personal achievement (28)
27	Begin or end school (26)
28	Change in living conditions (25)
30	Trouble with boss (23)
33	Change in schools (20)
36	Change in social activities (18)
41	Holiday (13)
42	Christmas (12)
43	Minor violations of the law (11)

KEY TERMS

Daily hassles The 'irritating, frustrating, distressing demands that to some degree characterise everyday transactions with the environment' (Kanner et al., 1981).

Daily uplifts The minor positive experiences of everyday life, e.g. receiving a compliment at work or feeling good about one's appearance.

The five most common hassles and uplifts (Kanner et al., 1981)	
Hassles	Uplifts
Concerns about weight 52.4%	Relating well with spouse/lover 76.3%
Health of a family 48.1%	Relating well with friends 74.4%
Rising prices of common goods 43.7%	Completing a task 73.3%
Home maintenance 42.8%	Feeling healthy 72.7%
Too many things to do 38.6%	Getting enough sleep 69.7%

* The percentage shown indicates how many people selected each item as a hassle/uplift.

Sources of stress: daily hassles

Daily hassles are relatively minor events in the course of a normal day, such as everyday work concerns, a disagreement with a colleague, or missing the bus. Lazarus (1980) proposed that these are more relevant to stress levels than the relatively rare life events. **Daily uplifts**, like a smile from a stranger or an email from a long-lost friend, may counteract the damaging effects of stress.

◎ Explaining the effect of daily hassles

Accumulation: the additive effect of minor daily stressors accumulates to cause stress reactions such as anxiety and depression (Lazarus, 1999).

Amplification: chronic stress from major life changes (e.g. divorce) makes people more vulnerable to daily hassles (e.g. squabbling children). The minor stressors amplify the experience of stress and deplete the person's resources for coping.

◎ Key study: Kanner et al. (1981)

How? The Hassles and Uplifts Scale (HSUP) was completed monthly for nine months by 100 participants aged 45–67. They also completed a life events scale, a measure of anxiety and depression, and a scale assessing positive and negative emotion.

Showed? The five most common hassles and uplifts are shown in the table opposite. (These differ from those selected by student participants, who stressed by having too much to do.) There was a significant negative correlation between frequency of hassles and psychological well-being. Hassles were a better predictor of well-being than life events or uplifts.

◎ Other research on daily hassles

Bouteyre et al. (2007) found a positive correlation between scores on the hassles scale and the incidence of depressive symptoms in French psychology students starting university.

◎ Evaluation

Why daily hassles may have more impact than life changes

Flett et al. (1995) found that students rated people in scenarios experiencing major life events as more likely to seek and receive social support than people experiencing daily hassles. Daily hassles may be a greater source of stress because people receive less emotional support from others.

Reliability of recall

Retrospective reporting over a month may be biased and not always accurate. A diary method is better: Charles et al. (2013) studied 700 participants keeping daily diaries of hassles and negative feelings.

Problems with self-report

Social desirability bias affects the validity of findings. People may not want to admit negative experiences such as arguing with their children or feeling incompetent at work. This suggests that self-reports may offer a biased account of daily hassles.

Individual differences

Gender differences affect people's evaluation of events. Miller et al. (1992) found that females associate pets with uplifts (leisure, lack of psychological pressure), but males associate pets with hassles (time and money).

What does the research tell us?

Much research is correlational, and causation could be in either direction. A depressed person is more likely to interpret events negatively. However, the study by Charles et al. found that the hassles score predicted depression 10 years later, so the negative daily experience should be taken seriously.

Apply it

Scenario. People who reported a difficult day at work subsequently tended to report higher levels of stress on their commute home, and admitted shouting at other road users.

Using your knowledge of daily hassles and stress, explain the relationship between stress during the day and increased road rage on the commute home. (4 marks)

Application. A difficult day at work constitutes an experience of daily hassles, and according to Lazarus these frustrations accumulate so that the person can then respond badly to further stressors, such as heavy traffic or diversions on the way home. In addition, if the person is going through major life changes this can amplify the effect of minor hassles – so if they have a new job or even a promotion with more responsibility, this extra stress makes them more vulnerable to road rage on the way home.

Sources of stress: workplace stress

Stress causes illness and absenteeism, which costs the UK economy £6.5 billion a year (Shearer, 2013). Work satisfaction is a key element of happiness, and unchallenging work (work underload) can also be stressful.

The job-strain model
This model proposes that the workplace creates stress in two ways:
- High **workload** – creating greater job demands
- Low **job control** – over deadlines, procedures, etc.

Key study: The Whitehall study – Marmot *et al.* (1997)
How? 10,000 UK civil servants were followed from 1985, measuring workload, sense of job control and social support. Coronary heart disease (CHD) was assessed after 11 years.

Showed? Highest-grade workers (e.g. accountants) had higher workload and sense of job control than lower-grade workers (e.g. administrative staff). High workload was not associated with CHD but low job control was. Low job control with high workload (high job strain) was strongest in younger workers and not reduced by high levels of social support.

Key study: Swedish sawmill – Johansson *et al.* (1978)
How? 28 manual workers were divided into high-risk (high workload, low control) and low-risk groups, matched for education and experience. Adrenaline levels in their urine were recorded daily, with self-reports of job satisfaction and illness.

Showed? The high-risk group had higher illness rates, higher adrenaline levels and reported more sense of social isolation than the low-risk group.

Is workload more important in creating stress than job control?
Kivimäki *et al.* (2002) found that, in 800 Finnish workers, those with high 'job strain' were 2.2 times more likely to die from CHD than those with low 'job strain'. This effect disappeared if workload or job control were considered separately, or if occupational group (related to socioeconomic status) was taken into account.

Evaluation
Individual differences
Lazarus's transactional approach offers a fuller explanation: that the person's perceived ability to cope affects their perception of stress in the workplace. Schaubroeck *et al.* (2001) found that some workers are *less* stressed by having no control or responsibility, and have better immune responses.

Work underload
When people are in jobs beneath their capabilities, or given tasks lacking any creativity or challenge, they report low job satisfaction and significant absence due to stress-related illness (Shultz *et al.*, 2010). However, the highest levels of stress-related illness were still in employees reporting work overload.

Validity
Many studies use questionnaires, so validity is affected by social desirability bias. Keenan and Newton (1989) found that interviews revealed stressors not included in questionnaires, e.g. time-wasting job demands. Conversely, questionnaires contain items which are seldom mentioned, e.g. role conflict and ambiguity. Interviews may be more valid.

Workplace stress and mental health
When combined with other problems such as difficulties at home, workplace stress can increase the risk of depression. Certain features of the workplace are needed for good mental health, described by Warr (1987) as 'vitamins'. These include variety, personal control, physical security and social contact.

The evolution of work and workplace stressors
Work environments are changing with new technology, so research is rapidly outdated. This means that research into the influence on work and stress may tell us very little about how people cope with the stressful nature of modern work practices.

KEY TERMS
Job control The extent to which a person feels they can manage aspects of their work, such as deadlines and work environment.

Workload The amount of effort and/or activity involved in a job. It is quite often discussed as 'job demand', i.e. the amount required for a person to do during their working day.

Workplace stress Aspects of our working environment (such as work overload or impending deadlines) that we experience as stressful, and which cause a stress reaction in our body.

Apply it
Scenario. Tom is at college and works in a call centre in the evenings, which he finds very boring and frustrating as he has to cold call home owners, who are often quite rude to him. He has to meet targets for numbers of contacts, but people usually put the phone down before he has explained why he is calling. He tries to do his homework at the weekend but is often too tired to concentrate.

Using your knowledge of workplace stress, explain why Tom is struggling to do his homework at the weekend. (4 marks)

Application. Tom is under pressure at work as he has to meet targets, so this gives him a high workload, and it is difficult to make the contacts so this gives him low job control. High workload and low job control combine to make high job strain and this causes stress, according to the Swedish sawmill study by Johansson. This makes Tom tired. Tom is at risk of becoming physically ill and is too tired to do his homework because his experience of work is negative. If he was having work satisfaction he might feel happier and have more energy, but he finds his work very boring and frustrating.

KEY TERMS

Hassles and Uplifts Scale (HSUP) A self-report scale. Hassles and uplifts are scored on a 3-point scale for severity and frequency. The two scores are reported separately.

Physiological measures of stress Any method that is based on the body's physical response to stress and thus related to effects of the SAM pathway or HPA system.

Skin conductance response A measurement of the electrical conductivity of the skin, which is increased when sweat is produced as part of the sympathetic response.

Social Readjustment Rating Scale (SRRS) A self-report scale to assess life events over a set period of time. There are 43 events on the scale, each of which is related to a certain number of life change units (LCUs).

LINK

See p.85 for example items from the SRRS.

LINK

See p.84 for the physiology of stress.

Measuring stress: self-report scales and physiological measures

○ Self-report scales

These are questionnaires measuring people's perception of their stress. Despite some limitations (see evaluation) they are popular in research.

Social Readjustment Rating Scale (SRRS): Holmes and Rahe (1967) developed this scale by analysing 5,000 patient records and finding 43 common life events reported by patients as issues in their lives. Four hundred people scored them according to how much readjustment they would require by an average person compared to marriage, which was given a score of 50. The average scores gave life change units (LCUs) for each life event. To complete the scale, the individual selects events that have occurred within a set period of time, and the LCUs are added up.

Hassles and Uplifts Scale (HSUP): Kanner et al. (1980) generated a list of 117 hassles and 135 uplifts relating to work, health, family, the environment and chance occurrences. To complete the scale for a particular time period, the hassles are rated on a 3-point scale for severity and uplifts are rated for frequency.

○ Physiological measures

Skin conductance response: Arousal of the sympathetic nervous system leads to production of adrenaline and noradrenaline. These cause physiological responses, increasing heart and breathing rates, blood pressure and sweating. Sweat increases the electrical conductance of the skin, especially in the palms of the hands which contain many sweat glands. A very small voltage (0.5V) is passed through two electrodes on the index and middle fingers, measuring conductance.

Physiological measures of stress: Blood pressure and heart rate can be monitored as a measure of sympathetic arousal. Cortisol, produced in response to ongoing stressors, can be measured in saliva or urine.

○ Evaluation

Criticisms of the SRRS

Events have different meanings for different people, e.g. a divorce may be less stressful if the marriage was unhappy. However, Holmes and Rahe argued that negative and positive events are stressful. Some items only apply to adults, and modified versions have been produced. The scale ignores social support, which moderates the negative effects of stress. The Life Stressors and Social Resources Inventory (LISRES) addresses this.

Criticism of the HSUP scale

The original scale contained health-related items, which would create a spurious correlation with illness, and have now been removed to improve validity. Self-report scales are vulnerable to response bias, where a participant prefers to answer positively, or tends to select items from the right rather than the left. The scale is very long – 250 items – and respondents don't maintain concentration, resulting in poor test–retest reliability (.48 for hassles, .60 for uplifts). A shorter version of 53 items has been produced.

Physiological measures are more appropriate in some situations

They avoid social desirability and response set bias, and can be used with young children and animals, but the subjective perception of stress is ignored – stress is not just physiological.

Non-specific response

Sympathetic arousal can be caused by many emotions: fear, anger, sexual arousal and a sense of being treated unfairly. Temperature, humidity and medication can also change the skin conductance.

Other applications

The polygraph or lie detector uses skin conductance, but results are not reliable as so many other factors affect conductance. Also psychopaths lack emotional responsiveness and can lie without any physiological signs.

Apply it

Scenario. Janette is interested in the stress levels of students taking exams.

Outline and evaluate methods Janette could use to measure students' stress levels. (16 marks)

Application extract… Janette could use multiple methods, to gain a variety of measures of stress. She could measure the students' skin conductance before, during and after the exam, although the equipment might be intrusive, so it would be difficult to measure during the exam. She could attach heart rate or blood pressure monitors to students to provide continuous data during the exam. She could measure cortisol in their saliva before and after exams. These physiological measures depend on other factors, however, so …

In order to test the students' own perception of their stress levels, it would be better to use self-report measures. The SRRS and HSUP scales could be used to test the students' general levels of stress, to see whether life events or hassles and uplifts affect their response to exam stress. However, these scales …

Individual differences in stress: personality

Personality is a set of characteristic behaviours, attitudes and general temperament that remain relatively stable over the course of a person's life and distinguish one individual from another.

Type A and B personality

Friedman and Rosenman were medical doctors working with CHD patients.

They proposed that **Type A personalities** display competitiveness and achievement striving, impatience, hostility and aggressiveness. These characteristics would lead to raised blood pressure and stress hormones, causing CHD.

Type B personalities lack these characteristics, so are patient, relaxed and easy-going, decreasing risk of CHD.

Key study: Friedman and Rosenman (1959, 1974)

How? The Western Collaborative Group (WCG) interviewed 3,000 Californian men aged 39–59, excluding any with existing signs of CHD. Interviewers were deliberately provocative, such as speaking very slowly so that Type As would want to interrupt.

Showed? After eight and a half years, 257 participants had developed CHD. Twice as many Type As had suffered heart attacks as Type B. Type As also had higher blood pressure, and twice as many had died of cardiovascular problems. (Type As were also more likely to smoke and have a family history of CHD.)

Type C personality

Type C individuals suppress negative emotions and are unassertive, likeable, helpful people. They cope with stress by ignoring their own physical and emotional needs. This behaviour has been linked to cancer, because chronic stress affects the immune system.

Key study: Morris *et al.* (1981)

How? 75 women attending a London cancer clinic over a two-year period were interviewed. They were asked about expression of affection, unhappiness or anger. The interviewer was blind to their diagnosis.

Showed? Women with breast lumps which were found to be cancerous reported that they experienced and expressed far less anger (fitting Type C) than those whose lumps were non-cancerous.

Evaluation

Further evidence from the WCG study

Ragland and Brand (1988) followed up the WCG men 22 years later. 15% had died of CHD. Age, smoking and high blood pressure were risk factors, but there was no relationship with Type A personality. Perhaps Type A men changed their behaviour after the first study was published.

The key component of Type A

Hostility is the key factor. Myrtek (2001) reviewed 35 studies in a meta-analysis, finding an association between CHD and hostility but no other components of Type A personality. This suggests that not all factors in the Type A personality are linked to negative health outcomes.

Gender bias

The WCG sample was all men, and Type A characteristics are typically masculine. Friedman *et al.* (1986) studied 800 men and women who had experienced CHD. Participants receiving cardiac and Type A counselling were less likely to have further CHD problems (13%) than those just receiving cardiac counselling (28%).

Direct effects of personality

Nemeroff and Musselman (2000) found that depressed people had 41% more sticky blood platelets than normal people. These block arteries and increase risk of heart attacks. Prozac caused mood improvement and reduced the number of platelets. So did a placebo, showing that the mood, not the drug itself, caused the improvement.

Challenges to the concept of Type C

Greer *et al.* (1979) found that women with a 'fighting spirit' were more likely to recover from cancer. However, Giraldi *et al.* (1997) found no association between psychosocial variables (emotional suppression or a 'fighting spirit') and cancer progression. They did find more stressful life events in the months before a cancer diagnosis.

KEY TERMS

Type A personality Someone who experiences constant time pressure, competitiveness in work and social situations, and is easily frustrated by other people and becomes angry.

Type B personality Someone with an easy-going, relaxed and patient approach to life.

Type C personality Someone with extreme emotional suppression and a desire to please others.

Apply it

Scenario. Liam has a degree in Psychology, and has started work in the Human Resources department of a city trading company employing 80% male traders. Liam wants to improve their health and well-being. He has noticed that many seem to be very competitive and stressed, and wonders whether their Type A personality is putting them at risk of heart disease.

How could Liam help the traders improve their health and well-being? (4 marks)

Application. If the traders are male and competitive, they could fit the Type A personality profile, so they would be at risk of heart attacks, according to the findings of the WCG study. If they are stressed, it could cause high blood pressure, leading to cardiovascular disease. Liam could provide relaxation classes or counselling to help them to be less stressed, or address workplace issues like lack of job control to help reduce stress. In particular, the traders may need to be less hostile, as hostility is the biggest risk factor for coronary heart disease. He should strongly advise them not to smoke, as this is an even bigger factor according to Ragland and Brand's follow-up study of the WCG men.

KEY TERM

Hardiness A style of personality which provides defences against the negative effects of stress. The characteristics are: having control over one's life, commitment (i.e. a sense of involvement in the world) and challenge (i.e. life changes are opportunities rather than threats).

Individual differences in stress: hardiness

◉ The hardy personality

Kobasa and Maddi (1977) identified a 'hardy' personality type, which protects against the negative effects of stress. It is characterised by:

- **Control** – hardy people see themselves as in control of their lives.
- **Commitment** – they are involved with the world and have a strong sense of purpose.
- **Challenge** – they see life's challenges as problems to overcome rather than threats, and enjoy change as an opportunity for development.

◉ Key study: Kobasa (1979)

How? 800 executives from a utility company in the US were asked about life events they had experienced in the last three years (using the Social Readjustment Rating Scale), and any illness in that period. 86 high stress/low illness men and 75 high stress/high illness men were identified. They completed personality tests on control, commitment and challenge.

Showed? High stress/low illness men scored high on all three characteristics of the hardy personality. Hardy people can be stressed without becoming ill.

◉ Other research

Maddi (1987) found that two-thirds of employees of a US telephone company suffered stress during a period when many colleagues were made redundant. The remaining third 'thrived', and had more **hardiness** characteristics.

Lifton *et al.* (2006) found that US university students were more likely to complete their degree if they scored high for hardiness, and low hardiness scores were more common in students who dropped out.

◉ Evaluation

Problems of measurement

Much research used long self-report scales with awkward wording. The Personal Views Survey (Maddi, 1997) has improved on these, but still shows poor internal reliability for the challenge component.

Direct effects

Hardiness may affect the autonomic nervous system directly. Maddi (1999) found that hardy individuals had lower blood pressure than those with low hardiness. Contrada (1989) found that Type B people who were also hardy had the lowest blood pressure.

Real-world application

Maddi has developed hardiness training, which is more effective than relaxation/meditation or social support (Maddi *et al.*, 1998) in increasing hardiness and job satisfaction, while decreasing strain and illness severity. It has been used in business, education and the military.

Hardiness and negative affectivity (N-A)

High N-A individuals are more likely to report distress, dissatisfaction, failures and negative aspects of themselves and the world. N-A correlates with hardiness, so 'hardy individuals' may just be low in N-A (Watson & Clark, 1984). Funk (1992) argued that negativity leads to the ill effects of stress.

Is hardiness a personality type?

Sandvik *et al.* (2013) assessed 21 hardy Navy candidates and found those with lower challenge scores also showed a weaker immune response, so challenge may be the key component. However, Rotter's (1966) work shows that people with high internal locus of control feel stress less. Cohen *et al.* (1993) found the people who felt their lives were unpredictable and uncontrollable were twice as likely to develop colds as those who felt in control. So control may be the key factor. If only one factor is key, hardiness is not really a personality type.

Apply it

Scenario. Lydia and Silas are being interviewed for a company which wants to recruit 'hardy' employees. Lydia says she works better on her own, whereas Silas says that in a team his colleagues 'would be there to help if things went wrong'. Lydia explains that, 'After my family, my job is the most important thing in my life', while Silas says, 'There are more important things in life than work.' Finally, when asked about the stresses of high-pressure work, Lydia claims she 'relishes' the challenge, whereas Silas asks whether there was private health insurance.

Using your knowledge of the hardy personality, and the desire of this company to appoint someone who is suitably 'hardy', which candidate should be appointed and why? (4 marks)

Application. Lydia shows characteristics of control (working better on her own), commitment (the job is really important to her) and challenge (relishing it), so she is a hardy personality. Silas shows the opposite: low control (depending on colleagues to rescue him if things go wrong), low commitment (there are more important things…) and low challenge (he seems to think about getting ill when he is asked about high-pressure work), so he would score low on hardiness overall, and would be more at risk of getting ill or leaving as he wouldn't be able to cope with the pressure. They should appoint Lydia.

Managing and coping with stress: drug therapies

Drug therapies for stress aim to reduce anxiety by targeting the physiology of the stress response. Anti-anxiety drugs are a biological approach to stress management.

○ Benzodiazepines (BZs)

Benzodiazepines (BZs), e.g. librium and diazepam, slow down the activity of the central nervous system.

BZs and GABA: BZs enhance the action of GABA, a neurotransmitter which binds to receptors, opening channels to increase the flow of chloride ions into the post-synaptic neuron. Chloride ions make the neuron resistant to excitation by other neurotransmitters, slowing down its activity. BZs bind to sites on the GABA receptor and boost the effect of GABA, allowing even more chloride ions to enter. As a result, the person feels calmer and less anxious.

BZs and serotonin: Serotonin can have an arousing effect on the brain. BZs reduce any increased serotonin activity, reducing anxiety.

○ Beta blockers (BBs)

Beta blockers target the sympathomedullary response to stress, blocking sites which would normally be activated by adrenaline and noradrenaline.

Sympathetic arousal: Stress activates the SAM pathway, triggering production of adrenaline and noradrenaline from the adrenal medulla. These have an immediate effect on target organs, especially the heart muscle, leading to increased heart rate and blood pressure, as well as increased breathing rate and sweating. Beta blockers bind to beta-receptors in target organs, preventing the action of adrenaline and noradrenaline. As heart rate, etc. do not increase, the person feels calmer.

Other uses: BBs are also taken by people with coronary heart disease (CHD) to dampen their sympathetic arousal and reduce wear and tear on the heart. Stage performers can also take the drug to control their anxiety, as it doesn't affect the brain. However, it is a banned substance for athletes.

○ Evaluation

Effectiveness

In a randomised controlled trial of 250 people, Kahn *et al.* (1986) found that BZs were significantly better than a placebo for treating anxiety and stress. However, Schweizer *et al.* (1991) found that beta blockers reduced heart rate during a maths test (compared to a placebo), but not all kinds of beta blocker reduced the feeling of stress.

Ease of use

Pills are easy to take, so take less time and effort than psychological therapies. As a result, drug therapies tend to be effective because people are more inclined to continue with them.

Problems with addiction – BZs

Patients taking even low doses of BZ show withdrawal symptoms when they stop taking them. It is recommended that they should be limited to four weeks, although they are still used for long-term treatment. They are not suitable for treating everyday stress, but are used for anxiety disorders like OCD or phobias.

Side effects

BZs can produce 'paradoxical' symptoms: increased agitation, panic, aggressiveness and cognitive effects (impaired memory). BBs do not usually produce side effects, although they have been linked to increased risk of diabetes.

Treating the symptom rather than the problem

When a person stops taking the drug, the problem often recurs. It may be preferable to use a treatment that deals with underlying issues, particularly as drug therapies introduce new problems like side effects and addiction.

KEY TERMS

Benzodiazepines A class of drug used to treat stress and anxiety. They facilitate the action of the neurotransmitter GABA in quietening down neurons in the brain.

Beta blockers Decrease stress and anxiety by blocking the effects of adrenaline and noradrenaline, which are part of the sympathomedullary response to stress.

LINK

See p.83 for the SAM pathway.

Apply it

Scenario. Rosanne is a music student who has started experiencing extreme anxiety when she is preparing for a concert. She shakes, sweats and feels sick.

Explain how possible biological treatments could help Rosanne. (6 marks)

Application. If Rosanne is anxious just before a concert, beta blockers could help her. They reduce the effect of adrenaline and noradrenaline on her target organs, so she would not feel her heart beating faster, her palms sweating or the sick feeling. This would help her get through the performance without shaking. Alternatively, if she has developed generalised anxiety which is affecting her preparation some time before the performance, she may benefit from benzodiazepines (BZs) which target the central nervous system. They enhance the action of GABA, by increasing the flow of chloride ions into post-synaptic neurons, dampening down the activity of the brain, and this will make Rosanne feel calmer. She could use these for a few weeks to help her get over her performance anxiety.

KEY TERM

Stress inoculation therapy A type of CBT which trains people to cope with anxiety and stressful situations more effectively by learning skills to 'inoculate' themselves against the damaging effects of future stressors.

Managing and coping with stress: stress inoculation therapy

A psychological therapy targeting the underlying problem, with the assumption that the symptoms will then go away.

◉ The principles behind stress inoculation therapy (SIT)

SIT is a form of cognitive behavioural therapy (CBT) developed by Meichenbaum (1985) to help people develop coping systems to deal with future stress. Although the causes of stress cannot often be changed, people can change the way they think about stress. Positive thinking leads to positive attitudes and feelings, which reduce the stress response.

◉ How it works

1. **Conceptualisation phase:** The therapist allows the client to tell their story, identifying current maladaptive strategies. The client is taught to perceive threats as problems to be solved, and to break them down into components that can be coped with. The client reconceptualises (thinks differently about) their problem.
2. **Skills acquisition, rehearsal and consolidation:** Coping skills are selected to match the client's preferences and problems, and are practised in the clinic before transferring them to real life. Skills include positive thinking and coping self-statements, relaxation, social skills, attention diversion, using social support and time management. Cognitive skills encourage the client to think differently. Behavioural skills involve practising new behaviours. Skills are rehearsed using imagery (imagining how to deal with stressful situations), modelling (watching and imitating) and role play.
3. **Application and follow-through:** Clients practise using coping skills in increasingly stressful situations. They may be asked to help train others. Booster sessions can be offered.

Apply it

Scenario. Jade is very anxious about starting university. She has been at a small school since she was five, and tends to avoid busy places like shopping centres, as they make her feel stressed.

Explain how a psychologist might use stress inoculation therapy to treat Jade. (6 marks)

Application. In the conceptualisation phase, the psychologist would encourage Jade to talk about her worries, and how she copes with stress currently. She would identify maladaptive behaviours like avoiding shopping centres. Jade would start to reconceptualise her problem by breaking it down into parts, like meeting new people, going to lectures and finding her way round the campus. Next, the psychologist would teach Jade coping skills like positive self-statements, 'Relax – you're in control' or 'You can develop a plan to deal with it', and will help Jade to imagine how she can use these at university in different stressful situations. She could also use role play to practise meeting new people, or how to go into a lecture theatre and choose a seat. Finally, in the application stage Jade will rehearse her new skills in real life, maybe by going to a shopping centre, and get follow-up once she starts university to help her generalise the skills.

Examples of coping self-statements

Preparing for a stressful situation:
- You can develop a plan to deal with it.
- Don't worry; worry won't help anything.

Confronting and handling a stressful situation:
- One step at a time – you can handle it.
- Relax – you're in control. Take a slow breath.

Coping with the feeling of being overwhelmed:
- Keep the focus on the present.
- Label your fear 0 to 10 and watch it change.

Reinforcing self-statements:
- It worked – you did it.
- It wasn't as bad as you expected.

◉ Evaluation

Effectiveness

Meichenbaum (1977) compared SIT with systematic desensitisation for a snake phobia. Both therapies reduced the phobia, but SIT also helped clients to deal with a second phobia. SIT has been used effectively in many situations: parents whose children are undergoing medical procedures; law students dealing with academic stress; and to reduce stress in public speaking.

The hello–goodbye effect

Evaluating the effectiveness of SIT depends on subjective reports from clients. They may exaggerate their problems initially to make sure they get help, and may be grateful for help at the end, and so minimise any remaining issues.

Preparation for future stressors

SIT gives the client skills and confidence to deal with future problems, giving long-lasting effectiveness. This contrasts with drug therapy which only addresses current symptoms.

A challenging therapy

SIT is time-consuming and requires high motivation, taking 8–15 sessions plus follow-up sessions for up to a year. Some people may not want to invest this much time, or don't like discussing feelings, or don't want to make the effort to change the way they think. If they don't complete the therapy, this reduces its effectiveness.

Unnecessarily complex

The cognitive elements could be more important than practising skills, so the therapy could be simplified and shortened. A 20-minute version has been used in preparing people for surgery. A key ingredient is probably relaxation, which reduces sympathetic arousal and makes people feel less stressed.

Managing and coping with stress: biofeedback

Biofeedback uses physiological information (heartbeat or blood pressure) and psychological conditioning. It helps people cope with biological and psychological aspects of stress. The client learns to exert voluntary control over involuntary functions controlled by the autonomic nervous system (ANS).

⚙ How it works

Relaxation: The client is taught relaxation techniques to reduce the activity of the sympathetic nervous system and activate the parasympathetic nervous system. This reduces heart rate, blood pressure, etc.

Feedback: The client receives information about their ANS activities via EMG (electromyography – responding to muscle tone), skin conductance (measuring sweating), EEG (measuring electrical activity in the brain), heart rate or breathing rate. The information is converted to light, sound or a screen image. The client practises relaxation and observes the change in ANS activity.

Operant conditioning: The reduction in ANS is rewarding and unconsciously reinforces the relaxation behaviour.

Transfer: The client learns to relax in real stressful situations.

⚙ Demonstration of biofeedback

Miller and DiCara (1967) tested biofeedback in 24 paralysed rats. Twelve were rewarded (by direct stimulation of the brain's pleasure centre) when their heart rates slowed down, and the other 12 when their heart rate increased. The heart rates slowed or speeded up accordingly, demonstrating involuntary learning by operant conditioning.

⚙ Evaluation

Research support
Gruber and Taub (1998) trained four monkeys to raise and lower body temperature and reduce muscle tension using biofeedback. This demonstrates that biofeedback does not require conscious thought. Many studies have shown the effectiveness of biofeedback in humans, e.g. Lewis *et al.* (2015): biofeedback training decreased heart rate in military personnel.

Operant conditioning may be irrelevant
Miller and DiCara's (1967) results were not replicated by other researchers, and DiCara refused to share his data, then ended his life by suicide. It is now believed that he fabricated his data. Relaxation may directly reduce sympathetic activity, or make people feel more in control, rather than working via unconscious operant conditioning.

Continued popularity
Biofeedback is used for many conditions including post-traumatic stress disorder (PTSD), migraines and asthma. Bradley (1995) showed that it is superior to relaxation alone for treating tension headaches, but this may be a placebo effect as people believe that the electrical equipment must be helping them.

Strengths
Biofeedback is a non-invasive technique, so can be used with children who cannot use drug treatments or the more cognitively demanding stress inoculation therapy. It reduces sympathetic arousal by relaxation, and doesn't just treat symptoms.

Limitations
It requires expensive equipment, and takes at least a month. It takes some effort as well as specialist supervision. If relaxation is the main benefit, that could be taught without the costly biofeedback therapy.

KEY TERM

Biofeedback A method of stress management that involves a person learning to control aspects of autonomic functioning through the use of operant conditioning.

🐾
Apply it

Scenario. Darius is a soldier who has been suffering from PTSD for three years as a result of horrific experiences serving in the Iraq war. He presents with extreme anxiety attacks, flashbacks and nightmares. He has asked his doctor for drugs to help him, but his doctor would like him to try biofeedback first.

Explain why Darius's doctor is recommending biofeedback treatment for Darius. (4 marks)

Application. Darius has a long-term stress disorder, so long-term drug use could lead to dependency or addiction. Biofeedback, however, is non-invasive so would not cause withdrawal symptoms, unlike drugs which could have side effects while they are being taken, and withdrawal symptoms when he stops. Darius's doctor wants him to avoid these unpleasant effects of drugs, and hopes that biofeedback could be just as effective. It would reduce the activity of Darius's sympathetic nervous system, so that his anxiety symptoms don't cause the physiological symptoms of heart racing, breathlessness, sweating, etc., and this would help him to feel more relaxed.

KEY TERMS

Avoidance-oriented coping A way to cope with stress by behaving in ways that distance yourself from the problem.

Emotion-focused coping A way to cope with stress by tackling the symptoms of stress, e.g. the anxiety that accompanies stress.

Problem-focused coping A way to cope with stress by tackling the factor(s) causing the stress, often in a practical way.

Tend-and-befriend response An adaptive response to stress in female animals, related to protecting offspring (tend) and relying on the social group for mutual defence (befriending).

Apply it

Scenario. Sally and Jack work in the same council parking office. It is a stressful job, as they have to deal with a large number of difficult, and often abusive, telephone calls from people who are clearly unhappy about having received a parking ticket.

Using your knowledge of gender differences in coping with stress, explain how Sally and Jack are likely to cope with the specific stressors associated with their work role. (4 marks)

Application. Sally and Jack are dealing with the same work-related stressors, but they may use different strategies. Peterson found that women tend to use more emotion-focused coping, to try to reduce their emotional response, so Sally may eat chocolate or talk to a friend when she is stressed – women are also more likely than men to use social support to deal with stress. Peterson found that men often use problem-focused coping, so Jack may try to pass difficult calls onto a manager or distance himself by refusing to engage. However, men also sometimes use emotion-focused coping.

Individual differences in stress: gender differences

Physiological explanations for gender difference

Taylor (2000) proposed the **tend-and-befriend response** to stress, suggesting it is more adaptive for females, to maximise the survival of self and offspring, as females invest more in raising young. This response is controlled by oxytocin, the 'love hormone' which is released during breastfeeding and promotes feelings of bonding. Males also produce oxytocin, but have more testosterone than females, which counteracts the bonding effect of oxytocin, producing a more aggressive response.

Psychological explanations for gender difference

Lazarus and Folkman (1984) distinguished between **problem-focused** and **emotion-focused coping** styles. Stress can be managed by tackling the problem itself, but when this is not possible an alternative approach is to reduce the stress response (emotion-focused). The gender difference is seen in the Peterson *et al.* (2006) study below.

Stress experienced and coping: Some research suggests men and women have to cope with different stressors, leading to different coping styles. This is role constraint theory. Matud (2004) found that Spanish men listed relationship, finance and work stress as greatest (requiring a problem focus) but women listed family and health-related stress (requiring an emotion focus).

Key study: Peterson *et al.* (2006)

How? 1,000 men and women seeking fertility treatment completed the 'Ways of Coping Questionnaire' (Lazarus & Folkman).

Showed? Women used emotion-focused strategies, like confrontive coping: trying to change the situation in order to reduce the emotional impact. They were more likely than men to seek social support. Men used problem-solving and also distanced themselves from the problem. However, men also used some emotion-focused coping.

Evaluation

Not simply a tend-and-befriend response by females

It is adaptive for women to be aggressive, to protect their offspring. Female animals are aggressive towards threatening intruders, and will also flee if their young are sufficiently mobile. Females use a wide repertoire of strategies as appropriate and are not restricted to the 'tend and befriend' response to stressful situations.

Lack of research support for coping focus

Most studies do not support gender differences in coping, e.g. Hamilton and Fagot (1988) found no differences in male and female undergraduates' coping styles over eight weeks. The model may be too simplistic: Endler and Parker (1990) identified a third strategy, **avoidance-oriented coping**.

Confounding variables

Coping styles vary with the type of stressor, and women are more likely to receive social support than men, which reduces the amount of stress they experience (see p.95). Women would therefore select coping strategies such as social support more than would men.

Other methodological issues

Research depends on self-report measures, and women may be more willing than men to admit to emotion-focused coping (social desirability bias). Scales are completed retrospectively and are unreliable, as memories of past stress may be affected by current stress levels.

Changing roles and lives of men and women

Gender differences in coping probably relate to lifestyle differences rather than innate factors. Traditionally, men experienced more work-related stress than women, but as women gain equality in the workplace they also experience more stress. Women in non-traditional work roles (e.g. lawyers, bus drivers, engineers) have higher levels of stress hormones than women in traditional roles (Frankenhauser, 1986).

The role of social support in coping with stress

◉ Sources of social support
Family and friends may be sources of stress or of support. Social networks give a safety net of relationships: Nabi *et al.* (2013) surveyed 400 students; number of Facebook friends correlated with stronger perceptions of social support, lower stress levels and less physical illness. Dickinson *et al.* (2011) suggested that, for older people, reduced social contact may be an important factor in ill health.

◉ Different kinds of support
Instrumental support: Offers of tangible help such as money or a lift to the doctor; a problem-solving approach. This can include information support; giving advice (Schaefer *et al.*, 1981). Can be offered by friends and family, or strangers.

Emotional support: Emotion-focused, e.g. listening, giving advice about how to reduce the emotional impact of stress. Less likely to be offered by strangers.

Esteem support: Making someone feel better about themselves, e.g. through expressions of confidence. This increases their self-worth and self-efficacy about being able to cope, reducing feelings of stress.

◉ Explaining the effects of social support
The buffering hypothesis: Social support is more important at times of stress, when friends protect one from the negative effects of stress by offering instrumental support.

Direct physiological effects: Social support increases relaxation via the autonomic nervous system.

◉ Key study: Kamarck *et al.* (1990)
How? Female student participants carried out a stressful mental task, while their physiological reactions were monitored. Some were alone; others brought a close female friend, who touched their wrist during the task.

Showed? Participants with a friend present showed lower physiological arousal (e.g. heart rate) than those who were alone. For some tasks, this difference was only seen for Type A personalities, supporting the buffering hypothesis.

◉ Evaluation
Gender differences
A review by Lucknow *et al.* (1998) found, in 25 of 26 studies, that females were more likely to use social support than men. However, studies generally measure emotional support; men use more problem-focused support. Findings from single-sex studies should not be generalised.

Cultural differences
Bailey and Dua (1999) found that Asian students use collectivist coping strategies (implicit support). Anglo-Australian students use individualist strategies (explicit, instrumental support). The longer the Asian student remains in Australian culture, the more they use individualist coping styles.

Distinguishing types of social support
Definitions are inconsistent. House (1981) suggested emotional support includes esteem support and group belonging (a collectivist concept). Schaefer *et al.* (1981) list emotional, tangible and informational support as the three main categories. Many researchers simply distinguish between tangible and social/emotional support.

Pets can provide support
'Social' support refers to one's own species, but pets also reduce stress. Pets reduce blood pressure in children reading aloud and buffer the elderly against life event stresses (Allen, 2003). Talking to pets may help more than talking to people. Benefits may result from not feeling alone.

Relative importance of social support
Kobasa *et al.* (1985) found that social support was the least important factor in reducing stress levels and hardiness was most important. The benefits, in terms of physical and psychological health, depend on the quality of the relationship; strained relationships can increase stress (Kiecolt-Glaser & Newton, 2001).

KEY TERMS
Emotional support Focused on trying to find ways to reduce feelings of anxiety associated with stress.

Esteem support Increasing a person's sense of self-worth so they can feel more confident about coping with both instrumental and emotional issues.

Instrumental support When direct aid and actual material services are offered.

Apply it
Scenario. Some universities provide a 'puppy room' for students to cuddle puppies during exam periods.

How might the puppy room help students during their exam period? (4 marks)

Application. Students would be stressed during exams, and cuddling puppies could reduce stress by helping to calm down the sympathetic nervous system. Cuddling produces oxytocin, which is associated with a 'tend-and-befriend' response rather than a 'fight-or-flight' response, so the students will feel calmer. Students can talk to the pets and will not experience any strain in these relationships, whereas other students may also be stressed at exam time and could make things worse.

Chapter 9
Aggression

Paper 3, Section D, option 1. 4.3.8 Aggression

- Neural and hormonal mechanisms in aggression, including the roles of the limbic system, serotonin and testosterone. Genetic factors in aggression, including the MAOA gene.
- The ethological explanation of aggression, including reference to innate releasing mechanisms and fixed action patterns. Evolutionary explanations of human aggression.
- Social psychological explanations of human aggression, including the frustration–aggression hypothesis, social learning theory as applied to human aggression, and de-individuation.
- Institutional aggression in the context of prisons: dispositional and situational explanations.
- Media influences on aggression, including the effects of computer games. The role of desensitisation, disinhibition and cognitive priming.

Key terms (highlight each cell when you can define the term confidently)

Neural, hormonal and genetic influences	Ethological and evolutionary explanations	Social psychological explanations	Institutional aggression	Media influences on aggression
Limbic system	Ethological explanations	Frustration–aggression hypothesis	Institutional aggression	Desensitisation
Serotonin	Fixed action pattern	Social learning	Dispositional explanations	Disinhibition
Testosterone	Innate releasing mechanism	De-individuation	Situational explanations	Cognitive priming
Genetic factors	Evolutionary explanations			
MAOA				

Content checklist

1. In each 'describe', 'apply' and 'evaluate' cell tick when you have produced brief notes.
2. Once you feel you have a good grasp of the topic add a second tick to the cell.
3. When you feel you have complete mastery of the topic and would be able to answer an exam question without the aid of notes highlight the cell.

I am able to ...	Describe	Apply	Evaluate
Neural mechanisms in aggression, including the roles of the limbic system and serotonin			
Hormonal mechanisms in aggression, including the role of testosterone			
Genetic factors in aggression, including the MAOA gene			
The ethological explanation of aggression, including innate releasing mechanisms and fixed action patterns			
Evolutionary explanations of human aggression			
The frustration–aggression hypothesis			
Social learning theory and human aggression			
De-individuation and aggression			
Institutional aggression in prisons; dispositional and situational explanations			
Media influences on aggression, including the effects of computer games			
The role of desensitisation, disinhibition and cognitive priming			

Neural influences

◎ The limbic system

The **limbic system** coordinates behaviours that satisfy motivational and emotional urges, such as aggression and fear.

The **amygdala** evaluates the emotional importance of sensory information and prompts an appropriate response. Stimulation of the amygdala causes an animal to respond with aggression. Surgical removal means the animal no longer responds to stimuli that would have previously led to rage.

The **hippocampus** is involved with the formation of long-term memories, allowing an animal to compare a current threat with similar past experiences. Impaired hippocampal function causes the amygdala to respond inappropriately to sensory stimuli, resulting in aggressive behaviour (e.g. Boccardi *et al.*, 2010).

◎ Serotonin

Serotonin inhibits the firing of the amygdala. Low levels of serotonin remove this inhibitory effect, so that individuals are less able to control impulsive and aggressive behaviour (the 'serotonin deficiency hypothesis'). Dexfenfluramine alters serotonin levels and thus increases aggressive behaviour (Mann *et al.*, 1990).

Hormonal influences

◎ Testosterone

Testosterone influences aggression due to its action on brain areas involved in controlling aggression. Removing the source of testosterone in different species typically results in much lower levels of aggression. At an age when testosterone concentrations are at their highest (21–35), there is an increase in male-on-male aggressive behaviour (Daly & Wilson, 1998). Changes in testosterone levels influence aggressive behaviour by increasing amygdala reactivity during the processing of social threat, e.g. angry facial expressions.

◎ Evaluation of neural influences

Evidence for the role of the amygdala in aggression

Reduced amygdala volume can predict the development of persistent aggression. Pardini *et al.* (2014) found that males with lower amygdala volumes exhibited higher levels of aggression. This suggests that lower amygdala volume compromises the ability to evaluate the emotional importance of sensory information and makes a violent response more likely.

Evidence for the role of the hippocampus in aggression

Raine *et al.* (2004) provided support for the role of the hippocampus in aggressive behaviour. Compared to violent offenders who had escaped conviction, offenders who been caught had acted more impulsively. The researchers discovered hippocampal asymmetries in this group, suggesting an impaired ability of the hippocampus and the amygdala to work together. This meant that emotional information was not processed correctly, leading to inappropriate violent responses.

Research support for the serotonin deficiency hypothesis

Duke *et al.* (2013) provided support for the serotonin deficiency hypothesis as an explanation for aggressive behaviour. They carried out a meta-analysis of 175 studies, which found a small inverse relationship between serotonin levels and aggression. However, this was only true for 'other-reported' (rather than 'self-reported') aggression, suggesting that the relationship between serotonin and aggression is more complex than originally thought.

Evidence from studies of non-human species

Raleigh *et al.* (1991) found that vervet monkeys fed on experimental diets high in tryptophan (which increases serotonin levels in the brain) exhibited decreased levels of aggression, and individuals fed on diets that were low in tryptophan exhibited increased aggressive behaviour. This suggests that the difference in aggression could be attributed to differences in their serotonin levels.

◎ Evaluation of hormonal influences

Inconsistent evidence

Despite many studies showing a positive relationship between testosterone and aggression, other studies found no such relationship. For example, positive correlations have been reported between levels of testosterone and self-reported levels of aggression among male prison inmates (Albert *et al.*, 1994), but no correlation was found between testosterone levels and *actual* violent behaviour. This suggests that the relationship between testosterone and aggression in humans remains unclear.

Aggression or dominance?

In animals, the influence of testosterone on dominance behaviour might be shown through aggressive behaviour, but in humans, testosterone can have more varied effects. For example, Eisenegger *et al.* (2011) found testosterone could make women act 'nicer' rather than more aggressively, depending on the situation. This suggests that, rather than directly increasing aggression, testosterone promotes status-seeking behaviour, of which aggression is one type.

KEY TERMS

Limbic system A system of structures lying beneath the cortex (i.e. subcortical), including the amygdala, hippocampus and hypothalamus. The region is associated with emotional behaviour.

Serotonin A neurotransmitter implicated in many different behaviours and physiological processes, including aggression, eating behaviour, sleep and depression.

Testosterone A hormone produced mainly by the testes in males, but also occurring in females. It is associated with the development of secondary sexual characteristics in males (e.g. body hair), but has also been implicated in aggression and dominance behaviours.

Apply it

Scenario. Rhodri is a man in his early sixties. He has always been active and hates the thought of getting older. He is told he has low testosterone levels so decides to try having testosterone injections. A worrying side effect is that he finds himself feeling more aggressive and recently got into a fight at a local pub.

Explain what is happening to Rhodri. (3 marks)

Explanation. Testosterone influences aggression because of its action in brain areas controlling aggressive behaviour. Because Rhodri has recently started having testosterone injections, this could explain his increased feelings of aggression and his increased levels of aggression. Testosterone also increases amygdala reactivity in the processing of social threat, so he might have misinterpreted the ambiguous actions of someone in the pub, leading to a fight with them.

KEY TERMS

Genetic explanations The likelihood of behaving in a particular way is determined by a person's genetic make-up, i.e. it is inherited from parents.

MAOA Monoamine oxidase A (MAOA) is an enzyme that, among other things, regulates the metabolism of serotonin in the brain.

Apply it

Scenario. Carl is in prison for repeated assault charges. While in prison he meets a relative who is also in prison for the same kind of offences. Carl never knew his biological family because he was adopted as a baby due to physical abuse from his parents. The relative tells him that Carl's biological father was also 'doing time' at another prison, and proceeds to tell him of the violent history of all his biological relatives.

With reference to Carl, outline and evaluate the genetic explanations of aggression. (16 marks)

Explanation extract... Carl's aggressive tendencies can be explained in terms of the genetics of aggression. For example, a study by Hutchings and Mednick (1975) found that a significant number of adopted boys with criminal convictions also had biological parents with convictions for criminal violence. It is also possible that members of Carl's biological family share the MAOA-L variant of the MAOA gene. Individuals with this variant have been found to be significantly more likely to grow up to exhibit anti-social behaviour if they had been maltreated as children (Caspi *et al.*, 2002), which is consistent with the reason for Carl's adoption. ...

Genetics and aggression

Twin studies
If MZ twins are more alike (compared to DZ twins) in terms of their aggressive behaviour, then this should be due to genes rather than environment. Using comparisons of adult twin pairs, Coccaro *et al.* (1997) found that nearly 50% of the variance in direct aggressive behaviour (i.e. aggression towards others) could be attributed to genetic explanations.

Adoption studies
If a positive correlation is found between aggressive behaviour in adopted children and aggressive behaviour in their biological parents, a genetic, rather than an environmental, effect is implied. Hutchings and Mednick (1975) found that a significant number of adopted boys with criminal convictions had biological parents with convictions for criminal violence, providing evidence for a genetic effect.

MAOA and aggression
The role of MAOA: MAOA regulates the metabolism of serotonin in the brain, and low levels of serotonin are associated with aggressive behaviour. A study of a Dutch family found that many of its male members behaved in a particularly violent and aggressive manner. These men were found to have abnormally low levels of MAOA and a defect in the MAOA gene (Brunner *et al.*, 1993).

MAOA-H and MAOA-L: Caspi *et al.* (2002) discovered a variant of the gene associated with high levels of MAOA (MAOA-H) and a variant associated with low levels (MAOA-L). Those with the MAOA-L variant were significantly more likely to grow up to exhibit anti-social behaviour but *only* if they had been maltreated as children. MAOA-L is much more frequent in populations with a history of warfare, with about two-thirds of people in these populations having this version of the gene.

Evaluation
Problems of sampling
Many studies in this area have focused exclusively on individuals convicted of violent crime. However, convictions for violent crime are few compared to the vast number of violent attacks by individuals that never result in a conviction. They therefore represent just a small minority of those regularly involved in aggressive behaviour. This means that it is difficult to draw meaningful conclusions from such studies.

Difficulties in determining the role of genetic factors
The connection between genetic factors and aggression is not straightforward because of problems determining what is, and what is not, a product of genetic inheritance. For example, it is difficult to establish genetic contributions to aggressive behaviour because more than one gene usually contributes to a given behaviour, and there are many non-genetic influences on the manifestation of aggressive behaviour.

Problems of assessing aggression
Many studies of aggression have used self-reports of aggressive behaviour, whereas other studies have made use of observational techniques. Studies using self-reports tend to show more genetic influences for aggression, whereas observational ratings tend to show significantly *less* genetic contribution and a greater influence of environmental factors. These inconsistencies make it difficult to accurately assess the relative contributions of genetic and environmental factors in aggression.

Evidence for the influence of the MAOA gene
Supporting evidence comes from Tiihonen *et al.* (2015). They studied Finnish prisoners, revealing that the MAOA low-activity genotype (MAOA-L) in combination with another gene (the CDH13 gene) was associated with extremely violent behaviour. There was no substantial evidence for either of these genes among non-violent offenders, indicating that this combination of genes was specific for violent offending only.

The MAOA gene might explain gender differences in aggressive behaviour
MAOA research can explain the uneven rates of violence for males and females. The MAOA gene is linked to the X chromosome. When men inherit an X-linked abnormal MAOA gene, they are more likely to be affected by it, whereas women inheriting the same gene are generally unaffected (as they also have a second 'normal' X chromosome). This could explain why males typically show more aggressive behaviour than females.

Ethological explanations of aggression

Fixed action patterns and innate releasing mechanisms

Members of the same species have a repertoire of stereotyped behaviours which occur in specific conditions and which do not require learning, i.e. **fixed action patterns** (FAPs). FAPs are produced by a neural mechanism known as an **innate releasing mechanism** (IRM) and are triggered by a specific sign stimulus. Tinbergen's research (1952) showed that a male stickleback produces a fixed sequence of aggressive actions in response to the sign stimulus of another male's red underbelly.

Characteristics of FAPs include the fact they are *stereotyped* (the behaviour always occurs in the same way), independent of individual experience (it is innate with no learning involved) and each FAP has a *specific trigger* (sign stimulus).

The 'hydraulic model' (Lorenz, 1950)

Each FAP has a reservoir of 'action-specific energy' (ASE) that builds up over time. The appropriate sign stimulus causes the IRM to release this energy and the animal then performs the FAP. The FAP may also be produced in the absence of the sign stimulus if the level of ASE is sufficiently high.

Ritualistic aggression

Aggressive behaviour may be ritualised in the form of threat displays. These are intended to make an opponent back down without actual fighting. Anthropologists have found evidence of the use of ritualised aggression in tribal warfare in human cultures. Gardner and Heider (1968) described how the Dani of New Guinea engaged in highly ritualised patterns of intergroup hostility.

Wolves and doves

Lorenz (1952) claimed that hunting species must have instinctive inhibitions that prevent them using their natural weapons against members of their own species. Non-hunting species have no such natural weapons, and therefore have not developed the same inhibitions against hurting their own kind. Because humans do not have powerful natural weapons, we have not developed strong instinctive inhibitions against killing one another.

Evaluation

Criticisms of an 'instinctive' view of aggression

Lehrman (1953) argued that Lorenz had underestimated the role of environmental factors in the development of species-typical aggressive behaviour patterns. These environmental factors, largely the result of learning and experience, interact with innate factors in complex ways. This suggests, claims Lehrman, that behaviour is not as 'fixed' as implied by the term fixed action pattern.

Do humans have fixed action patterns for aggression?

Eibl-Eibesfeldt (1972) identified a number of human FAPs or human 'universals', e.g. smiling as a sign of greeting. However, because the environment in which humans exist changes so rapidly, Eibl-Eibesfeldt suggests that FAPs such as aggression are no longer adaptive in modern times. This suggests that, although animal species may respond aggressively to specific sign stimuli, human behaviour is far more varied and less predictable.

A problem for the hydraulic model

Lorenz argued that when levels of ASE reached a critical point, this led to performance of a FAP, and a reduction in biological energy. However, this argument was challenged by von Holst (1954), who showed that performance of an aggressive behaviour could itself provide a further stimulus, which, rather than reducing the likelihood of further aggressive behaviour (due to a lowered level of ASE), made it more likely.

The benefits of ritualised aggression

The advantage of ritualised aggression preventing conflicts escalating into dangerous physical aggression is evident in human cultures. Among the Yanomamö people, chest pounding and club fighting contests can settle a conflict short of actual violence (Chagnon, 1992). This shows that, even in violent cultures such as the Yanomamö, rituals can reduce actual aggression and prevent injury or death of the combatants.

Killing conspecifics is not that rare

A problem for the **ethological explanation** concerns the claim that predator species must have instinctive inhibitions that prevent them using their natural weapons against members of their own species. However, this is not borne out by evidence. In some predator species, the killing of conspecifics is common, e.g. male lions will kill the cubs of other males, and male chimpanzees will routinely kill members of another group.

KEY TERMS

Ethological explanation Stresses the adaptive value of animal behaviours. Ethologists study the behaviour patterns of animals in their natural environments.

Fixed action patterns A repertoire of stereotyped behaviours, which occur in specific conditions (i.e. in response to specific triggers) and which do not require learning.

Innate releasing mechanism A neural network that, when stimulated by the presence of a sign stimulus, communicates with motor control circuits to activate the fixed action pattern associated with that sign stimulus.

Apply it

Scenario. On television, a presenter lives with different tribes in the Amazonian rainforest. One tribe in particular is renowned for its violent behaviour, particularly when members of other tribes come into their territory. However, the presenter is at pains to point out that much of this is ritualistic, in the form of war dances and threat displays, rather than actual violence.

How might this form of behaviour be explained in terms of the ethological explanation of aggression? (3 marks)

Explanation. This explanation claims that species have a repertoire of stereotyped fixed action patterns that occur in specific situations and are triggered by a sign stimulus. For this tribe, the ritualistic displays might be the fixed action pattern to the sign stimulus of enemies entering their territory. These threat displays are intended to make opponents back down without actual fighting. Anthropologists have found evidence of such ritualised aggression in tribal warfare in human cultures.

KEY TERM

Evolutionary explanations Focus on the adaptive nature of behaviour, i.e. modern behaviours are believed to have evolved because they solved challenges faced by our distant ancestors and so became more widespread in the gene pool.

Evolutionary explanations of human aggression

An **evolutionary explanation** of aggression is based on the premise that the human brain is a product of natural selection. Aggression is a strategy that would have been effective for solving a number of adaptive problems among early humans. Solving these problems enhanced the survival and reproductive success of the individual, and as a result this mental module would have spread through the gene pool.

◉ Sexual competition

Ancestral males would have had to compete with other males for access to females. Individuals who used aggression would have been more successful in acquiring mates and passing on their genes to offspring. This would have led to the development of a genetically transmitted tendency for males to be aggressive towards other males. Puts (2010) argues that various male traits (e.g. greater muscle mass) seem to imply that competition with other males did take place among ancestral males.

◉ Sexual jealousy

Male aggression can occur as a result of sexual jealousy, which arises as a result of paternal uncertainty. As a result, men are always at risk of *cuckoldry*, the reproductive cost inflicted on a man as a result of his partner's infidelity. The adaptive functions of sexual jealousy would have been to deter a mate from sexual infidelity, minimising the risk of cuckoldry. Buss (1988) suggests that sexual jealousy may lead to the use of violence to prevent a partner from straying, as well as violence towards a perceived love rival.

◉ Aggression in warfare

An evolutionary explanation claims that any behaviour associated with warfare would have evolved because of the adaptive benefits for the individual and their offspring. For example, male warriors in traditional societies tend to have more sexual partners and more children, suggesting a direct reproductive benefit linked to their aggression. Displays of aggressiveness and bravery in battle also increase warriors' status, meaning that these individuals are more likely to share the benefits associated with that status.

◉ Evaluation

Gender differences in aggression may be better explained by socialisation
Prinz (2012) argues that gender differences in aggressive behaviour may be better explained by different socialisation experiences, e.g. parents physically punish boys for bad conduct, which could increase male physical violence. Girls adopt other, more social forms of aggression rather than physical aggression. This challenges the view that males alone have evolved aggression as a way of dealing with rivals, as females have simply developed a *different* form of aggression.

Aggressive behaviour may not always be adaptive
One problem with seeing aggressive behaviour as an effective way to meet the challenges of social living is that aggressive behaviour can be more *mal*adaptive than adaptive in some cases (e.g. leading to injury or social ostracism). However, Duntley and Buss (2004) claim the benefits of aggression must only have outweighed the costs *on average* relative to other strategies in the evolutionary past.

Support for the link between aggression and status
The claim that aggression confers status is supported by evidence that the most violent gang members often have the highest status among their peers (Campbell, 1993). Males display sensitivity to affronts to their status, and many acts of violence result from one male perceiving a slight to his status from another (Buss, 2005). This suggests that aggression is an important way of gaining status among males and a consequence of threats to that status.

Gender bias in evolutionary explanations of aggression
Evolutionary explanations for aggression in warfare demonstrate a gender bias because women do not increase their fitness through aggression as much as men do. Women have considerably less to gain from fighting and considerably more to lose (through loss of their reproductive capacity). Our understanding of the physical aggressive displays typically found in warfare, therefore, is limited to the behaviour of males rather than females.

Limitations of evolutionary explanations of aggression
Explanations of aggression that are based on mating success, sexual jealousy or the acquisition of status in warfare fail to explain the extreme levels of cruelty that are often found in human conflicts. For example, they do not tell us why humans torture their opponents when they have already been defeated. Watson (1973) suggests this is more a consequence of de-individuation than evolutionary adaptations.

Apply it

Scenario. Petra is preparing an assignment on domestic violence against women for her General Studies project.

What aspects of the evolutionary explanation of aggression might she incorporate into her report? (4 marks)

Explanation. A problem for early males would have been to avoid cuckoldry, the reproductive cost as a result of his partner's infidelity. Sexual jealousy would have arisen as a consequence of this threat. Buss (1988) suggests that sexual jealousy might have led to the use of violence to prevent a partner from straying. If successful, this mental module would have become widespread in the gene pool because males who were successful would have been better able to pass on their own genes. In similar situations nowadays, when a male suspects his partner of infidelity he may use violence against her to avoid the costs of cuckoldry.

The frustration–aggression hypothesis

Dollard *et al.* (1939) claimed frustration leads to the arousal of an aggressive drive, which then leads to aggressive behaviour, which consequently has a cathartic effect on the individual. Frustration increases when our motivation to achieve a particular goal is very strong and when there is nothing we can do about it, e.g. Brown *et al.* (2001) surveyed British holidaymakers stranded in Calais as a result of a blockade of the port by French fishing boats, and found an increase in hostile attitudes towards the French as a result of the passengers' frustration.

Justified and unjustified frustration
Pastore (1952) distinguished between justified and unjustified frustration, arguing that it was mainly the latter that produces anger and aggression. Pastore found that participants expressed much lower levels of anger when a bus with an 'out of service' message (justified frustration) failed to stop at a bus-stop than when a bus without this message failed to stop (unjustified frustration).

Displaced aggression
When people are frustrated, they experience a drive to be aggressive towards the object of their frustration. If it is impossible to behave aggressively towards the source of frustration, this drive is inhibited. Dollard *et al.* assumed that aggression is sometimes displaced from the source of the frustration on to someone or something else.

A revised frustration–aggression hypothesis (Berkowitz, 1989)
Berkowitz's revised **frustration–aggression hypothesis** argued that frustration is only one of many different types of unpleasant experience that can lead to aggression. These unpleasant experiences create 'negative affect' in the individual, and it is this, claims Berkowitz, that triggers the aggression, rather than frustration alone. Under this reformulation of the frustration–aggression hypothesis, the nature of the frustrating event is less important than how negative is the resulting affect.

Evaluation
Aggression is not an automatic consequence of frustration
Aggressive behaviour may be only one possible response to frustration. An individual *may* respond to frustration with aggression if it has been effective for them before or if they have observed it being effective in others. Rather than frustration always leading to aggression, an individual *learns* to produce aggressive actions and also learns the circumstances under which they are likely to be successful.

Lack of research support for the central claims
Critics of the frustration–aggression hypothesis argue that many of its claims had no support. The concept of catharsis, that aggression reduces arousal and so reduces aggressive feelings, has not been supported by research. Bushman (2002) found that behaving aggressively is likely to lead to *more* rather than less aggression in the future, as aggressive behaviour keeps aggressive thoughts active in memory.

Not all aggression arises from frustration
Frustration is only one of a large number of aversive events that can lead to aggression. A study of baseball found that, as temperatures increased, so did the likelihood that pitchers displayed aggressive behaviour towards the batters (Reifman *et al.*, 1991). This supports the *revised* frustration–aggression hypothesis in that extreme temperatures are aversive stimuli that make people angry, which then increases the likelihood of aggression.

Real-world application: frustration and mass killings
The frustration–aggression hypothesis has been used as an explanation of mass killings. Staub (1996) suggests these are often rooted in the frustration caused by social and economic difficulties. These frustrations typically lead to scapegoating and then discrimination and aggression against this group (e.g. Jews after the First World War). This shows that widespread frustration can have violent consequences for a scapegoated group.

Real world-application: sports violence
Priks (2010) found supporting evidence for the frustration–aggression hypothesis in a study of violent behaviour among Swedish football fans. Priks found that supporters were more likely to act aggressively and fight with opposition supporters when their team performed worse than expected. This finding suggests that supporters become more aggressive when their expectations of good performance are frustrated, thus supporting the frustration–aggression hypothesis.

KEY TERM
Frustration–aggression hypothesis This sees aggression being the consequence of frustration, defined as 'any event or stimulus that prevents an individual from attaining some goal and its accompanying reinforcing quality'.

Apply it
Scenario. The TV news carries a report of protestors blocking major roads and access routes to airports by chaining themselves together across the roads. This leads to aggressive outbursts aimed at the protestors from travellers and other road users.

With reference to these incidents, outline and evaluate the frustration–aggression explanation of aggression. (16 marks)

Explanation extract… Dollard *et al.* (1939) claimed that frustration leads to the arousal of an aggressive drive, which then leads to aggressive behaviour. Frustration increases when our motivation to achieve a particular goal is very strong and when there is nothing we can do about it. Because the protestors prevented people from completing their journeys, this was experienced as frustration. Many people would have been prevented from catching flights – therefore their frustration would have been very strong. Pastore (1952) distinguished between justified and unjustified frustration, arguing it was mainly the latter that produces anger and aggression. Many road users expressed their anger against the protestors, suggesting that they perceived this as unjustified frustration. …

KEY TERM

Social learning theory Learning through observing others and imitating behaviours that are seen to be rewarded.

Social learning theory (SLT)

Social learning theory (SLT) suggests that we learn by observing the aggressive behaviour of others.

Observation

Children primarily learn their aggressive responses through *observation* – watching the behaviour of role models with whom they identify and then *imitating* that behaviour.

Vicarious reinforcement

By observing the *consequences* of aggressive behaviour for others, a child gradually learns something about what is considered appropriate (and effective) conduct in the world around them.

Mental representation

For social learning to take place, the child must form mental representations of events in their social environment, together with expectancies of future outcomes. These mental representations (the script) then become internalised. Once established in childhood, this pattern of aggression can become a way of life.

Production of behaviour

Maintenance through direct experience

If a child is rewarded (i.e. gets what he or she wants or is praised by others) for a behaviour, he or she is likely to repeat the same action in similar situations in the future.

Self-efficacy expectancies

In addition to forming expectancies of the likely outcomes of their aggression, children also develop confidence (or not) in their ability to carry out the necessary aggressive actions to resolve conflicts.

Key study: Bandura *et al.* (1961)

How? Male and female children aged between three and five were exposed either to adult models interacting aggressively (both physically and verbally) with a Bobo doll or to non-aggressive models. Children were then allowed to interact with the Bobo doll.

Showed? Children in the aggression condition reproduced physically and verbally aggressive behaviour resembling that of the model. Children in the non-aggressive group exhibited virtually no aggression towards the doll. Boys reproduced more imitative physical aggression than girls, but they did not differ in their imitation of verbal aggression.

Evaluation

Lack of realism in research

Early research on social learning relied heavily on Bandura's Bobo doll studies. However, there are significant methodological problems with the Bobo doll studies. A doll is not a living person, and does not retaliate when hit. This raises questions about whether these studies tell us much about the imitation of aggression towards other human beings (who are likely to retaliate).

Research support for social learning theory

Gee and Leith (2007) believed that ice hockey players born in North America were more likely to have been exposed to aggressive models of aggression and less likely to have been punished for their aggressive play compared to players born in Europe. In line with SLT predictions, they found that players born in North America were much more likely to be penalised for aggressive play and fighting than players born in other countries.

Explaining inconsistencies in aggressive behaviour

A strength of SLT is that it can explain inconsistencies in an individual's use of aggressive behaviour. The expectation of consequences in any particular situation determines the likelihood of aggression being used in that situation. As a result, this means that we can predict whether or not aggression is likely in a particular situation by knowing its expected consequences.

Cultural differences in aggression

SLT can be used to explain cultural differences in aggression. Among the !Kung San people, aggression is comparatively rare because of child-rearing practices which do not involve physical punishment or reinforcement of aggressive behaviour. The absence of direct reinforcement of aggression and the absence of aggressive models means there is little opportunity or motivation for children to acquire aggressive behaviours.

The consequences of social learning

The belief that aggressive behaviour can be learned through social learning has raised concerns about aggressive models in young people's lives. ACT Against Violence educates parents about the dangers of providing aggressive role models. After completing the programme, parents demonstrated increases in positive parenting and discontinuation of physical punishment, showing that the power of social learning can be used to *decrease* aggressive behaviour (Weymouth & Howe, 2011).

Apply it

Scenario. Kelly has noticed that since her three-year-old son has started preschool he has become a lot more aggressive in his behaviour towards other children.

Explain this change in behaviour in terms of the social learning theory of aggression. (4 marks)

Explanation. Children primarily learn their aggressive responses through observation, watching the behaviour of role models with whom they identify and then imitating that behaviour. Kelly's son would have learned by observing and imitating the aggressive behaviour of the older children. By observing the consequences of their behaviour, he would have learned what is appropriate behaviour in that situation. He might have seen other children getting what they wanted by being aggressive, so would have learned through vicarious reinforcement.

De-individuation

The psychological state of de-individuation is aroused when individuals join crowds or large groups, giving them a 'cloak of anonymity' that diminishes any personal consequences for their actions. Factors that contribute to this state of de-individuation include anonymity and altered consciousness due to drugs or alcohol.

The process of de-individuation

People refrain from acting aggressively because of social norms inhibiting this behaviour and because they are easily identifiable. Being anonymous reduces inner restraints and increases behaviours that are usually inhibited. In a crowd, each person is faceless and anonymous – the larger the group, the greater the anonymity. There is a diminished fear of the negative evaluation of actions and a reduced sense of guilt. Research has shown that individuals who believe their identities are unknown are more likely to behave in an aggressive manner.

Research on de-individuation

Zimbardo et al.'s Stanford prison study (1972) found that participants who played the role of guards (in a de-individuated state) acted aggressively towards other participants who were in the role of prisoners. The guards also wore mirrored sunglasses to accentuate their de-individuated state. Other researchers have found that wearing mirrored sunglasses makes people feel greater anonymity, which increases the experience of de-individuation (Zhong, 2010).

Key study: Zimbardo (1969)

How? Groups of females were required to deliver electric shocks. Half wore lab coats and hoods that hid their faces, sat in separate cubicles and were never referred to by name. The other participants wore normal clothes, wore name tags and were introduced by name. They were able to see each other when seated at the shock machines.

Showed? Participants in the de-individuation condition were more likely to press a button they believed would give shocks to a 'victim'. They held it down for twice as long as the identifiable participants.

Evaluation

Gender differences

Cannavale et al. (1970) found that male and female groups responded differently under de-individuation conditions. An increase in aggression was obtained only in the all-male groups and not in all-female groups. One possible reason is that males tend to respond to provocation in more extreme ways than females and that these tendencies are magnified under de-individuation conditions (Eagly, 2013).

Anonymity and de-individuation

Rehm et al. (1987) found support for Zimbardo's de-individuation concept through an investigation of the effect of increased anonymity on aggressive behaviour in games of handball. Teams that wore the same-coloured shirts showed significantly more aggressive acts than teams that wore their own differently coloured shirts. The results support the claim that de-individuation through increased anonymity leads to more aggressive acts.

Inconclusive support for de-individuation

A meta-analysis of studies of de-individuation (Postmes & Spears, 1998) concluded there is insufficient support for the major claims of de-individuation theory. For example, they found that disinhibition and anti-social behaviour are *not* more common in large groups and anonymous settings. Rather, they found that de-individuation increases people's responsiveness to situational norms, which could also lead to increased *pro*social behaviour.

Real-world application: the baiting crowd

Mann (1981) used de-individuation to explain the concept of the 'baiting crowd'. An analysis of 21 suicide leaps reported in US newspapers showed that, in nearly half of these, baiting had occurred. These incidents tended to occur at night, when the crowd was large and some distance from the victim, all features likely to produce a state of de-individuation in members of the crowd.

Cultural differences

Support for the deadly influence of de-individuation comes from Watson (1973). He collected data on the extent to which warriors in 23 societies changed their appearance (e.g. through war paint) prior to going to war and the extent to which they killed, tortured or mutilated their victims. Societies where warriors changed their appearance were more destructive towards their victims compared to those who did not change their appearance.

KEY TERM

De-individuation A psychological state in which individuals have lowered levels of self-evaluation (e.g. when in a crowd or under the influence of alcohol) and decreased concerns about evaluation by others.

Apply it

Scenario. In his cultural history class, Connor learns about the violence in Northern Ireland in the eighties and nineties. In one incident, a large group of masked youths took to the streets of Belfast at night and threw petrol bombs and bricks at the security forces.

With reference to this incident, outline and evaluate the de-individuation explanation of aggression. (16 marks)

Explanation extract... A state of de-individuation arises when individuals join crowds or large groups, giving them a 'cloak of anonymity' that diminishes any personal consequences for their actions. This incident describes how the 'large group' of youths were 'masked' and the incident took place 'at night'. These are factors associated with de-individuation. In large groups there is a diminished fear of negative evaluation of actions and a reduced sense of guilt. Research has shown that individuals who believe their identities are unknown are more likely to behave aggressively. This would explain why these youths felt safe to act violently towards the security forces, because their identity was hidden by their masks. ...

KEY TERMS

Dispositional explanations Emphasise the causes of a particular behaviour as being due to the enduring characteristics of the individuals involved rather than any aspect of the situation they are in.

Institutional aggression Refers to aggressive acts that are found in particular violent institutions such as prisons.

Situational explanations Emphasise the causes of a particular behaviour as being due to the context in which it occurs rather than any enduring characteristics of the individuals involved.

Apply it

Using insights from the dispositional explanation of prison violence, consider what steps might be taken to minimise institutional aggression in prisons. (4 marks)

Explanation. Drury and DeLisi (2011) found that individuals who had been members of gangs prior to imprisonment were significantly more likely to engage in violence while in prison. Prisoners might be screened for gang membership when entering prison, and any members of violent street gangs could be kept in special units where their contact with other prisoners is minimised. Other dispositional characteristics that have been found to relate to aggressive behaviour in prison include anger and low levels of self-control (DeLisi *et al.*, 2003). Prisoners could be given anger management sessions and be taught self-control to minimise the likelihood of them getting into fights with other prisoners.

Situational explanation: the deprivation model

Institutional aggression is seen as the product of the stressful conditions of the prison itself (e.g. the loss of liberty), which are linked to an increase in violence. Some inmates cope with these conditions by engaging with violence against other prisoners or against staff. A study of prison inmates (Kimmet & Martin, 2002) found that most violent situations in prisons were to do with the need for respect and fairness, avoiding exploitation by appearing weak or as a way of expressing loyalty and honour.

The role of prison characteristics

In order to understand institutional aggression, we need to consider the situational context where violence takes place. These include overcrowding (Ministry of Justice Report, 2014), heat and noise (Griffin & Veitch, 1971), and job burnout (Maslach *et al.*, 2001).

Dispositional explanation: the importation model

Irwin and Cressey (1962) claim that inmates bring with them to prison their violent pasts and draw on their experiences in an environment where toughness and physical exploitation are important survival skills. Prisoners are not 'blank slates' when they enter prison, and many of the normative systems developed on the outside are 'imported' into prison. Cultural belief systems such as 'the code of the street' define how some individuals behave once in prison, particularly when this code relates to gang membership.

Gang membership

Within prison environments, gang membership is consistently related to violence and other forms of anti-social behaviour. Drury and DeLisi (2011) found that individuals who had been members of gangs prior to imprisonment were significantly more likely to commit various types of misconduct in prison, including murder, hostage taking and assault with a deadly weapon.

The role of dispositional characteristics

Other **dispositional explanations** that have been found to relate to aggressive behaviour in prison include anger, anti-social personality style and impulsivity (Wang & Diamond, 1999), and low levels of self-control (DeLisi *et al.*, 2003).

Evaluation of the dispositional explanation

Research support for the importation model

Mears *et al.* (2013) tested the view that inmate behaviour stems in part from the cultural belief systems that they import with them into prison. Their findings supported the argument that a 'code of the street' belief system affects inmate violence. This effect was particularly pronounced among those inmates who were involved in gangs prior to being in prison.

Challenges to the importation model

Evidence from DeLisi *et al.* (2004) challenges the claim that pre-prison gang membership predicts violence while in prison. Inmates with prior street gang involvement were no more likely than other inmates to engage in prison violence. However, the lack of any association can be explained by the fact that violent gang members tend to be isolated from the general inmate population, restricting their opportunities for violence.

Evaluation of the situational explanation

Research support for the deprivation model

There is substantial research evidence to support the claim that violence is used to relieve the deprivation experienced in prisons. McCorkle *et al.* (1995), in a major study of US prisons, found that **situational explanations** such as overcrowding, lack of privacy and the lack of meaningful activity all significantly influenced inmate-on-inmate assaults and inmate-on-staff assaults.

Challenges to the deprivation model

The link between situational factors and institutional aggression is challenged by research by Harer and Steffensmeier (1996). They collected data from more than 24,000 inmates from 58 prisons across the US, and concluded that race, age and criminal history were the only significant predictors of prison violence, whereas none of the deprivation variables were significant in this respect.

Real-world application: HMP Woodhill and the deprivation model

Prison Governor David Wilson reasoned that if most violence occurs in environments that are hot, noisy and overcrowded, then it should be possible to significantly reduce prison violence by reducing these three factors. Making these changes at HMP Woodhill virtually eradicated assaults on prison staff and other inmates, providing powerful support for the claim that situational variables are the main cause of prison violence (Wilson, 2010).

Violent films and TV

Laboratory and field experiments
A consistent finding is that those who watch violent scenes subsequently display more aggressive behaviour than those who do not. Bjorkqvist (1985) found that compared with children who viewed a non-violent film, those who watched a violent film were subsequently rated much higher on measures of physical aggression.

Longitudinal studies
Huesmann et al. (2003) studied children aged six to ten and then again 15 years later. They found habitual early exposure to TV violence predicted adult aggression later in life. This relationship persisted even when the possible effects of socioeconomic status, intelligence and differences in parenting styles were controlled.

Meta-analyses
Bushman and Huesmann (2006) carried out a meta-analysis of 431 studies, 264 involving children and 167 involving adults. They found significant effect sizes for exposure to media violence on aggressive behaviours, thoughts and feelings. The short-term effects of violent media were greater for adults than for children, whereas the long-term effects were greater for children than for adults.

Violent computer games

Experimental studies
These have found short-term increases in levels of physiological arousal, hostile feelings and aggressive behaviour following violent game play. Anderson and Dill (2000) found that participants blasted opponents with white noise for longer after playing a violent game compared to those who played a slow-paced puzzle game.

Longitudinal studies
Anderson et al. (2007) surveyed children aged seven to nine at two points during the school year. Children who had high exposure to violent video games became more verbally and physically aggressive and less prosocial. Adachi and Willoughby (2013) suggest the longitudinal link found between violent video games and aggression may be due to their competitive nature.

Key study: Greitemeyer and Mügge (2014)
How? Greitemeyer and Mügge carried out a meta-analysis of 98 studies to investigate how playing violent and prosocial games influenced aggressive and prosocial behaviour (e.g. aggression and helping) as well as aggressive and prosocial cognitions and emotions (e.g. anger and empathy).
Showed? Violent video game use was linked to an increase in aggressive outcomes *and* a decrease in prosocial outcomes. Prosocial games were linked to a *reduction* in aggressive behaviour and an increase in prosocial, cooperative behaviour.

Evaluation
Media violence research: overstating the case
Very few studies have actually measured aggression against another person. Ferguson and Kilburn (2009) note that, when aggression towards another person or violent crime is the measure of aggression used in research, the relationship between exposure to media violence and aggressive behaviour is actually close to zero.

Simple questions but complex answers
Livingstone (1996) claims answering questions about **media influences** is not a simple matter. Effects research has mostly tended to use unrepresentative samples (e.g. male students) and then made generalisations about all viewers. Livingstone argues that there is a need for better methodologies in more natural viewing conditions.

Failure to consider other causal variables
Many studies fail to account for other variables that explain why some people display aggressive behaviour and why those same people may choose to play violent computer games. Ferguson et al. (2009) found that the effects of violent media content on aggressive behaviour disappears when other potential influences such as trait aggression and family violence are taken into consideration.

Problems with research on the effects of computer games
A weakness of experiments in this area is that researchers must use measures of aggressive behaviour (e.g. noise blasts) that have no relationship to real-life aggression. A problem for longitudinal studies is that participants may be exposed to other forms of media violence (e.g. on television) during the course of the study, so the effect from violent video game exposure alone is uncertain.

Game difficulty rather than content may lead to aggression
Przybylski et al. (2014) suggest aggressive behaviour may be linked to a player's experiences of frustration during a game rather than the game's violent storyline. They found it was the difficulty players had in completing the game that led to frustration and aggression. The researchers argue that even non-violent games can leave players feeling aggressive if they are poorly designed or too difficult.

KEY TERM
Media influences Changes in behaviour that are attributed to exposure to media such as TV or computer games.

Apply it
Scenario. Toby loves nothing better than an evening in playing *Call of Duty*. When his parents suggest he might like to do something 'more healthy' he becomes abusive towards them and they observe he is a lot less friendly and helpful to other members of the family.

Consider whether Toby's parents might be right in blaming violent computer games for his aggressive behaviour. (4 marks)

Explanation. Research by Greitemeyer and Mügge (2014) concluded that violent video game use was linked to an increase in aggressive outcomes *and* a decrease in prosocial outcomes. This is consistent with the observation that Toby was becoming more aggressive after playing them and displaying lower levels of prosocial behaviour towards other members of his family. However, Przybylski et al. (2014) found it was the difficulty players had in completing the game that led to frustration and aggression, so Toby's aggression might be more to do with his inability to master the game than being the victim of its violent storyline.

KEY TERMS

Cognitive priming Refers to a temporary increase in the accessibility of thoughts and ideas. For example, violent media activate thoughts or ideas about violence, which activate other aggressive thoughts through their association in memory pathways.

Desensitisation Explanations based on this assume that, under normal conditions, anxiety about violence inhibits its use. Media violence may lead to aggressive behaviour by removing this anxiety.

Disinhibition Exposure to violent media legitimises the use of violence in real life because it undermines the social sanctions that usually inhibit such behaviour.

The role of desensitisation, disinhibition and cognitive priming

Desensitisation

Anxiety about violence normally inhibits its use. Media violence removes this anxiety by representing aggression and violence as 'normal'. Someone who becomes desensitised to violence may therefore perceive it as being more acceptable and as a result be more likely to engage in violence themselves. They are less likely to notice violence in real life, feel less sympathy for the victims of violence and have less negative attitudes towards violence, all of which would increase the likelihood of aggressive responses in real life (Mullin & Linz, 1995).

Disinhibition

Watching or playing violent media can legitimise the individual's use of violence in their own lives because it undermines the social sanctions that usually inhibit such behaviour. Disinhibition can have an immediate effect and a long-term effect. Violence on TV or in a computer game triggers a state of physiological arousal, which leads to a greater probability of behaving aggressively. In this aroused state, inhibitions are temporarily suppressed by the drive to act. In the longer term, when violence is justified or left unpunished on television, the child feels less inhibited about behaving aggressively again.

Cognitive priming

When people are exposed to violent media, this activates violent thoughts, which activate other aggressive thoughts through their association in memory pathways. Prolonged exposure to violent media results in a lowered activation threshold for these aggressive thoughts, allowing them to be accessed more readily and so used to process and interpret information. Zelli *et al.* (1995) found that cognitive priming by aggressive stimuli influenced individuals to make hostile attributions about the behaviour of other people, increasing the likelihood of aggressive behaviour.

Evaluation of desensitisation
Research support for desensitisation

Carnagey *et al.* (2007) tested the claim that individuals would show less physiological arousal to violence in the real world after exposure to computer game violence. Participants who had previously played the violent computer game had a lower heart rate and skin conductance response while viewing the filmed real-life violence compared to participants who had played a non-violent game. This demonstrated physiological desensitisation to violence, as predicted by this explanation.

The good and bad of desensitisation

Desensitisation can be adaptive for individuals, e.g. desensitisation to the horrors of combat makes troops more effective in their role. However, desensitisation to violence may also have detrimental effects. Bushman and Anderson (2009) found that violent media exposure can reduce helping behaviour to others in distress. They claim that people exposed to media violence become 'comfortably numb' to the suffering of others and are consequently less helpful.

Evaluation of disinhibition
The disinhibition effect depends on other factors

For example, younger children are more likely to be affected because they are drawn into high-action violent episodes without considering the motives or consequences of the violence (Collins, 1989). This demonstrates that the relationship between media violence and disinhibition is not a straightforward one, and is mediated by a number of individual and social characteristics.

Negative consequences make disinhibition more likely

Goranson (1969) showed people a boxing match where there were two alternative endings. Participants who did not see the negative consequences (the loser dies) were more likely to behave aggressively after viewing the fight than those who did see the consequences. This supports the claim that disinhibition is more likely where the negative consequences are not made apparent to viewers.

Evaluation of cognitive priming
Research support for cognitive priming

Bushman (1998) tested the hypothesis that exposure to violent media makes aggressive thoughts more accessible to viewers. Participants who watched a violent film subsequently had faster reaction times to aggressive words than did those who had seen a non-violent film. Video content did not, however, influence reaction times to non-aggressive words. This suggests that exposure to violent media primes memories related to aggression.

Priming is less likely with less realistic media

Atkin (1983) suggests that film or game realism is an important factor in the relationship between exposure to violent media and the priming of aggressive thoughts and behaviours. The fictional violence in some computer games, for example, may not have the same priming effects as games with more realistic violence, and therefore would not be as likely to produce aggressive behaviour.

Apply it

Scenario. After Toby has been playing violent computer games, he finds that he no longer seems to be bothered about watching scenes of devastation and war on television. It 'washes over' him, whereas it used to make him very anxious and upset. He also fails to stop the bullying of younger children in his road, just walking by without a second glance.

Using your knowledge of 'desensitisation', 'disinhibition' and 'cognitive priming', explain which one best fits Toby's behaviour. (3 marks)

Explanation. Media violence removes anxiety about aggression by representing it as 'normal'. Desensitised individuals are less likely to notice violence in real life and feel less sympathy for the victims of violence (Mullin & Linz, 1995). This would explain why Toby is no longer anxious or upset when he watches violence on the TV, and why he no longer appears to feel sympathy for the younger children who are being bullied in his street.

Chapter 10

Forensic psychology

Paper 3, Section D, option 2. 4.3.9 Forensic psychology

- Problems in defining crime. Ways of measuring crime, including official statistics, victim surveys and offender surveys.
- Offender profiling: the top-down approach, including organised and disorganised types of offender; the bottom-up approach, including investigative psychology; geographical profiling.
- Biological explanations of offending behaviour: a historical approach (atavistic form); genetics and neural explanations.
- Psychological explanations of offending behaviour: Eysenck's theory of the criminal personality; cognitive explanations; level of moral reasoning and cognitive distortions, including hostile attribution bias and minimalisation; differential association theory; psychodynamic explanations.
- Dealing with offending behaviour: the aims of custodial sentencing and the psychological effects of custodial sentencing. Recidivism. Behaviour modification in custody. Anger management and restorative justice programmes.

Key terms (highlight each cell when you can define the term confidently)

Defining and measuring crime	Offender profiling	Biological explanations	Psychological explanations: Eysenck	Psychological explanations: cognitive	Psychological explanations: differential association	Psychological explanations: psychodynamic	Dealing with offender behaviour
Official statistics	Top-down approach	Atavistic form	*Extraversion*	Cognitive distortions	Differential association theory	*Affectionless psychopathy*	Custodial sentencing
Victim surveys	Disorganised type	Genetic explanations	*Neuroticism*	Hostile attribution bias		*Maternal deprivation*	Recidivism
Offender surveys	Organised type	Neural explanations	*Psychoticism*	Minimalisation		*Superego*	Behaviour modification
	Bottom-up approach			Level of moral reasoning			Anger management
	Investigative psychology						Restorative justice programmes

Content checklist
1. *In each 'describe', 'apply' and 'evaluate' cell tick when you have produced brief notes.*
2. *Once you feel you have a good grasp of the topic add a second tick to the cell.*
3. *When you feel you have complete mastery of the topic and would be able to answer an exam question without the aid of notes highlight the cell.*

I am able to ...	Describe	Apply	Evaluate
Ways of measuring crime: official statistics, victim and offender surveys			
Offender profiling: the top-down approach, including organised and disorganised types of offender			
Offender profiling: the bottom-up approach, including investigative psychology; geoprofiling			
Biological explanations of offending behaviour: a historical approach (atavistic form)			
Biological explanations of offending behaviour: genetics and neural explanations			
Psychological explanations of offending behaviour: Eysenck's theory of the criminal personality			
Psychological explanations of offending behaviour: cognitive explanations; level of moral reasoning and cognitive distortions, including hostile attribution bias and minimalisation			
Psychological explanations of offending behaviour: differential association theory			
Psychological explanations of offending behaviour: psychodynamic explanations			
Dealing with offender behaviour: the aims and psychological effects of custodial sentencing. Recidivism			
Dealing with offender behaviour: behaviour modification in custody. Anger management			
Dealing with offender behaviour: behaviour modification in custody. Restorative justice programmes			

KEY TERM

Crime Refers to any behaviour that is unlawful and punished by the state. It is an act that is harmful to an individual, group or society as a whole.

Defining crime

The definition of **crime** is a social construct – related to the dominant morals and values of a particular culture at a particular time. For example, in the UK, homosexuality was illegal until 1964 and remains illegal in some countries, e.g. Egypt and Saudi Arabia.

Ways of measuring crime

◎ Official statistics

The Home Office annually publishes any incident reported to the police or offences observed or discovered by the police. The National Crime Reporting Standard (NCRS) records any reported incident, even if it is not recorded as a crime. Statistics can make historical comparisons to identify trends, e.g. whether knife crime is increasing or decreasing.

In the US the FBI produces the annual Uniform Crime Reports which record instances of crime reported to local and state enforcement agencies. However, not all governments publish crime statistics, e.g. China and Burma. This is a concern for the UNICR (United Nations Interregional Crime and Justice Research Institute) which monitors crime statistics around the world.

◎ Victim surveys

The Crime Survey for England and Wales (CSEW) began in 1982. Since 2001 the survey has been repeated yearly with a randomly selected sample of about 50,000 households. Those aged 16 and over are interviewed using a fixed set of questions relating to general attitudes (e.g. 'In your view what are the major causes of crime in Britain today?') and specific events ('both reported and unreported' (e.g. 'During the last 12 months have you or anyone in your household been a victim of vehicle theft?').

Victim surveys are also used in other countries such as the US National Crime Victimization Survey and the European Union International Crime Survey (EU ICS).

◎ Offender surveys

In 2003, the Offending, Crime and Justice Survey (OCJS) surveyed people in England and Wales aged 10–65 living in private households. Subsequently, an annual subsample of 5,000 10–25-year-olds was carried out, with over 95% of respondents taking part over four years. Questions focused on criminal behaviour and relevant contextual data to understand the extent of offending, anti-social behaviour and drug use.

◎ Evaluation

Defining crime: universal concepts

Despite some behaviours being universally regarded as unacceptable – murder, rape and theft – cultural variations can be seen in the laws. For example, the French concept of a 'crime passionnel' (crime of passion) may result in a more lenient sentence for murder if the court decides that the offender was driven by a strong and unplanned impulse.

Official statistics only represent part of criminal activity

Official statistics only show crimes which make it through the 'crime funnel'. Crimes may go unreported because the victim does not feel the police will take it seriously, may wish to avoid stigma or may not even be aware a crime has been committed. Walker *et al.* (2006) found only 24% of crime victims mentioned in the British Crime Survey were reported to the police ('dark figure' of crime).

Victim surveys can potentially provide information about the 'dark figure' of crime

However, this measurement relies on the honesty of those interviewed. Some may still be reluctant to mention crimes experienced, especially if the crime has stigma attached (e.g. rape) or the person feels the crime is too trivial (e.g. minor graffiti). Nonetheless, victim surveys may be more consistent when making comparisons over time, unlike official statistics which vary with changes in laws and reporting practices.

Victim surveys: samples may be biased

Although random sampling is used to obtain a representative sample, only about 75% of households contacted take part, meaning the final sample is biased (those willing to respond may be more available and/or have an interest in upholding the law). The use of Royal Mail's list of addresses as a sampling frame can also bias the sample, e.g. those of no fixed address may be more vulnerable to becoming a victim of crime but are not included.

The crime survey may underestimate the level of crime as the number of crimes any one individual is able to report is capped at five. A domestic abuse victim may experience more incidents in any year but this would not be reported. Farrell and Pease (2007) suggest this cap means as many as three million incidents may not be included in the overall figures.

Offender surveys may lack accuracy

We might expect that people may underplay their criminal involvement and other behaviours (such as drug use). However, Hales *et al.*'s (2007) longitudinal analysis of the OCJS found participants reported that they had answered the survey honestly.

Apply it

Scenario. Researchers decided to use official statistics to investigate whether trends in violent crime differed from trends in non-violent crime over a five-year period.

Explain **one** *limitation of using this way of measuring crime. (2 marks)*

Explanation. Not all crimes will be reported to police and so the official statistics may only represent a part of criminal activity. For example, some victims of domestic violence may be afraid to approach the police and so these violent crimes would be underrepresented in official statistics.

The top-down approach

This approach involves the intuitive application of the profiler's prior knowledge – the profiler has a 'feel' for the kind of person who committed the crime – to produce a profile of the most likely offender. There are six main stages in the top-down process (Douglas *et al.*, 2006).

1. Profiling inputs
The crime scene (photographs, sketches), information about the victim (employment, habits, relationships) and the crime (weapon, cause of death, autopsy report) along with trivial details are collected. To avoid bias, no suspects are considered at this stage.

2. Decision-making process
The profiler organises data into meaningful patterns, e.g. murder type – mass, spree or serial murders; time factors – length of time taken, time of day; and location factors – one or multiple locations? For example, kidnapped from one location but murdered elsewhere.

3. Crime assessment
Crimes by an **organised type of offender** refer to a planned crime with a specifically targeted victim, the body is transported from the scene, the weapon usually hidden and violent fantasies may be acted out. **Disorganised type of offender** relates to unplanned crimes, random selection of (and little engagement with) the victim and any sexual acts performed after death, and many clues such as blood, semen and fingerprints are found at the scene.

4. Criminal profile
In **offender profiling**, the profiler hypotheses about the offender's background, habits and beliefs. For example, organised offenders are thought to be generally high in intelligence, socially and sexually competent, usually live with a partner and follow their crimes in the media. The profile created anticipates how the offender will respond to various investigative efforts and, once apprehended, interview techniques.

5. Crime assessment
Police are given the written report, and persons matching the profile are evaluated. If new evidence is generated and/or no suspect is identified the profiler returns to step 2.

6. Apprehension
If a suspect is apprehended, the entire profile-generating process is reviewed. Each stage is checked to ensure the conclusions reached were legitimate and to consider how the process may be revised for future cases.

Evaluation
Use of FBI methods are supported by practising police officers
Copson (1995) found, of 184 US police officers questioned, 82% said the technique was operationally useful and over 90% said they would use it again. While the technique may not result in actual identification of the offender, the top-down approach offers investigators a different perspective, opens up new lines of enquiry and may even prevent wrongful conviction (Scherer & Jarvis, 2014).

The basis of the method may be flawed
Interviews with 36 of the most dangerous and sexually motivated murderers were used to develop the classifications of organised/disorganised type of offender. The individuals, including Ted Bundy and Charles Manson, were highly manipulative and so may not be the most reliable source of information. Furthermore, their approach and rationale may be very different to more 'typical offenders'.

Profiling is harmful 'junk science'
The process of top-down analysis is not based on any science or theory. The Barnum effect – where ambiguous descriptions can be made to fit any person/situation – may explain the believability of profiles. Profiles can be harmful in that inaccurate profiles might mislead investigations or smart offenders may deliberately mislead profilers by leaving false clues at the crime scene.

Measuring the accuracy of the approach
If the profile created closely matches the actual offender's characteristics then the profile could be said to be useful. However, such judgements may be unreliable. Alison *et al.* (2003) found that over 50% of police officers given an account of the offender, along with the profile used in the case, judged the profile to be generally or very accurate – even though half of the police officers saw a 'fake' account of the offender.

Distinguishing between organised and disorganised types
Descriptions of the two types often include phrases such as 'tends to be …'. This might imply offenders are more likely to fall along a continuum instead of fitting into a distinct category. Douglas *et al.* (1992) suggested introducing a 'mixed offender' category, but critics argue this is a dustbin category. Canter *et al.*'s (2004) analysis of murders committed by over 100 US serial killers found a number of subsets of organised-type crimes and little evidence for disorganised types.

KEY TERMS
Disorganised type of offender The crime scene is left with many clues such as fingerprints, there is little evidence of engagement with the victim, and the offender has lower intelligence and competence.

Offender profiling A method of working out the characteristics of an offender by examining the characteristics of the crime and crime scene.

Organised type of offender This type of offender commits a planned crime and may engage in violent fantasies with the victim. They are of high intelligence and socially competent.

Top-down approach (Also known as crime scene analysis.) First used by the FBI in the US, the top-down approach was developed as a way of trying to solve bizarre and extreme murder cases. Through analysis of previous crimes, a profile of the offender is created which is then used to narrow the field of possible suspects. Unlike the bottom-up approach, the top-down approach relies on the intuition and beliefs of the profiler.

Apply it
Scenario. A psychologist was analysing police reports of a range of crime scenes. Based on the reports she categorised the offenders as either organised or disorganised.

Explain the common features found in the crimes of organised types of offender and the common features found in those of disorganised types of offender. (3 marks)

Explanation. The crime scenes of disorganised offenders would contain clues such as blood, semen and fingerprints. It is likely the offender selected the victim at random and would have shown little engagement with the victim. Organised offenders would have planned their crime and targeted a specific victim. They may hide any weapons used in the offence and will have transported the body from the scene.

KEY TERMS

Bottom-up approach A data-driven approach where statistical techniques are used to produce predictions about the likely characteristics of an offender. Compared to top-down, the bottom-up approach is regarded as more scientific and logical as inferences (profiles) are driven by actual data rather than from judgements of the profiler (as occurs in the top-down approach).

Geographical profiling A form of bottom-up profiling based on the pattern shown by the location or locations of a series of crimes. Geographical profiling analyses the locations of connected crimes to consider where they were committed, the spatial relationships between each crime, and how this might relate to the offender's place of residence.

Investigative psychology A form of bottom-up profiling based on psychological theory.

The bottom-up approach

◎ Investigative psychology

Canter's approach consists of three main features:

Interpersonal coherence

The consistency of behaviour means elements of the crime and everyday behaviour should correlate. Behaviour can change over time, so looking at how crimes differ across a period of time may offer clues.

Forensic awareness

The behaviour of the offender may reveal past experience of police techniques. Davis *et al.* (1997) found rapists who conceal fingerprints often had previous burglary convictions.

Smallest space awareness

Salfati and Canter (1999) used analysis to find correlating patterns of behaviour in 48 crime scenes and offender characteristics from 82 UK stranger murders. Three underlying themes were identified.

- *Instrumental opportunistic*: murder is an instrument to obtain or accomplish something via the easiest opportunity for the offender.
- *Instrumental cognitive*: the offence is planned due to concerns of detection.
- *Expressive impulsive*: uncontrolled acts in the heat of strong emotions.

◎ Geographical profiling

The offender's choice of location can be a vital clue to their identity. For example, offenders are more likely to commit a crime near where they live or habitually travel to.

Circle theory

Canter and Larkin (1993) suggest most offenders have a kind of imagined circle (a spatial mindset) in which they commit their crimes. *Marauders* are offenders whose home is within the geographical area in which their offending occurs. *Commuters* travel to other areas and commit crimes within a defined space (circle).

Criminal geographical targeting (CGT)

A computerised system based on Rossmo's formula produces a '3D' map of spatial data relating to time, distance and movement to and from crime scenes. This 'jeopardy surface' uses different colours to indicate the likely closeness of the offender's residence to the crime scene.

◎ Evaluation

More scientific than top-down approaches?

Bottom-up approaches have the potential to be objective and systematic due to their statistical techniques and computer analysis. However, techniques rely on data gathered from offenders who have been caught so tell us little about behaviour in unsolved crimes. Underlying assumptions linking items of data may also be flawed, e.g. Rossmo's formula has been criticised for ignoring personality characteristics.

Is investigative psychology useful?

Copson (1995) found that while 75% of police officers surveyed (from 48 UK police forces) said the profiler's advice had been useful, only 3% said the advice had helped identify the actual offender. Furthermore, the maximum number of investigations per year using profiling was only 75 cases. While **investigative psychology** may not be useful in catching the actual offender, the support it offers to the investigation makes it worthwhile.

Is circle theory useful?

Of the 45 sexual assaults studied by Canter and Larkin (1993), 91% of offenders were identified as marauders. If almost all offenders are marauders, then the distinction between this type and commuters is not particularly useful. Petherick (2006) argues that if an offender's home base is not actually in the centre of the circle time may be wasted looking in the wrong place. The use of circles may also be too simplistic as in cities patterns may form another shape.

Is geographical profiling generally successful?

Geographical profiling can prioritise house-to-house searches or identifying an area where DNA could be collected. However, it cannot distinguish between multiple offenders in the same area and does not consider other influential factors. Critics question whether it offers much more insight than the traditional method of pins on a map. In 2001 the Vancouver Police Department dismissed Rossmo as it felt his methods did not enhance police outcomes.

The danger of focusing on one profile

In 1992 forensic psychologist Paul Britten helped police create a profile of Rachel Nickell's murderer. The profile led to the identification of Colin Stagg. After a considerable amount of time and money was wasted trying to convict Stagg, it turned out the actual murderer was Robert Napper, who had originally been ruled out of the investigation for being taller than the profile suggested.

Apply it

Scenario. A team of police officers were using a geographical profile to investigate a spate of muggings in their local community.

What should they consider regarding the usefulness of the profile for their investigation? (3 marks)

Explanation. The police should remember that while a geographical profile can help identify possible areas to conduct house-to-house enquiries, they should not eliminate other locations if they do not fit the profile. The offender's home base may not be in the centre of the circle and elements of the landscape may not necessarily form a circle. While previous police investigations have found geographical profiling useful – 75% of officers stated it was of use (Copson, 1995) – it often does not lead to identification of the actual offender.

Criminal personalities

Early approaches tended to identify different personality types based on physical characteristics of the head or body (soma). It assumes their innate physiological make-up causes their criminality.

Atavistic form

Lombroso (1876) proposed offenders possessed similar characteristics to lower primates, citing they displayed such features as an asymmetrical face, excessive jaw, unusual ears (either very small or sticking out) and excessive arm length. Lombroso also linked different features to different crimes, e.g. stating that thieves had twisted up-turned noses while murderers' noses were beak-like (aquiline) or rose like a peak from swollen nostrils.

Empirical evidence

Lombroso and his team conducted over 50,000 live and post-mortem examinations making precise measurements of skulls and other features (anthropometry – the measurement of humans). In one study of 383 convicted criminals 21% had one atavistic trait and 43% had at least five.

Environmental influences

Lombroso later proposed inherited **atavistic forms** (nature) interacted with a person's physical and social environment (nurture) to determine behaviour. He moved away from the atavistic form as the only explanation for criminality and identified three types of criminal: *born criminals* – the atavistic type; *innate criminals* – suffering from mental illness; and *criminaloids* – those whose mental characteristics predisposed them to criminal behaviour under certain environmental circumstances.

Somatotypes

Kretschmer's (1921) study of over 4,000 criminals led him to propose four main body types and associated criminal behaviour:

• Leptosome or asthetic – tall and thin; petty thieves
• Athletic – tall and muscular; violent crimes
• Pyknic – short and fat; crimes of deception and occasional violence
• Dysplastic or mixed – range of types; crimes against morality.

Evaluation

Contribution to the science of criminology

Before Lombroso, it was assumed that crime was a choice which could be deterred with punishment. Lombroso argued a more humane view was needed when dealing with criminals as biology and environment may remove the option of free will. Today we may criticise his conclusion but we can admire his use of empirical observation and detailed measurement which raised the possibility of the scientific study of criminality.

Lombroso's research lacked adequate controls

Lombroso did not study non-prisoners to the same extent as convicted criminals, so we cannot accept the claim that criminals possess specific physical characteristics. Goring (1913) compared 3,000 convicts with a group of non-convicts. Other than the convicts being slightly shorter, no physical differences were reported.

Lombroso's study of criminality is gender biased

Lombroso did not study women directly yet claimed that, despite being less evolved than men, women were less likely to become criminals. He felt women's passivity, low intelligence and maternal instinct neutralised their negative traits of jealousy and insensitivity to pain. He saw women who did commit crimes as possessing masculine characteristics that, while in a man were beneficial, turned women into 'monsters'.

Evidence of somatotypes

While Kretschmer's evidence was never submitted for scrutiny (so it is unclear if it was actually based on fact), later research has offered some support. Glueck and Glueck (1970) found 60% of delinquents were mesomorphs (athletic type). Shelton's (1949) study of 200 young adults concluded that delinquents tended to be mesomorphs. These findings support the notion of innate criminal types identified by their physical features.

Later theories also link personality type with criminal behaviour

Notions of a basic criminal type have just become more sophisticated. For example, Eysenck's theory of a criminal personality is based on large data sets generated through rigorous research (see p.114). Genetic explanations of criminality (see p.112) imply some people are born to be criminals. Lombroso himself later argued that the atavistic (inherited) form was not the only basis of criminality, which is in line with the view of an interaction between nature and nurture.

(see p.114)
(see p.112)

KEY TERM

Atavistic form An early explanation for criminal behaviour, suggesting that certain individuals are born with a criminal personality and this innate personality is a throwback to earlier primate forms. Turvey (2011) identified 18 different characteristics that make up the atavistic type.

Apply it

Scenario. Sally enjoys reading books about famous criminal cases and enjoys watching true-life crime documentaries. When speaking to her friend she explained that criminals have a 'look' about them and claims she could probably predict people with criminal tendencies just by observing their appearance.

With reference to Sally's comments, discuss the historical approach to explaining offender behaviour. (16 marks)

Explanation extract… By stating that criminals have a 'look', Sally could be seen to support the atavistic form which claims criminals are 'throwbacks' to lower primates. The physical traits Sally may look for when trying to predict possible criminals include unusually sized ears, a chin that either recedes or is excessively long and exaggerated cheekbones. In his study of 383 convicted criminals Lombroso found 43% had five or more atavistic traits, which may explain why Sally feels criminals have a 'look' about them. However, because Lombroso did not study non-prisoners we cannot be certain these features are not also found in non-criminal populations. …

KEY TERMS

Epigenetics Refers to the material in each cell of the body that acts like a set of 'switches' to turn genes on or off.

Genetic explanations The likelihood of behaving in a particular way is determined by a person's genetic make-up, i.e. it is inherited from parents.

Neural explanations Involve areas of the brain and nervous system and the action of neurotransmitters in controlling behaviour.

Genetic and neural explanations

Modern research methods have provided more insight into the mechanisms that underlie criminal traits. However, neural explanations may not necessarily link to genetic explanations as biological abnormalities can result from life experiences.

◑ Genetic explanations

Raine's (1993) review of research into delinquent behaviour found concordance rates of 52% for MZ twins (genetically identical) and 21% for DZ twins (50% shared genes). As evidence suggests MZ twins may be treated more similarly than DZ twins, concordance rates may reflect genetic and environmental similarity.

Candidate genes

Monoamine oxidase A (MAOA): Brunner *et al.* (1993) analysed the DNA of 28 male members of a Dutch family who had histories of impulsive and violent criminal behaviours. They found they shared a particular gene that led to abnormally low levels of MAOA.

Cadherin 13 (CDH13): Tiihonen *et al.* (2015) studied 900 offenders, finding evidence of low MAOA activity as well as low activity from the CDH13 gene. They estimated that abnormalities in these two genes are responsible for 5–10% of all violent crime in Finland.

Diathesis–stress

Epigenetics proposes genes are 'switched' on or off by epigenomes, which have been affected by environmental factors. Caspi *et al.*'s (2002) longitudinal study of 1,000 New Zealanders found that, when assessing levels of anti-social behaviour at 26 years of age, 12% of men with low MAOA genes (nature) had experienced maltreatment in childhood (nurture) and were responsible for 44% of the violent convictions recorded.

◑ Neural explanations

Neural explanations consider how brain structures and neurotransmitter levels may be different in criminals. Differences may be due to nurture or may be inherited (nature).

Regions of the brain

Harmon (2012) found 8.5% of the US population have a brain injury compared to 60% of the US prison population.

Prefrontal cortex – Brain imaging studies found murderers, psychopaths and violent individuals showed reduced functioning in the prefrontal cortex (Raine, 2004). Lowered activity in this area is associated with impulsiveness and loss of control.

Limbic system – Raine *et al.* (1997) found that, when compared to matched controls, murderers found not guilty by reason of insanity showed abnormal asymmetries in the limbic system, especially the amygdala – there was reduced activity on the left and increased activity on the right.

Neurotransmitters

Serotonin – Serotonin inhibits the prefrontal cortex; therefore, low levels may predispose individuals to impulsive aggression and criminal behaviour.

Noradrenaline – High levels are associated with activation of the sympathetic nervous system and the fight-or-flight response, and thus linked to aggression. Low levels reduce people's ability to react to perceived threats.

◑ Evaluation

Research support from adoption studies

Adopted children who had a biological parent with a criminal record had a 50% greater risk of also having a criminal record at age 18. Adopted children whose biological mother did not have a criminal record had a 5% risk (Crowe, 1972). However, genes may only be marginally more significant. Mednick *et al.* (1987) found that, out of 14,000 adoptees studied, 15% of sons adopted by criminal families went on to offend compared to 20% whose biological parents were criminals.

Deterministic views of criminal behaviour cannot be ruled out

Lawyers for murderer Stephen Morley (unsuccessfully) claimed his family history of violence suggests he was 'born to kill'. Tiihonen *et al.* found those with the defective CDH13 gene were 13 times more likely to show repeated violent behaviour. However, not everyone with this gene becomes an offender; while criminality cannot be solely due to genetics, studies such as Caspi's suggest it is harder for some to avoid criminal violence due to both their biology and environment.

Most research focuses on violent or aggressive behaviour

Biological explanations may just account for violent crimes and psychopathy. Blonigen *et al.* (2005) found support for a genetic basis of this personality type when studying 600 twins. Furthermore, research on neurotransmitters often uses non-human animals, and as such it is aggression not criminality that is being studied. This undermines the usefulness of such information for understanding non-violent offending. Finlay (2011) points out that because crime is socially constructed it is difficult to argue that criminal behaviour is simply due to biological factors.

Neural studies identify correlations, not cause and effect

Are abnormalities in brain areas or neurotransmitter levels the cause of offending behaviour, or the result of it? It is possibly a false relationship, e.g. is someone who grew up in a violent household or engages in risky behaviour more likely to suffer a head injury? As with genetic evidence, there is not 100% correspondence with any brain area or neurotransmitter, so data cannot be used to predict who might become an offender.

Real-world application

Identifying neural abnormalities could lead to potential treatments, e.g. prisoners could be given diets that would enhance serotonin levels with the aim of decreasing aggression. Artificial sweeteners are high in phenylalanine and low in tryptophan, both of which make the production of serotonin difficult.

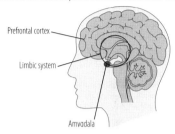

Prefrontal cortex

Limbic system

Amygdala

Apply it

Scenario. Jake has been excluded from school a number of times for aggressive behaviour. The headmaster remembers teaching Jake's father and uncle who, in his opinion, were 'nothing but trouble'. His experiences with Jake's family have led him to conclude that some people are born with criminal tendencies.

With reference to the headmaster's experiences, discuss the biological explanations of offending behaviour. (16 marks)

Explanation extract… Jake's family has a history of offending behaviour, which has led his headmaster to suggest the cause of Jake's aggression originates from within him. He could be referring to genetic explanations as Jake and his first-degree (father) and second-degree (uncle) relatives also show criminal behaviour. This claim is supported by Brunner *et al.* who found male members of a Dutch family who had a history of impulsive and criminal behaviour shared a gene that led to abnormally low levels of MAOA. MAOA regulates the metabolism of serotonin which, in low levels, is associated with aggressive behaviour. …

KEY TERMS

Extroversion Refers to outgoing people who enjoy risk and danger because their nervous systems are under-aroused. They are characterised by positive emotions but may get bored easily.

Neuroticism Refers to people with a negative outlook who are easily upset. Their lack of stability results from an overactive response to threat (fight-or-flight).

Psychoticism Refers to an aggressive, anti-social person who lacks empathy and has little regard for the welfare of others. This may be related to high levels of testosterone.

Eysenck's theory of the criminal personality

Eysenck (1967, 1978) proposed that character traits tended to cluster along three dimensions: extroversion–introversion, neuroticism–stability, and psychoticism–normality. Each dimension, assessed by the Eysenck Personality Questionnaire (EPQ), is normally distributed: about 68% of people fall within one standard deviation of the mean.

Biological basis

Eysenck (1982) claimed 67% of the variance of traits is due to genetic factors.

Extroversion is determined by overall level of arousal in the nervous system. Extroverts are under-aroused, so seek external stimulation to increase their cortical arousal. Due to over-arousal, introverts seek to reduce or avoid stimulation.

Neuroticism is determined by level of stability/reactivity of the sympathetic nervous system. A neurotic person is slightly unstable and reacts/gets upset quickly. Stable people have a more unreactive nervous system; they are calm under pressure.

Psychoticism has been linked to higher levels of testosterone, which explains why more men are found at this end of the spectrum.

Link to criminal behaviour

Extroverts' search for arousal may lead them to engage in dangerous activities. Neurotics' instability makes them prone to overreaction in situations of threat, which may explain some criminal behaviour. Traits of aggression and lack of empathy associated with psychoticism are easily linked to offending. Criminality is explained as the outcome of innate personality and socialisation, e.g. when a 'normal' person is punished the likelihood of repeating the behaviour is reduced (operant conditioning). Eysenck claimed that those high in extroversion and neuroticism are less easily conditioned and so do not learn to avoid anti-social behaviour.

Evaluation

Is personality genetic?

Twin studies support a biological basis to personality type. Zuckerman (1987) found a +.52 correlation for MZ twins compared to +.24 for DZ twins on neuroticism. For extroversion, figures were +.51 (MZ) and +.12 (DZ). However, although this shows there is a considerable genetic component, it is not as high as claimed by Eysenck. For example, a +.51 correlation means that about 40% of the variance in these traits is due to genetics.

Personality may not be consistent

Any regularity of behaviour is likely to be due to the fact we often tend to be in similar situations. The situational perspective suggests people's personality may change across different situations, e.g. a person may be relaxed and calm at home but neurotic at work. Mischel and Peake (1982) asked family, friends and strangers to rate 63 students in a number of situations and found almost no correlation between traits displayed. This suggests the notion of a 'criminal personality' is flawed.

Personality tests may not be reliable

The EPQ asks respondents to select traits that apply to them, e.g. 'Are you rather lively?' For many people the answer is 'sometimes', but the questionnaire forces a 'yes' or 'no' response. Social desirability bias may also reduce truthfulness of answers. To counteract this, lie scales are included. These are sets of questions such as: 'Are all your habits good and desirable?' People who repeatedly answer 'yes' to these questions are probably being dishonest and so their data is discarded.

Can we predict delinquency based on personality?

Dunlop et al. (2012) found both extroversion and psychoticism, as well as lie scales, were good predictors of delinquency. Delinquency was assessed by recording minor offences committed in the previous 12 months (e.g. theft, traffic offences), though armed robbery was included. Van Dam et al. (2007) found only a small group of male offenders in a juvenile detention centre scored highly in extroversion, neuroticism and psychoticism.

Is Eysenck's theory useful?

Eysenck's theory was foremost a personality theory rather than an explanation of offending behaviour. While there is some merit in the concept of certain traits being found in criminals it is difficult to know how to use this information. For example, it is not close enough to use as a means of identifying those likely to engage in offending behaviour. However, it may help in the treatment of offenders, e.g. paying greater attention to conditioning experiences to ensure that those high in extroversion and neuroticism do learn from their experiences.

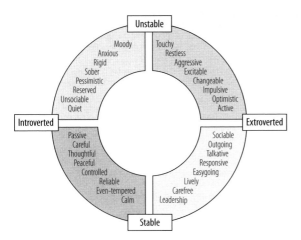

Apply it

Scenario. Jharred's job as a prison guard involves managing a range of different people currently serving custodial sentences. He believes that while their age and backgrounds may differ the people in his care all share similar personality characteristics; they are often aggressive and lack empathy.

With reference to Jharred's views, briefly outline Eysenck's theory of the criminal personality. (4 marks)

Explanation. Eysenck's personality theory suggests those high in extroversion, neuroticism and psychoticism may be more likely to engage in criminal activities than those high in introversion, stability and normality. Extroverts' search for stimulation may lead them to partake in dangerous activities, while a raised level of testosterone may lead to the aggressive, anti-social actions of someone who lacks the ability to empathise with others. Jharred seems to be describing psychoticism, suggesting that, as well as a lack of empathy and aggression, the prisoners in his charge may also show traits of egocentrism, impulsivity and a lack of concern about others' welfare. Jharred's comments reflect Eysenck's view that there is a biological basis to personality as he states 'regardless of age and background', suggesting personality is innate.

KEY TERMS

Cognitive distortion Thinking that has a bias, such as what is perceived by a person does not match reality. Two examples of cognitive distortion are hostile attribution bias and minimalisation.

Hostile attribution bias When a person automatically attributes malicious intentions to another. These negative attributions then lead to more aggressive behaviour.

Minimalisation Underplaying the consequences of an action to reduce negative emotions such as feeling guilty.

Moral reasoning Thinking in a consistent and logical way about right and wrong, with reference to socially agreed principles.

Apply it

Scenario. David has served a number of short-term prison sentences for theft. He claims his crimes are not serious as he only targets wealthy properties and never takes any items that could belong to children or those that may have sentimental value such as jewellery. He argues any items he steals can easily be replaced as they will be covered by home insurance.

Using your knowledge of cognitive distortions, explain David's offending behaviour. (4 marks)

Explanation. Cognitive distortions are a form of irrational thinking. In this case David has twisted the reality of his crimes so that they no longer represent the actual truth: David is under-exaggerating his offending behaviour, which allows him to rationalise it. He has minimalised the impact his burglaries have on victims by justifying his choice of items to steal (no children's items or those with sentimental value) and the families he targets (wealthy households who are able to replace the items he takes). This helps David accept the consequences of his behaviour and reduces any negative feelings he may experience, e.g. guilt.

Cognitive explanations

The following explanations focus on **cognitive distortions** and the way thinking about right and wrong affects behaviour (**moral reasoning**).

Cognitive distortions

A form of irrational thinking where the person's perception of events is wrong but they think it is accurate, allowing them to deny or rationalise their behaviour.

Hostile attribution bias

Violent people may have a **hostile attribution bias**, i.e. they tend to perceive ambiguous actions by others as being hostile, leading them to respond in hostile ways themselves. For example, in 1999 two Columbine teenagers shot and killed a number of their fellow students who they felt had bullied them.

Minimalisation

Minimalisation explains how negative interpretations of offending behaviour can be reduced. This helps them accept the consequences of their behaviour and reduce any negative emotions experienced. For example, a shoplifter may feel stealing from a successful supermarket chain has very little effect on the business.

Level of moral reasoning

Kohlberg (1969) proposed a stage theory of moral development. People progress through these stages (from pre-conventional to conventional, then post-conventional) as a consequence of biological maturity and environmental experiences, e.g. opportunities to take the perspective of another person.

Moral reasoning and offending behaviour

Kohlberg found that only about 10% of adults reach the **post-conventional** stage (they define morality in terms of abstract principles that apply to all societies and situations). The most common level is **conventional** (criminal behaviour is justified if it helps maintain relationships or society, e.g. protecting family). Criminals are likely to be at the **pre-conventional** level (believe breaking the law is justified if rewards outweigh the costs/if punishment can be avoided).

Most people reach the pre-conventional level by age 10. This fits with the idea of criminal responsibility: in England and Wales children under 10 cannot be charged with a crime as it is believed they don't understand the idea of moral responsibility.

Evaluation

Research support for cognitive distortions

55 violent offenders viewed emotionally ambiguous faces varying in intensity of either anger, happiness or fear. Compared to a matched control group, offenders were more likely to interpret expressions of anger as aggression. Misinterpreting non-verbal cues may partly explain aggressive-impulsive behaviour (Schönenberg & Aiste, 2014).

Kennedy and Grubin (1992) found sex offenders often downplayed their offending, e.g. suggesting the victim's behaviour contributed to the crime. Others simply denied that a crime had been committed. However, Maruna and Mann (2006) suggest this minimalisation is not isolated to criminals. Most people try to blame events on external sources to protect the self.

Reducing cognitive distortions

Heller et al. (2013) used cognitive behavioural techniques with young men from mainly disadvantaged groups in Chicago. Across 13, one-hour sessions techniques were used to reduce judgement and decision-making errors. Compared to a control group, a 44% reduction in arrests was reported.

Research support for moral reasoning

Colby and Kohlberg (1987) reported that the sequence of stages seems universal. A survey of 128 male juvenile offenders using the Offending Motivation Questionnaire found 38% did not consider the consequences of their actions and 36% were confident they would not be caught (Gudjonsson & Sigurdsson, 2007), suggesting a pre-conventional level of reasoning. In addition, Chen and Howitt's (2007) assessment of 330 male adolescent offenders (aged 12–18) from Taiwan found those with more advanced reasoning were less likely to be involved in violent crimes.

Limitations of Kohlberg's theory

Krebs and Denton (2005) suggest moral principles may be overridden by more practical factors such as opportunity for financial gain. Their analysis of real-life moral decisions showed moral principles were used to justify behaviour *after* it had been performed. Kohlberg is also criticised for only using male samples, and Gilligan (1982) suggests the theory is focused on the male perspective of justice rather than caring.

Real-world application

Kohlberg observed children raised on Israeli kibbutzim were more morally advanced. This led him to suggest that belonging to a democratic group and being involved in making moral judgements facilitated moral development. He and Gilligan set up *Just communities* in schools and one prison, where members defined and resolved disputes to encourage moral development.

Differential association theory

Sutherland (1939) suggests a mathematical formula could be developed to predict whether or not someone would turn to crime based on the frequency, duration and intensity of their social contacts.

What is learned?
A potential criminal is someone who, as a child, has learned pro-criminal attitudes from others. Children also learn which crimes are acceptable and desirable in their community as well as learning specific methods for committing crimes (some crimes require technical knowledge, e.g. credit card fraud, while others are simple, e.g. stealing from a local shop).

Who is it learned from?
Attitudes and behaviour are learned from friends, family and the wider neighbourhood. The extent to which criminal involvement is supported/opposed (differential social organisation) determines differences in crime rates from one area to another. Individuals or social groups may not be deviant themselves but may still hold deviant attitudes or accept these attitudes in others.

How is it learned?
Frequency, length and personal meaning of social associations will determine the degree of influence. A child may be directly reinforced for deviant behaviour, e.g. praise, or be punished for such behaviour by family and peers. Role models provide opportunities to model behaviours. Role models who are successful criminals provide indirect, vicarious reinforcement.

Sutherland proposed nine key principles
1. Criminal behaviour is learned, not inherited.
2. It is learned through association with others.
3. The association is with intimate personal groups.
4. What is learned are techniques and attitudes/motivations.
5. This learning is directional – either for or against crime.
6. Offending occurs if favourable attitudes outweigh unfavourable ones.
7. Differential associations vary in frequency/intensity for each individual.
8. Criminal behaviour is learned through the same process as any other behaviour.
9. General 'need' (e.g. for money) does not explain offending as not everyone with those needs turns to crime.

Evaluation
Major contribution
Rather than 'blaming' individual factors, this theory highlighted the role of social factors in offending behaviour. This has real-world implications because learning environments can be changed, unlike genes. Sutherland also introduced the concept of 'white-collar crime' – non-violent crimes by business and government professionals such as fraud, bribery and forgery.

Support for differential association theory
Osbourne and West (1979) found that 40% of sons whose fathers had criminal convictions had committed a crime by the age of 18, compared to 13% of sons of non-criminal fathers (such findings can, however, be explained in terms of genetics). Akers et al.'s (1979) survey of 2,500 male and female adolescents found that peers were the most important influence on drinking and drug taking. Differential association, reinforcement and imitation combined to account for the 68% variance in marijuana use and 55% variance in alcohol use.

Methodological issues
Data is correlational so does not tell us anything about cause and effect: it could be that offenders seek out other offenders as they share similar interests, which would explain why offenders are likely to have peers who also offend. It is also difficult to isolate learned from inherited influences, making the theory untestable. Likewise, it is not clear from this research what balance of unfavourable to favourable associations would tip the balance such that a person becomes a criminal.

Only a partial account of offending behaviour
Social learning influences may explain 'smaller' crimes but not violent and impulsive offences. However, 'smaller' crime is more common, e.g. in England and Wales in 2014, there were 500 murders compared to 400,000 burglaries (ONS, 2015). The theory also can't explain why most offences are committed by young people; Newburn (2002) found 40% of offences are committed by under 21s. By contrast, Eysenck's theory can explain this in terms of a desire for risk-taking as an aspect of criminal behaviour.

The diathesis–stress model may offer a better account
A more complete explanation may be to combine social factors with vulnerability factors, e.g. innate genetic ones or early experience (maltreatment). Others have suggested attachment problems in early childhood may make a child vulnerable to deviant peer influences in adolescence at a time when individuals tend to have a need for risk-taking.

KEY TERM
Differential association theory An explanation of offending behaviour in terms of learning theory, how interactions with others lead to the formation of attitudes about crime (which may be more or less favourable), as well as acquiring specific knowledge about how to commit crimes.

Apply it
Scenario. Gemma's friends regularly use pirate sites to download music and films. They know it is illegal but can't really see the harm as everyone seems to be doing it. Gemma has recently begun using the sites herself.

How would differential association theory explain Gemma's behaviour? (4 marks)

Explanation. As people in Gemma's social network condone the use of illegal sharing sites she sees the crime as acceptable within her circle of friends and so is likely to want to access music and films in this way too. She states that 'her friends regularly use pirate sites', which suggests the intensity and frequency of the learning experiences are sufficient to influence her own behaviour. Gemma has learned techniques to enable her to access films and music without purchasing them herself from her peers. Her peers are role models who have been successfully using these sites without consequence, increasing the likelihood Gemma will also imitate their actions.

KEY TERMS

Affectionless psychopathy A behaviour disorder in which the individual has no ability to experience shame or guilt, and lacks a social conscience and a sense of responsibility. This means that they may find it 'easier' to commit crimes.

Maternal deprivation The loss of emotional care that is normally provided by a primary caregiver.

Psychodynamic explanation Refers to any theory that emphasises change and development in the individual, particularly those theories where 'drive' is a central concept in development. The key elements of explanations are that early experiences coupled with innate drives create the adult personality.

Superego The superego embodies our conscience and is our moral compass, as well as notions of the ideal self. It develops between the ages of three and six. The superego is likely to be involved in offending behaviour because it is concerned with right and wrong.

Apply it

Scenario. A psychologist was interested in researching the life experiences of prisoners prior to their offending. He identified a number of individuals who had experienced periods of time when they were separated from their primary caregivers. Further interviews revealed many prisoners had a tendency to act in impulsive ways and showed little regard for others.

With reference to the above scenario, describe and evaluate psychodynamic explanations of offending behaviour. (16 marks)

Explanation extract... Bowlby's 44 juvenile thieves study suggests prolonged mother–infant separation leads to long-term emotional consequences. 39% of the thieves had experienced early separations compared to a control group, none of whom had experienced separations. The psychologist in the scenario seems to have found similar evidence. The scenario also suggests that offenders show affectionless psychopathy (identified by Bowlby), as it mentions they 'showed little regard for others'. The psychologist may also have identified some prisoners with a weak superego: 'a tendency to act in impulsive ways'. Freud suggests that, during the phallic stage, failure to identify with a same-sex parent (possibly because of separations experienced) can lead to the development of a weak superego. Therefore, these individuals have little control over their anti-social behaviour. ...

Psychodynamic explanations

John Bowlby was a Freudian psychiatrist whose theory of **maternal deprivation** was based on psychodynamic principles. Other **psychodynamic explanations** emphasise the role of the **superego** in moral behaviour.

Maternal deprivation

Bowlby (1951, 1953) claimed prolonged mother–infant separations (before two and a half) could have lasting emotional consequences if no substitute mother-figure is present. He also felt there was a continuing risk up until the age of five. Bowlby identified **affectionless psychopathy** as a potential long-term consequence, which is related to the notion of a psychopath.

Explaining delinquent behaviour

In his work at London's Child Guidance Clinic, Bowlby observed that many of the delinquent thieves had experienced frequent separations and displayed affectionless psychopathy. He compared 44 thieves with 44 control patients and found that none of the control patients had experienced early separations but 39% of the thieves had. He also found 86% of the affectionless thieves (12 out of 14) had experienced frequent separations compared to 17% (5 out of 30) of other thieves.

The superego

Freud proposed personality develops from three components.

1. The **id** operates according to the pleasure principle, representing primitive desires.
2. The **superego** functions as our moral compass, causing guilt when rules are broken.
3. The **ego** is anchored in the external world (the reality principle).

Weak or underdeveloped superego

Around four years of age the superego develops as an outcome of the Oedipus complex (boys) or Electra complex (girls) during the phallic stage. Failure to identify with the same-sex parent, or absence of a same-sex parent, can lead to development of a weak superego. The individual has little control over anti-social behaviour and acts in ways to gratify the instinctual id impulses.

Harsh or overdeveloped superego

A very strong identification with a strict parent will cause excessive feelings of guilt and anxiety. Any time id impulses are acted on, the offender would feel bad. They wish to be caught as punishment would reduce the guilt felt.

Deviant superego

Identification with the same-sex parent means the child takes on the parent's moral attitudes. Identifying with a criminal parent may result in adoption of the same deviant attitudes.

Evaluation

Important consideration of emotion

Explanations such as cognitive distortions and moral reasoning tend to ignore how emotion affects behaviour. The psychodynamic approach addresses this and includes how anxiety and/or feelings of rejection may contribute to offending. It also recognises the influence of biological factors and early childhood experiences in personality development, both of which are key aspects of other theories.

Only an association, not a causal relationship

Bowlby's 44 thieves study cannot conclude that prolonged separation caused emotional problems. It might be that discord in the home resulting from separations also caused the affectionless nature of some children. Alternatively, it could be argued that the affectionless personality of the child causes the separations (e.g. difficult children may be more likely to be placed in care).

Real-world application

Treatment of emotional problems in delinquents is slow and difficult, so it is better to avoid early separations. Along with James and Joyce Robertson, Bowlby showed that children could cope reasonably well with separations as long as alternative emotional care was available.

Gender bias in Freud's research

Freud proposed that women develop a weaker superego than men because they do not identify as strongly with the same-sex parent. He felt the resolution of the Electra complex is less satisfactory partly because he believed there was little reason for anyone to identify with women because of their low social status. These views represent an alpha bias. If Freud were correct then women would commit more crimes than men, something that is not supported by crime statistics.

Approaches should be combined to explain offending behaviour

Farrington *et al.* (2009) conducted a 40-year longitudinal study with 400 South London boys. They found the most important risk factors at age 8–10 for later offending were family history of criminality (could be genetics and/or differential association), risk-taking personality (Eysenck), low school attainment, poverty and poor parenting (psychodynamic approach).

Custodial sentencing

◎ Aims of custodial sentencing

To protect the public: incapacitation: Violent offenders and psychopaths who cannot control their behaviour need to be separated from wider society.

To punish the offender/prevent recidivism The behaviourist principle that punishment decreases the likelihood of behaviour being repeated. Punishment or threat of punishment may not work, but many believe it is why most people don't commit crimes.

To deter others: If the law was seen as less serious, more people may be willing to commit crimes. Social learning theory suggests we learn indirectly from observing the consequences of others' behaviour.

To atone for wrongdoing: retribution: Provides the victim and family/friends a sense of justice as the offender is seen to pay for their behaviour.

To rehabilitate offenders: Education/therapy taking place in prison may have fewer distractions, and incentives may be offered to those who participate.

◎ Psychological effects of custodial sentencing

De-individuation: Zimbardo's Stanford Prison study (1973) demonstrates how prison and guards' uniforms lead to a loss of individual identity which is associated with increased aggression and inhumane treatment of others.

Depression, self-harm and suicide: Abramson et al. (1989) suggest offenders may feel helpless in the frightening prison environment over which they have little control and hopeless about their future. The Howard League for prison reform reported 10,000 incidents of self-harm in 2008. Young men in the first 24 hours of imprisonment are at greatest risk of suicide.

Overcrowding and lack of privacy: The number of prisoners has increased but not the number of prisons. Data from the Ministry of Justice (2012) suggest 25% of prisoners are in overcrowded accommodation which affects the psychological states of inmates. Calhoun (1962) found rats who experienced overcrowding displayed increased aggression, hypersexuality, stress and physical illness.

Effects on the family: Children with a parent in prison are affected financially and psychologically. Parents in prison may feel guilt and suffer separation anxiety (Glover, 2009).

◎ Evaluation

High rates of recidivism suggest custodial sentencing doesn't work
Behaviourists state immediate punishment is most effective. But sentencing is not instant, so the offender might see the sentence as punishment for being caught rather than for the offence itself. In addition, people often commit crimes in highly emotional states and so are unable to consider the consequences of being caught. Severity of punishment also doesn't seem to be a deterrent as murder rates in US states with a death penalty are no lower than rates in other states (Amnesty International, 2015).

Benefits of custodial sentencing may be limited
Incapacitation only applies to a small number of dangerous prisoners so does not reduce recidivism rates. There are ways to achieve *retribution*, e.g. restorative justice (see p.122), which potentially changes attitudes to reoffending. Offenders cannot be forced to participate in *rehabilitation* programmes, and if they do take part involvement may be superficial.

Prisons as a training ground for crime
Differential association theory (see p.117) suggests offending may increase due to associating with others who hold pro-crime attitudes. Prisoners can also learn how to be more successful criminals. Latessa and Lowenkamp (2006) claim that placing those at low risk of reoffending with those deemed a high risk makes reoffending more likely. Imprisonment may also lead to low self-esteem, reduced empathy for others and anger towards the system, which increases risk of offending (Pritkin, 2009).

Individual differences in recidivism
Walker et al. (1981) found length of sentence made little difference to reoffending rates of habitual offenders. However, rates of recidivism appear to vary with age and crimes – younger people are more likely to reoffend; those convicted of theft and burglary are more than twice as likely to reoffend than those committing drug and sexual offences (Home Office, 2005). This suggests sentencing should be targeted in different ways for different groups of offenders.

The benefits of non-custodial sentencing
Alternatives include probation, electronic monitoring, fines, community service and anti-social behaviour orders. These avoid some of the problems occurring in prison, e.g. de-individuation, inmate culture and suicide. Evidence suggests cautions are a more effective deterrent than arrests (Klein et al., 1977), and the Home Office (1995) found those sentenced to community rehabilitation are less likely to reoffend (this may be because less serious offenders are given community sentences).

KEY TERMS

Custodial sentencing A custodial sentence refers to cases where the court has decided the offender is to be held in prison or some other closed community like a psychiatric hospital.

De-individuation A psychological state in which individuals have lowered levels of self-evaluation (e.g. when in a crowd or under the influence of alcohol) and decreased concerns about evaluation by others.

Recidivism This is when a person reoffends after receiving some form of punishment for previous offences. The Prison Reform Trust (2014) reports that 46% of adults and 67% of under 18s are reconvicted within one year of release.

Apply it

Scenario. Ian, a father of two young children, has received numerous cautions and fines for driving offences. He was recently arrested for speeding and driving a car without an MOT or insurance. His court case is coming soon and he is worried the magistrate will give him a custodial sentence.

What psychological effects might Ian experience if he is sent to prison?
(4 marks)

Explanation. Prisons face increasing pressure from a growing prison population. In 2012, the Ministry of Justice reported that 25% of prisoners are in overcrowded accommodation. This means Ian may have to share a cell, which could have a negative impact on him psychologically. Ian may feel helplessness on entering prison and hopeless about his future, both of which could lead to depression. He may also be at risk of self-harming behaviour. Newton (1980) reported that self-harming was becoming part of inmate culture, so Ian may conform and engage in the behaviour. Ian may also feel guilt and separation anxiety as contact with his family will be greatly reduced.

Behaviour modification A therapeutic technique used to increase or decrease the frequencies of behaviour using operant conditioning.

Operant conditioning Learning through reinforcement or punishment. If a behaviour is followed by a desirable consequence, then that behaviour is more likely to occur again in the future.

Token economy A form of therapy where desirable behaviours are encouraged by the use of selective reinforcements. Rewards (tokens) are given as *secondary reinforcers* when individuals engage in correct/socially desirable behaviours. The tokens can then be exchanged for *primary reinforcers* – food or privileges. Token economy works well in a prison environment as rewards can be precisely manipulated.

Apply it

Scenario. Just after his 16th birthday, Aaron was arrested for knife crime and given a custodial sentence of six months. Initially Aaron's behaviour at the secure centre was very challenging, but staff's use of behavioural modification strategies improved his behaviour and hopefully reduced his risk of reoffending.

With reference to Aaron, describe and evaluate the use of behavioural modification in custody as a means of dealing with offender behaviour. (16 marks)

Explanation extract… The secure centre could use a token economy system to encourage Aaron to adopt desirable behaviour, e.g. if he made his bed on a daily basis and stood in line in the canteen he received tokens. The tokens are a secondary reinforcer as they can be redeemed for chocolate and cigarettes (primary reinforcers). This system may modify Aaron's behaviour as Cohen and Filipcjak (1971) found juvenile delinquents who had been trained with a token economy system were less likely to reoffend. However, to maintain Aaron's good behaviour, staff must remain consistent in the way they award tokens. …

Behaviour modification in custody

Behaviour modification techniques are based on behaviourist principles: both positive and negative reinforcement can be used to encourage desired behaviour with punishment being used to discourage undesirable behaviour.

Token economy

Reinforcement and punishment

Tokens, that can be traded for items such as tobacco, food or watching TV, are awarded when prisoners perform desired behaviours. Items are primary reinforcers and tokens are secondary reinforcers (they are repeatedly presented alongside the reinforcing stimulus – classical conditioning). Both rewards and target behaviours are clearly specified; this may be arranged in a hierarchy with some actions receiving more rewards than others. Undesirable behaviour can be punished by removal of tokens.

Shaping

Longer-term objectives or complex behaviours consisting of smaller components can be shaped through awarding tokens for progressively more complex behaviours, e.g. tokens are initially awarded for an easily achievable action, such as making their bed each day. Later on, tokens are received for being polite to prison guards.

Token economy research

How? Hobbs and Holt (1976) observed the use of token economy at Alabama Boys Industrial School, a state training school for delinquents aged 12–15. Staff received intensive training to identify and record target behaviours, recording data and working on logistical problems. The operation of the programme was assessed in weekly sessions. 125 males, living in four cottages, were observed. One cottage acted as a control group. Boys in the other three cottages were told the target criteria and how many tokens could be earned in each category. Each day boys were told how many tokens they had earned and once a week they could visit the store to trade tokens for food, toys and cigarettes. Tokens could also be saved for off-campus activities such as a visit home.

Showed? Before being given tokens the baseline mean percentages for social behaviour were 66%, 47% and 73% for each of the three cottages. This increased to 91%, 81% and 94% (an average increase of 27%). The control group showed no increase in the same time period.

Evaluation

Advantages of token economy

The token economy system is clearly defined and easy to implement. Trained psychologists are not needed as prison staff can think about what behaviours they wish to encourage to improve the prison environment. However, to be successful pre-planning is needed to set up a token economy and staff must use tokens consistently.

Success of token economy in prisons

Token economy has been used successfully in schools but is less effective in prisons. Token economy was popular in US prisons during the 1970s with most states using the system. While research showed socially approved behaviours could be increased and criminal behaviours decreased (Milan & McKee, 1976), good results did not persist and its popularity decreased. In the UK it was limited to young offenders' institutes (Culen & Seddon, 1981).

Short-term (behaviour in prison) versus long-term (behaviour after release) goals

Moyes *et al.* (1985) suggest token economy can have little effect on reoffending rates. Once rewards cease, the stimulus-response link is extinguished. Furthermore, behaviours learned in prison may not apply to the real world. If offenders lived in a half-way house an intermediate strategy could be employed where more 'natural' behaviours are rewarded – a strategy found to be successful with disabled adults (Stocks *et al.*, 1987).

Individual differences

Young delinquents have responded better to **operant conditioning** programmes than violent offenders. Cohen and Filipcjak (1971) found that juvenile delinquents who had experienced a token economy system were less likely to reoffend after one year. In contrast, Rice *et al.* (1990) found 50% of 92 males in a maximum security psychiatric hospital using token economy reoffended.

Ethical issues

Token economy may be seen to violate human rights as an individual's behaviour is being manipulated, not always with their consent. Hall (1979) suggests a solution would be to ask prisoners, officers and administrators to agree on the system and periodically review its use. Unfortunately, some prisoners cannot earn tokens as they are unable to control their behaviour and so may be denied privileges or even necessities. Finally, punishment in the form of removing tokens could be said to counteract the goals of rehabilitation and could even lead to the collapse of such systems (Nietzel, 1979).

Anger management

● Novaco (2011) identified three key aims for any anger management programmes

Cognitive restructuring – increase self-awareness and control over cognitive dimensions of anger; *regulation of arousal* – learning to control the physical state; and *behavioural strategies* – problem-solving, strategic withdrawal and assertiveness.

● Novaco's stress inoculation model (1975, 1977)

This drew on the stress inoculation approach (see p.92) which aims to 'vaccinate' against future 'infections'. Therapy is conducted in groups either inside prison or outside, e.g. during probation. There are three steps:

1. **Cognitive preparation.** Clients learn how anger can be adaptive/maladaptive, analyse their own anger patterns and identify provoking situations.
2. **Skill acquisition.** Clients learn skills to help manage anger, e.g. self-regulation, cognitive flexibility and relaxation, as well as improving communication skills to resolve conflicts assertively instead of aggressively.
3. **Application training.** Clients apply skills learned in controlled, non-threatening situations that previously made them angry. Extensive feedback is given from the therapist and group members. Later, clients apply skills in real-world settings.

● Anger management research

How? Ireland (2004) used a self-report questionnaire and prison officer assessments to identify pre-intervention anger in young male offenders. 50 offenders then took part in the programme (12 one-hour sessions over three days); 37 were placed on a waiting list.

Showed? Eight weeks later offenders were re-assessed using the same methods as before. The treatment group showed significant improvement, the control group showed no change.

How? Trimble *et al.* (2015) followed 105 offenders on probation who were required to attend an anger management programme consisting of nine weekly two-hour sessions. The sample included those whose anger and poor emotional control predisposed them to offending.

Showed? When compared to the pre-treatment score, outcomes suggested the programme significantly reduced the expression of anger and the amount of anger experienced.

● Evaluation

Success of anger management programmes

Taylor and Novaco (2006) report 75% improvement rates (based on six meta-analyses). Landenberger and Lipsey (2005) analysed 58 **cognitive behavioural therapy** studies, finding that the inclusion of an anger control element led to significant improvement in offenders. However, Howells *et al.* (2005) noted five meta-analytic studies which showed only moderate benefits, and Law (1997) reported a study where only one person improved.

The variability in anger programmes makes comparisons difficult

Some are quite brief, others span many years, some are run by psychologists, and others by less experienced prison staff. Variability also occurs with the type of offender and scope of the programme (some also target wider behavioural problems). Furthermore, self-report methods and observations are open to bias. The 'hello–goodbye' effect is a particular issue where offenders want to show the therapy worked so present themselves in a more positive light.

Limitations of anger management programmes

Some offenders don't like self-reflection and lack the motivation required to change attitudes and behaviours. Such individuals may drop out of voluntary programmes. Using the Anger Readiness to Change questionnaire prior to the programme avoids including offenders who will not benefit. An alternative is to offer drama-based programmes which are less reliant on verbal ability and are more engaging.

Short-term (anger in prison) versus long-term goals (recidivism)

Research reporting success in programmes often focuses on short-term goals. Difficulties in following up offenders means fewer studies have looked at the long-term effects. McGuire (2008) found some studies reporting a reduction in reoffending after one year compared to those just on probation. Success may be due to general therapeutic support rather than just anger management.

The relationship between anger and aggression and crime

Howells *et al.* (2005) concluded that 'anger is neither necessary nor a sufficient condition for aggression and violent crime', so anger management may be irrelevant. Loza and Loza-Fanous (1999) suggest studies showing a link between anger and crime are often lab-based using student samples. In their study of 300 male prisoners, no differences in anger were seen between violent and non-violent offenders. However, violent offenders may be better able to mask anger. Furthermore, anger management programmes may lead offenders to attribute violent behaviour to anger rather than taking personal responsibility.

KEY TERMS

Anger management A form of CBT specific to changing the way a person manages their anger. Techniques include cognitive restructuring, skill acquisition and behavioural training. Anger management has two aims: 1. In the short term, to reduce anger and aggression in prison. 2. The longer-term goal of rehabilitation and reduction of recidivism, especially in the case of violent prisoners.

Cognitive behavioural therapy
A combination of cognitive therapy (a way of changing maladaptive thoughts and beliefs) and behavioural therapy (a way of changing behaviour in response to these thoughts and beliefs). Cognitive behavioural therapy accepts the situation itself may not be changeable but a person can change the way they think about the situation and so change behaviour.

Apply it

Scenario. Shelly has a number of convictions for anti-social behaviour including a recent conviction for physically attacking someone in a pub when she thought they had deliberately bumped into her. While serving a custodial sentence Shelly is offered the opportunity to participate in an anger management programme.

What might prison officers tell Shelly about the programme? (4 marks)

Explanation. Prison officers could tell Shelly the programme will be a form of CBT which aims to change her maladaptive thoughts that led to aggressive behaviour. The programme will involve three steps. First, Shelly will learn about anger and she will identify her own anger patterns and situations that provoke anger such as thinking people are deliberately disrespecting her. Second, she will be taught skills to manage her anger, e.g. self-reflection, relaxation. Finally, she will role play these skills such as recreating the scene in the pub to practise alternative ways to behave. She will later apply these to real-life situations.

KEY TERM

Restorative justice A method of reducing and atoning for offending behaviour through reconciliation between offender and victim as well as the wider community. Offenders are often offered restorative justice as an alternative to a custodial sentence, if the victim agrees.

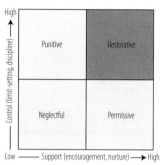

▲ Social discipline window.

Restorative justice programmes

Instead of punishing offenders, **restorative justice** programmes try to repair the harm done usually by victim–offender communication via letter writing, video conference or a face-to-face meeting. Carrabine *et al.* (2014) report, that over the last 20 years, restorative justice programmes have moved to the centre of the criminology field due to the failure of previous systems to reduce offending behaviour.

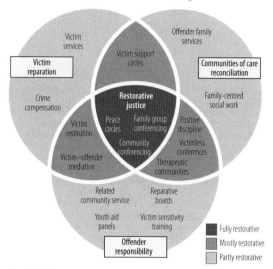

▲ Wachtel and McCold represent the way all the 'stakeholders' (victim, offender, community) can individually or jointly be supported. Full restorative justice requires the involvement of all three stakeholders: victim, offender and community.

◉ Key aims

Rehabilitation of offenders: The victim can explain the impact of the crime to help the offender understand the effects of their actions from another's perspective. This may reduce the possibility of reoffending. The offender is encouraged to take responsibility for the crime, which should have an effect on their future behaviour.

Atonement of wrongdoing: While offenders may offer compensation for their crime (money, unpaid community work) the 'atonement' is psychological – they are showing feelings of guilt. The victim can express distress, which gives the offender a chance to develop empathy.

Victim's perspective: The victim no longer feels powerless as they have a voice. The victim may also gain greater understanding of the offender, which reduces the victim's sense of being harmed.

◉ Wachtel and McCold's (2003) theory of restorative justice

The theory's starting point is that the focus should be on relationship, not punishment. Crime harms people and their relationships, so justice requires this harm to be healed. Unlike earlier models that just focused on the offender and victim, this theory suggests that the involvement of three 'stakeholders' is needed – the victim (seeking reparation), the offender (taking responsibility) and the community (achieving reconciliation). If only one stakeholder is involved, the process is not fully restorative, e.g. if the government pays financial compensation to the victim. If two are involved, it is mostly restorative, e.g. the offender received therapy.

Peace circles: This involves all stakeholders for full restoration. They aim to foster an environment of respect where the community offers support for the victims and also welcomes the offender to enable mutual understanding. Seated in a circle, a 'talk piece' is passed around so people can speak uninterrupted. A 'keeper' maintains an atmosphere of respect and articulates constructive solutions (Pranis *et al.*, 2003).

◉ Evaluation

Success from the victim's perspective

The UK Restorative Justice Council (2015) report 85% victim satisfaction from face-to-face meetings with their offender(s) for a range of crimes from theft to violent crime. Avon and Somerset Police reported 92.5% victim satisfaction when the victim had been the subject of violent crime (www.bbc.co.uk/news/uk-england-bristol-22024927). Dignan (2005) found victims had a greater sense of satisfaction than when cases go through court.

Success in terms of reduced offending

Sherman and Strang (2007) reviewed 20 studies of face-to-face meetings between offender and victim in the US, UK and Australia. All studies showed reduced reoffending. In one study of 142 males convicted of violence and property offences, reoffending rates were 11%, compared to a matched control group who served a short prison sentence and had a reoffending rate of 37%. The UK Restorative Justice Council (2015) report an overall figure of 14% reduction in reoffending rates.

Advantages over custodial sentencing

Restorative justice can also meet the aim of punishment. The offender finds facing the victim of their crime unpleasant, which may act as a deterrent, especially to those who have experienced it before. Using restorative justice as an alternative to prison avoids exposing offenders to deviant sub-cultures which may encourage reoffending. Financially, restorative justice is a superior method to sentencing. The Restorative Justice Council claims reduced reoffending means that £8 is saved for every £1 spent on the restorative process. The cost of restorative justice is sometimes funded by fines paid by offenders. Finally, the main reason for restorative justice is that custodial sentencing does not address the needs of the victim or promote offender accountability (Zehr, 2002).

Selecting victims and offenders

For restorative justice to be effective the offender has to admit to the crime, though Zahr (2002) claims it can take place without an offender's presence. Second, some crimes are not suitable. Finally, some victims may decline the offer. This means restorative justice can't be a global solution to dealing with offender behaviour.

Ethical issues

One major concern is that the victim may feel worse after meeting the offender. From the offender's perspective, making people face up to their wrongdoing can lead to abuses of power – victims may gang up on an offender, especially when that offender is a child; victims may also try to shame the offender, which is not the intention of the process. Programmes need to be carefully balanced to ensure benefit to both victim and offender.

Apply it

Scenario. A small group of adolescents has been causing trouble on Selina's housing estate. Over a period of months their anti-social behaviour escalated, leading to one of them pushing Selina over on her way home from the shops and kicking her shopping into the road. Police have asked Selina if she would be willing to meet with the young person who committed the offence.

Describe and evaluate restorative justice programmes with reference to Selina's experience. (16 marks)

Explanation extract... Restorative justice would involve Selina meeting with the young person who pushed her over to discuss the offence. This would help Selina reduce her sense of victimisation as she would no longer feel powerless. She may also gain a greater understanding of the young person's actions and may see that she wasn't specifically targeted. However, the process should be carefully managed to avoid Selina trying to shame the offender, as the offender is younger than her. By meeting Selina, the young person may come to understand the effects of their actions and develop empathy for Selina and other residents of the housing estate. This may reduce the possibility of further anti-social behaviour. ...

Chapter 11

Addiction

- Describing addiction: physical and psychological dependence, tolerance and withdrawal syndrome.
- Risk factors in the development of addiction, including genetic vulnerability, stress, personality, family influences and peers.
- Explanations for nicotine addiction: brain neurochemistry, including the role of dopamine, and learning theory as applied to smoking behaviour, including reference to cue reactivity.
- Explanations for gambling addiction: learning theory as applied to gambling, including reference to partial and variable reinforcement; cognitive theory as applied to gambling, including reference to cognitive bias.
- Reducing addiction: drug therapy; behavioural interventions, including aversion therapy and covert sensitisation; cognitive behavioural therapy.
- The application of the following theories of behaviour change to addictive behaviour: the theory of planned behaviour and Prochaska's six-stage model of behaviour change.

Key terms (highlight each cell when you can define the term confidently)

Describing addiction	Risk factors in development of addiction	Explanations for nicotine addiction	Explanations for gambling addiction	Reducing addiction	Application of theories of behaviour change
Addiction	Genetic	Dopamine	Learning theory	Drug therapy	Theory of planned behaviour
Physical dependence	Stress	Neurochemistry	Partial reinforcement	Behavioural interventions	Prochaska's six-stage model
Psychological dependence	Personality	Nicotine	Variable reinforcement	Aversion therapy	
Tolerance	Peers	Learning theory	Cognitive biases	Covert sensitisation	
Withdrawal syndrome		Cue reactivity		Cognitive behavioural therapy (CBT)	

Content checklist

1. In each 'describe', 'apply' and 'evaluate' cell tick when you have produced brief notes.
2. Once you feel you have a good grasp of the topic add a second tick to the cell.
3. When you feel you have complete mastery of the topic and would be able to answer an exam question without the aid of notes highlight the cell.

I am able to ...	Describe	Apply	Evaluate
Explain physical and psychological dependence, tolerance and withdrawal syndrome			
Risk factors in the development of addiction, including genetic vulnerability, stress, personality, family influences and peers			
Brain neurochemistry explanation for nicotine addiction including the role of dopamine			
Learning theory as applied to smoking behaviour, including reference to cue reactivity			
Learning theory as applied to gambling, including reference to partial and variable reinforcement			
Cognitive theory as applied to gambling, including reference to cognitive bias			
Reducing addiction: drug therapy			
Reducing addiction: behavioural interventions, including aversion therapy and covert sensitisation			
Reducing addiction: cognitive behavioural therapy			
Application of the theory of planned behaviour to addictive behaviour			
Application of Prochaska's six-stage model of behaviour change to addictive behaviour			

Describing addiction

● Physical dependence

People who have **physical dependence** on a particular substance need to take the drug in order to feel 'normal'. Physical dependence is demonstrated by the presence of unpleasant physical symptoms if the person suddenly abstains from the drug (**withdrawal syndrome**). The person depends on the drug to avoid these withdrawal symptoms and to function normally. Increased tolerance to the drug is also a characteristic of physical dependence, in that the user requires increased doses in order to obtain the desired effect.

An example of physical dependence: caffeine

Caffeine produces behavioural and physiological effects similar to other drugs of dependence (Meredith *et al*., 2013). Caffeine withdrawal syndrome (e.g. headaches, difficulty in concentrating) has been found in numerous studies. **Tolerance** to caffeine has also been demonstrated, in that among high-dose users of caffeine its effects are no longer different to a placebo. This tends not to be the case for low- or 'typical'-dose users.

● Psychological dependence

Psychological dependence occurs when a drug becomes a central part of an individual's thoughts, emotions and activities and produces a strong urge to use the drug, despite being aware of any harmful effects associated with its use. The person may experience cravings, an intense desire to repeat the experience associated with that activity. If the individual tries to abstain, they experience intense cravings to use the substance or engage in the behaviour. If these are not met, the person feels very anxious, and these feelings make ending the **addiction** extremely difficult. The desire to engage in the addictive behaviour again becomes so intense that it takes over their thinking completely.

Why does psychological dependence arise?

People experience differences between what they *think* (the rational information-processing system) and what they *feel* (the experiential system). The rational system operates according to culturally transmitted rules of reasoning. The experiential system drives us to behave in a particular way based largely on how that makes us *feel*. With psychological dependence, the experiential system has taken priority over the rational system.

● Tolerance

Over time, an individual no longer responds to the drug in the same way, so larger and larger doses are needed in order to feel the same effects as before. (i) In *metabolic tolerance*, enzymes that metabolise the drug do it more efficiently over time, making the effect weaker. (ii) Prolonged drug use leads to changes in *receptor density*, reducing the response to the normal dose of the drug. (iii) With *learned tolerance*, a user experiences reduced drug effects because they have learned to function normally when under the drug's influence.

Tolerance: an illustration (Isbell *et al*., 1955)

Prisoners were administered the same amount of alcohol daily over a 13-week period to keep them in a constant state of intoxication. However, over the course of the study, the men no longer appeared drunk despite receiving the same amount of alcohol. This was due to increased tolerance for the alcohol, i.e. the prisoners had learned to cope with the daily demands of living while under the influence of alcohol, and so no longer appeared to be drunk (*learned tolerance*).

● Withdrawal syndrome

If taking a drug such as heroin or nicotine is discontinued, withdrawal symptoms can occur. As the effect of the drug wears off, the person may experience symptoms such as increased anxiety, shakiness and irritability. The person may then take the drug again to relieve these symptoms. The appearance of withdrawal symptoms is an indication of the person's physical dependence on that drug. Just as tolerance is a consequence of the body adjusting to chronic drug use, withdrawal symptoms are a consequence of the body reacting to the cessation of the drug.

The two phases of withdrawal

Acute withdrawal begins within hours of drug cessation. Physical cravings are intense and persistent, as the body has yet to adjust to the loss of the drug it had become used to for so long.

Post-acute withdrawal can last for years after the person stops taking the drug. Addicts experience alternating periods of dysfunction and near-normality as the brain slowly re-organises and re-balances itself.

KEY TERMS

Addiction A state characterised by compulsively engaging in rewarding stimuli despite the associated adverse consequences.

Physical dependence Evident when an individual needs to take the drug in order to feel 'normal'. It can be demonstrated by the presence of withdrawal symptoms if the individual abstains from the drug.

Psychological dependence Occurs when a drug becomes a central part of an individual's thoughts, emotions and activities, resulting in a strong urge to use the drug.

Tolerance Means that an individual no longer responds to a drug in the same way, with the result that larger and larger doses are needed in order to experience the same effects as before.

Withdrawal syndrome Can occur when a drug on which an individual is physically dependent is discontinued. In such situations, withdrawal symptoms, such as shaking and anxiety, can occur, as the body attempts to deal with the absence of a drug's effects.

Apply it

Scenario. Ash got into heroin when he was just 17 and now spends all his money chasing his next fix. He used to be able to manage with just the occasional injection, but now needs higher and higher doses to get the same effect. He has tried to quit but feels anxious without his daily fix, and loses patience with those around him. He becomes desperate for the drug again to feel better.

With reference to withdrawal syndrome and tolerance, explain what is happening to Ash. (4 marks)

Explanation. Over time, drug users no longer respond to a drug in the same way, so larger and larger doses are needed in order to feel the same effects as before (tolerance). It is possible that enzymes in Ash's body metabolise the heroin more efficiently over time, making the effect of the drug weaker. If taking heroin is discontinued, withdrawal symptoms would occur. These include increased anxiety and irritability, which describes how Ash feels without heroin. Physical cravings are intense without the drug, as the body has yet to adjust to the loss. He would need to take heroin again to relieve these symptoms.

KEY TERMS

Genetic Inherited characteristics that are passed from parents to their children in the form of information carried on their chromosomes.

Personality The stable traits of a person that underlie consistencies in the way they behave over time and in different situations.

Stress A state of physiological arousal produced by demands from the environment (stressors).

Apply it

Scenario. Ryan returned from a tour of duty in Iraq in 2015, but since then he has found it difficult to hold down a job because of substance abuse. When he started taking drugs in order to deal with the traumatic memories of combat, his wife left him. He then started drinking as well and his addiction worsened.

Explain Ryan's behaviour in terms of the relationship between stress and addiction. (4 marks)

Explanation. Ryan is dealing with the traumatic stress of his tour of duty in Iraq by using drugs. Support for this claim comes from Robins *et al.* (1974), who found that 20% of US soldiers returning from the Vietnam War had developed dependence for heroin during their time in Vietnam. The self-medication explanation proposes that some individuals deal with stressful events in their life by engaging in behaviours that make them feel better or forget the stress. Ryan's use of alcohol appears to have been a way of him dealing with another stressful event in his life: the breakdown of his marriage.

Genetic vulnerability, stress and personality

◐ Genetic vulnerability

Slutske *et al.* (2010) interviewed pairs of twins to investigate the role of **genetic** and environmental factors in the development of gambling addiction. For example, MZ twins had a higher rate of both twins being pathological gamblers (if one was a pathological gambler) than DZ twins.

The dopamine receptor gene

Blum and Payne (1991) suggest that individuals who are vulnerable to drug addiction have abnormally low levels of the neurotransmitter dopamine and a decreased ability to activate dopamine receptors in the reward centre of the brain.

◐ Stress
Self-medication

This proposes that some individuals deal with stressful events in their life by engaging in behaviours that make them feel better or help them forget the **stress**. Research on drug abusers has shown that stress is one of the strongest predictors of relapse (Dawes *et al.*, 2000).

Traumatic stress

Robins *et al.* (1974) interviewed US soldiers within a year of their return from the Vietnam War and found 20% reporting that they had developed physical or psychological dependence for heroin during their time in Vietnam.

◐ Personality

Krueger *et al.* (1998) identified a number of **personality** traits (e.g. sensation seeking and impulsivity) that are commonly associated with addiction.

The addiction-prone personality (APP)

Barnes *et al.* (2005) found personality was a significant predictor of 'heavy' marijuana use. Studies using the APP scale have shown that this scale is an effective way of discriminating drug addicts from non-addicts, and predicting the severity of addiction and likelihood of remission during recovery.

Addiction and personality disorders

Research has shown a relationship between addiction and personality disorders. A review of research in this area (Verhheul *et al.*, 1995) found that the overall prevalence of personality disorders was estimated to be 44% in alcoholics, 70% for cocaine addicts and 79% for opiate addicts.

◐ Evaluation
Genetic differences in vulnerability to addiction

Although studies have supported the important role played by genetic factors in the development of alcoholism, research with women has produced inconsistent findings (McGue, 1997). Only two of five twin studies found greater concordance for alcoholism among female MZ twins than female DZ twins. This suggests that genetic factors are less important in the development of alcoholism in women.

Genetics and the diathesis–stress model

Genetic explanations can be given for why some people develop addictive behaviour, yet others with similar experiences do not. The A1 variant of the dopamine-receptor gene is associated with the development of cocaine dependence (Noble *et al.*, 1993) and nicotine dependence (Connor *et al.*, 2007). The exact nature of the addiction, however, is determined by environmental factors (diathesis–stress model).

If stress leads to addiction, does coping lead to abstinence?

Matheny and Weatherman (1998) found that coping with stress reduces the possibility of relapse. They carried out a follow-up study of smokers and found that there was a strong relationship between participants' use of stress-coping resources (e.g. tension control and perceived confidence in ability to succeed) and their ability to maintain abstinence from smoking once they had given up.

The role of stress varies by type of addiction

A limitation is that the relationship between stress and addiction varies according to type of addiction. The role of stress and drug addiction is fairly well established (e.g. Dawes *et al.*, 2000). However, support for the role of stress in other forms of addiction is not as convincing. For example, Arévalo *et al.* (2008) found no association between stress and alcohol addiction.

Support for the role of impulsivity

Research support for the influence of impulsivity in predicting later substance use and addiction comes from longitudinal studies. For example, Labouvie and McGee (1986) found that adolescents who progressed to heavier levels of alcohol abuse tended to score higher on impulsivity.

Personality: implications of an addiction-prone personality

An implication of the relationship between personality characteristics and addictive behaviours is that, by identifying vulnerable individuals in advance, help could be given to stop their behaviour developing into an addiction. This could reduce the enormous personal costs to those individuals and to society in their treatment.

Family influences

Social learning theory (Bandura, 1977) claims that behaviours are learned through the observation of those people with whom a person has the most social contact. For example, Reith and Dobbie (2011) demonstrated the importance of the family in the transmission of gambling behaviour.

Parental influences
Parents provide social models, e.g. adolescents with substance abusing parents are more likely to abuse substances (Biederman et al., 2000). Reith and Dobbie (2011) also found that patterns of gambling were transmitted within families in gendered ways, with males' first experience of gambling through their fathers, and females' through their mothers.

Authoritative parents show warmth but also exert appropriate control. This form of parenting is associated with the shaping of psychological resilience and emotional well-being in children, and lowered levels of substance abuse (Fletcher et al., 1995).

Peers

Peers exert their influence by introducing individuals to risky behaviours or pressuring them to take part. Social identity theory (Tajfel & Turner, 1986) suggests that a significant part of an individual's self-concept is formed as a result of the groups of which they are a part. As it is essential to be associated with the ingroup in order to be socially accepted, this makes individuals more likely to adopt their behaviours.

Social networks
Individual substance use may develop because of substance use within a particular network, e.g. Latkin et al. (2004) found that the probability of drug abuse was related to the number of members within an individual's social network who used drugs.

Indirect peer influence
Shakya et al. (2012) suggest peer influences may sometimes be expressed through indirect parental influence. Positive parenting may discourage substance abuse in adolescents and lead to reduced substance abuse in their friends.

Evaluation of family influences
Support for the role of family influences
Family characteristics most strongly associated with substance use were tolerant parental attitudes and sibling substance use (Bahr et al., 2005). Adolescents with parents who were tolerant of substance use were also more likely to interact with peers who smoked, drank or used illicit drugs. These findings suggest tolerant parental attitudes make it likely that adolescents seek the company of peers who endorse substance abuse.

Substance abuse may be due to *lack* of parental influence
Substance use may result from a *withdrawal* of parental involvement rather than any particular type of parent–adolescent interaction. Stattin and Kerr (2000) suggest adolescents might disclose too much information about their substance abuse, and parents, unable to deal with this, stop monitoring offspring they perceive as already beyond their control. Consequently, the adolescent continues to abuse and becomes more vulnerable to peer influences.

Intervention studies tend to ignore sibling influences
Feinberg et al. (2012) claim that failure to address sibling influences is likely to hinder efforts to reduce early substance use and later substance dependence. Interventions targeted only at the adolescent user or their parents could be undermined by sibling influences, given that older siblings are more likely to be the main source of influence for them.

Evaluation of peer influences
Support for peer influences through social media
Research on social media supports the claim that peer influences are an important influence on addictive behaviour. Litt and Stock (2011) found that teenagers who viewed peers' Facebook profiles that portrayed alcohol use are more likely to drink themselves. Litt and Stock's research suggests that exposure to social media alters adolescents' normative perceptions about substance use.

Peer influences may be overstated
However, the results of a study by De Vries et al. (2006) challenge the claim that peer influence is an important part of substance abuse. They suggest similarity in smoking behaviour among adolescents is more likely to be a consequence of friendship selection, i.e. smokers befriend other smokers rather than smokers influencing non-smokers to take up the habit.

Real-world application: reducing peer influences
Social norm interventions were developed to address the problem of adolescent alcohol abuse. Overestimations of problem behaviour in peers (e.g. patterns of alcohol or drug use) cause adolescents to increase their own drinking or drug use. Correcting these misperceptions (e.g. through media campaigns) will then result in a decrease in the problem behaviour and lessen the likelihood of later substance dependence.

KEY TERM
Peers Refers to individuals of the same age who possess common values and standards of behaviour. Peer groups tend to develop in middle childhood, when belonging to a group becomes more important for a child.

Apply it
Scenario. Casey has been using drugs since he was 14. In the early years he smoked cannabis with his friends, most of whom used drugs on a regular basis. Now at the age of just 23 he is addicted to class A drugs such as cocaine and heroin.

Explain Casey's addictive behaviour in terms of peer influences. (4 marks)

Explanation. Social identity theory suggests that an individual's self-concept is formed as a result of the groups of which they are a part. In order to be accepted by his peers, Casey would be more likely to adopt their behaviours. Latkin et al. (2004) found that the probability of drug abuse was related to the number of peers within an individual's social network who used drugs. Most of Casey's peer group already used drugs on a regular basis, which explains why he began experimenting with drugs, and why he is now addicted to class A drugs as his peer groups change.

KEY TERMS

Dopamine One of the key neurotransmitters in the brain, with effects on motivation and drive.

Neurochemistry Neural processes associated with the nervous system.

Nicotine The main active ingredient of tobacco. Nicotine is known to have a number of effects, including stimulant and relaxant effects.

Brain neurochemistry and nicotine addiction

Nicotine is the main active ingredient of tobacco. It can have a range of different effects, including tranquillisation, decreased irritability, increased alertness and even improved cognitive functioning. The finding that nicotine has both stimulant and relaxation effects is called the 'nicotine paradox', i.e. smoking can feel invigorating at some times and calming at others.

Dopamine and the brain's reward pathways

Nicotine becomes addictive because it activates areas of the brain that regulate feelings of pleasure, i.e. the 'reward pathways' of the brain. Nicotine attaches to neurons in the ventral tegmental area (VTA). These neurons trigger a release of **dopamine** in a brain region called the nucleus accumbens (NAc). As well as directly influencing the NAc to release dopamine, nicotine also stimulates the release of the neurotransmitter glutamate, which triggers an additional release of dopamine. This release of dopamine produces pleasure and a desire to repeat the behaviours that led to it.

Glutamate, GABA and MAO

Dopamine levels remain high after the direct nicotine stimulus ends, because of the action of glutamate and GABA. Nicotine causes glutamate to speed up dopamine release, but nicotine also prevents GABA from slowing it down after dopamine levels have been raised. This combination of dopamine release and the inhibition of GABA results in an increase in dopamine and an amplification of the rewarding properties of nicotine.

The development of nicotine addiction

Because the effects of nicotine disappear within a few minutes, this creates a need to continue the intake of nicotine throughout the day in order to get the dopamine 'rush'. The brain quickly becomes sensitised to nicotine, causing a nicotine-dependent state to develop. This state is associated with significant withdrawal symptoms when the smoker attempts to abstain from smoking, which can only be overcome by smoking another cigarette.

Evaluation: brain neurochemistry

Support for the nicotine–dopamine link

Support comes from the finding (Paterson & Markou, 2002) that a drug (gamma-vinyl GABA – GVG) reduces the surge of dopamine in the NAc that occurs after taking nicotine and consequently reduces its addictive tendencies. By counteracting any pleasurable experiences that may be gained by the increase in dopamine, this drug may offer a way of treating nicotine addiction.

Support for the role of glutamate and GABA

D'Souza and Markou (2013) blocked transmission of glutamate in rats, which resulted in a decrease in nicotine intake and nicotine seeking in the animals. This is consistent with explanations of the role of glutamate in nicotine addiction. Glutamate enhances the dopamine-releasing effects of nicotine – so blocking it would decrease those effects, making nicotine less rewarding.

Nicotine and Parkinson's disease

Support for the link between nicotine and dopamine comes from the treatment of patients with Parkinson's disease (PD), a neurodegenerative disorder characterised by a gradual loss of dopamine-producing nerve cells. Fagerstrom *et al.* (1994) treated two PD patients with nicotine gum and patches. They found significant changes in symptoms that were attributed to the increased levels of dopamine caused by the nicotine.

Implications: nicotine addiction and depression

Khaled *et al.* (2009) claimed that long-term smoking could have an adverse effect on mood because it alters brain **neurochemistry**. They found the incidence of depression was highest in long-term smokers and lowest in those who had never smoked. This was also the case in a Chinese study where smoking was associated with a greater risk of depression in males and females (Luk & Tsoh, 2010).

Nicotine affects men and women differently

Cosgrove *et al.* (2014) studied the brains of men and women using PET scans to measure the changing levels of dopamine when smoking. For women, there was a strong dopamine effect in the dorsal putamen, whereas men had a strong activation effect in the ventral striatum. This supports the claim that men and women smoke for different reasons – men for the nicotine effect itself, women to relieve stress and manage mood.

Apply it

Scenario. Tim is trying to give up smoking but finds that he has to sneak a cigarette several times a day. He claims it 'gives him a buzz' that he finds hard to give up.

With reference to Tim, outline and evaluate the relationship between brain neurochemistry and nicotine addiction. (16 marks)

Explanation extract... Nicotine, the main active ingredient of tobacco, activates the 'reward pathways' of the brain. It attaches to neurons in the ventral tegmental area, which trigger a release of dopamine in the nucleus accumbens. This would explain the 'buzz' that Tim experiences when he smokes, and why he finds it difficult to give this up. Tim admits he smokes several times a day. This is because the effects of nicotine disappear within a few minutes, so he needs to smoke frequently to continue the intake of nicotine throughout the day in order to get the dopamine 'rush' he appears to crave. ...

Learning theory and nicotine addiction

◉ Initiation
Social **learning theory** explanations of experimental smoking propose that young people begin smoking as a consequence of the social models they have around them who smoke (Kandel & Wu, 1995). Addictive substances and activities are immediately rewarding, which means they are learned quickly, which explains why people get 'hooked' on nicotine very quickly after starting to smoke. Inhaled nicotine enters the circulation rapidly and enters the brain within seconds. As a result, the individual feels a sudden 'rush', which reinforces the activity that produced it.

◉ Maintenance
When repeated many times, smoking becomes an established behaviour because of the positive consequences for the individual (i.e. positive reinforcement), e.g. they may learn that they can manipulate moods by smoking. Most people maintain their smoking habit to avoid withdrawal symptoms, which can occur if the person stops smoking. As the effect of the nicotine wears off, the person may experience symptoms such as increased anxiety, irritability or low mood. These withdrawal symptoms can be relieved if the person smokes another cigarette (i.e. negative reinforcement).

◉ Relapse: cue reactivity
Nicotine (UCS) increases the release of dopamine. The brain's response to this change in dopamine levels is to restore equilibrium by lowering dopamine levels back to normal (UCR).

Any stimulus associated with this nicotine input (e.g. smell of cigarette smoke) becomes a conditioned stimulus (CS), signalling that nicotine is on its way. With repeated associations, it is capable of producing the same response in the brain (**cue reactivity**).

This occurs even in the absence of the UCS, but the brain's response in the absence of nicotine means that dopamine levels are lowered *below* the optimum level. This is experienced as withdrawal symptoms, and the person is motivated to smoke again in order to feel better.

◉ Evaluation
Support for social learning explanations of smoking initiation
Many of the claims of social learning influences on the development of addictive behaviours have been supported by research evidence. Peer group influences have been found to be the primary influence for adolescents who experiment with smoking (DiBlasio & Benda, 1993). As predicted by explanations based on social learning, adolescents who smoked were more likely to 'hang out' with other adolescents who also smoked.

Support for smoking and mood manipulation
Research evidence has supported the claim that negative mood experiences often increase nicotine craving and risk of relapse among those trying to quit smoking. For example, Shiffman and Waters (2004) found that sudden increases in negative mood states were associated with relapse. These findings support the negative reinforcement explanation because of the greater likelihood of smoking during the experience of negative mood.

Support for the role of cue reactivity
Wiers *et al.* (2013) provided support for the importance of classically conditioned cues in nicotine cravings. Heavy smokers, ex-smokers and non-smokers were asked to respond to pictures of smoking-related and neutral cues with either an 'approach' or 'avoid' response. Heavy smokers showed a significant approach bias towards smoking-related cues compared to the other two groups, confirming that smoking cues play a significant role in nicotine addiction.

Gender differences in patterns of nicotine addiction
A limitation of learning theory explanations of nicotine addiction is that they fail to acknowledge the existence of gender differences. Research has shown that women are more likely than men to light up in stressful situations and their nicotine dependence grows more rapidly (Baewert *et al.*, 2014). Women also experience withdrawal effects sooner and have a harder time giving up the habit.

Implications for treatment
Drummond *et al.* (1990) proposed a treatment based on the cues associated with smoking. Cue exposure therapy (CET) involves presenting the cues without the opportunity to engage in the smoking behaviour. As a result, the association between the cue and smoking is extinguished. Unrod *et al.* (2014) demonstrated the effectiveness of this approach, with CET resulting in a progressive decline in cue-provoked craving.

KEY TERMS
Cue reactivity Objects and environments associated with a drug or behaviour become conditioned stimuli, so people experience greater craving and physiological arousal when exposed to the objects and environments associated with their addiction.

Learning theory Explanations (such as classical and operant conditioning) that explain behaviour in terms of learning rather than any inborn tendencies, physiological factors or cognitive reasoning.

UCS – Unconditioned stimulus
UCR – Unconditioned response
CS – Conditioned stimulus
CR – Conditioned response

Apply it
Scenario. Most of Harry's friends smoke cigarettes. Harry used to smoke and finds it difficult on nights out with his friends, because when they light up it makes him want to smoke again.

With reference to Harry, outline and evaluate the learning theory explanation of nicotine addiction. (4 marks)

Explanation. When people smoke cigarettes, nicotine increases the release of dopamine in the brain. When Harry is out with his friends and they start to smoke, the smoking-related cues of their cigarettes (e.g. the smell of the cigarette smoke) act as conditioned stimuli that, for Harry, predict the coming of nicotine. These cues are capable of producing the same conditioned response as nicotine, i.e. Harry's brain acts to lower dopamine levels back to normal. However, because Harry isn't actually smoking, this means that his dopamine levels are lowered below the optimum level and so Harry feels the urge to smoke again in order to feel better.

KEY TERMS

Learning theory Explanations (such as classical and operant conditioning) that explain behaviour in terms of learning rather than any inborn tendencies, physiological factors or cognitive reasoning.

Partial reinforcement Only some responses are reinforced, compared to full reinforcement where every response is reinforced. For example, responses may be reinforced every fifth time (regular interval) or at variable intervals.

Variable reinforcement A response is reinforced after an unpredictable number of responses. In variable ratio reinforcement, the delivery of reinforcement is unpredictable but averages out at a specific rate.

Apply it

Scenario. Matt and Gareth like nothing more than going to the casino to gamble on the fruit machines. Although neither seems to come away in profit at the end of the evening, they do experience the occasional win. Gareth admits part of the attraction is the whole casino experience.

Using learning theory explanations of gambling addiction, explain why Matt and Gareth continue to visit the casino to gamble, even though they end up losing. (4 marks)

Explanation. The use of variable reinforcement, where only a proportion of a player's responses are rewarded, has wins occurring after an unpredictable number of responses. It is the unpredictability of these wins that keeps Matt and Gareth gambling. They win 'occasionally', which is providing variable reinforcement, maintaining their gambling behaviour. Gareth admits that part of the attraction is the 'whole casino experience', which suggests that they are experiencing the casino itself as reinforcing. For example, flashing lights and ringing bells are likely to produce exhilaration for the gambler, which is why Matt and Gareth are driven to return to that environment again and again.

Learning theory explanations of gambling addiction

Behaviour that produces a rewarding consequence then becomes more frequent (operant conditioning). Gamblers playing slot machines may become addicted because of the physiological, psychological, social and financial rewards if they win (Griffiths, 2009).

Partial reinforcement

The sequence of outcomes in some forms of gambling (e.g. fruit machines) is determined by a **partial reinforcement** schedule, i.e. wins follow some bets, but not all. Behaviours acquired are slower to extinguish because of the uncertainty of reinforcement.

Variable reinforcement

A particular type of partial reinforcement, where only a proportion of a player's responses are rewarded, is known as **variable reinforcement**. Gambling machines use a particular type of variable reinforcement, known as variable-ratio reinforcement, with wins occurring after an unpredictable number of responses. It is the unpredictability of these rewards that keeps people gambling.

Gambling and its rewards

The 'big win' hypothesis

Many pathological gamblers report having a 'big win' early in their gambling career or an early prolonged winning streak. They continue to gamble because of a desire to repeat that early 'peak experience' (Aasved, 2003).

The 'near miss'

Near misses or losses that are 'close' to being wins create a brief period of excitement and thrill that encourage further gambling (Reid, 1986). Some fruit machines are designed to ensure a higher than chance frequency of near misses, as this form of reinforcement occurs at no expense to the casino.

The gambling environment

The casino itself is experienced as reinforcing. Flashing lights, ringing bells, etc. are all exciting for the gambler. The betting environment is full of conditioned stimuli, with exhilaration the conditioned response. These act as triggers for gambling as they have the ability to increase arousal (classical conditioning).

Evaluation

Learning theory can't explain all forms of gambling

It is difficult to apply the same principles to all different forms of gambling. For example, some forms of gambling have a short time-period between the behaviour and the consequence (e.g. scratch cards), whereas others (such as sports betting) have a much longer period between bet and outcome, and so have less to do with chance and simple conditioning and more to do with skill.

Fails to explain why only some people become addicted

There are problems with explaining addiction solely in terms of its reinforcing properties. Although many people gamble at some time during their lives and experience the reinforcements associated with this behaviour, relatively few become addicts. This suggests there are other factors involved in the transition from gambling behaviour to gambling addiction.

Support for the influence of partial reinforcement

Horsley *et al.* (2012) subjected high- and low-frequency gamblers to either partial or continuous reinforcement. After partial reinforcement, high-frequency gamblers continued to gamble for longer compared to low-frequency gamblers despite the lack of further reinforcement. The researchers concluded that this might be a result of increased dopamine function that is particular to high-frequency gamblers.

Reinforcement schedules may lead to irrational beliefs

There is support for the claim that an early big win can lead to persistence in gambling behaviour. Sharpe (2002) claimed the placement of early wins and the patterns of wins and losses within gaming sessions may lead to irrational thoughts generated by beliefs about being able to control the machine. The resulting overestimation of the chances to win and the underestimation of the possible losses encourage persistent gambling.

Different pathways to gambling addiction

'Behaviourally conditioned' gamblers may have begun gambling because of exposure to gambling through role models or peer groups. Their gambling can be explained in terms of social learning. The 'emotionally vulnerable' gambler uses gambling to relieve their aversive emotional states, suggesting that **learning theory** can explain some types of gambling addiction, but not all (Blaszczynski & Nower, 2002).

Cognitive theory and gambling addiction

◎ The role of cognitive biases

Irrational beliefs and distorted thinking patterns contribute to the development and maintenance of problem gambling. These are referred to as **cognitive biases**, and include:

The gambler's fallacy

The belief that completely random events such as a coin toss are somehow influenced by recent events, e.g. that runs of a particular outcome will be balanced out by the opposite outcome.

Illusions of control

These are demonstrated through the performance of superstitious behaviours, which the gambler believes helps them to manipulate the event outcome in their favour. Pathological gamblers show an exaggerated self-confidence in their ability to influence chance.

The 'near miss' bias

Near misses occur when an unsuccessful outcome is *close* to a win. Near misses appear to have some rewarding value for the gambler despite the lack of any monetary reinforcement associated with winning.

The recall bias

Pathological gamblers often suffer from a recall bias, i.e. the tendency to remember and overestimate wins while forgetting about, underestimating or rationalising losses (Blanco *et al.*, 2000).

◎ Key study: Cognitive bias in fruit machine gambling (Griffiths, 1994)

How? Griffiths (1994) studied whether regular gamblers thought differently to non-regular gamblers. He compared 30 regular gamblers who played fruit machines with 30 non-regular gamblers. Griffiths was interested in the gamblers' verbalisations as they played the machine.

Showed? Regular gamblers believed they were more skilful than they actually were and were more likely to make irrational statements during play. Most of the non-regular gamblers believed playing the game was 'mostly chance', whereas most of the regular gamblers believed success was due to skill, or equally chance and skill. They explained away losses by seeing 'near misses' as 'near wins', justifying their continuation.

◎ Evaluation

Research support for the role of cognitive biases

Ladouceur *et al.* (2002) found that 80% of gambling-related verbalisations made by problem gamblers would be classified as irrational. In contrast, research with recreational gamblers has not found the same high degree of cognitive biases. This lends support to the claim that irrational beliefs are what sustain the gambling habit and make people more vulnerable to developing a gambling addiction (Petry, 2005).

Implications for treatment

An implication of the cognitive explanation is that CBT might be helpful in reducing gambling addiction by correcting cognitive biases. For example, Echeburúa *et al.* (1996) found that CBT was effective in preventing relapse in gamblers who played slot machines. The researchers did acknowledge, however, that slot-machine pathological gamblers might not be representative of the larger population of problem gamblers.

Irrational thinking varies with type of gambling

Lund (2011) argues that some types of gambling are more likely than others to encourage cognitive biases. She found that cognitive biases were more likely in gamblers who preferred gambling machines and internet gambling. Lund concluded that mistaken ideas of skill and illusions of control are important in the development of cognitive biases, which in turn can lead to gambling addiction.

Awareness does not decrease susceptibility to cognitive bias

Research suggests that possessing relevant knowledge about probability and chance does not make people less susceptible to the cognitive distortions typically found in pathological gamblers. For example, Benhsain and Ladouceur (2004) found no difference between students trained in statistics and those in a non-statistical field in their susceptibility to irrational gambling-related cognitions.

Cognitive biases may have a biological basis

Research (Clark *et al.*, 2014) has shown that gambling addicts have a different pattern of brain activity compared to non-gamblers. This gives them the misguided belief that they are able to beat the odds in games of chance. If this region is damaged, people become immune to cognitive biases. This suggests that if cognitive biases have a neurological basis, then they could be treated with drugs that target specific regions of the brain.

KEY TERM

Cognitive biases Irrational beliefs that are unhelpful, illogical and inconsistent with our social reality, and which can lead us to behave in inappropriate ways.

Apply it

Scenario. Tom and Saif spend a lot of time playing the fruit machines. Tom is convinced that he is a skilled gambler and can 'play the system' to beat the machines. Saif has lost a lot of money in recent weeks, but only seems to remember the (relatively) few times he has won.

With reference to Tom and Saif's behaviour, outline and evaluate cognitive biases in gambling addiction. (16 marks)

Explanation extract… Tom is displaying the illusion of control in that he shows an exaggerated self-confidence in his ability to influence chance. Tom is a regular gambler, and Griffiths (1994) found that most regular gamblers who played fruit machines believed their success was due to skill rather than chance. Saif is displaying the recall bias: the tendency to remember and overestimate wins while forgetting about or underestimating losses (Blanco *et al.*, 2000). This is demonstrated by the fact that although overall he is losing money, he tends to overestimate the number of times he has won relative to the number of times he has lost. …

KEY TERM

Drug therapy Interventions that use medication in order to treat addiction. Drugs interact with receptors or enzymes in the brain to reduce cravings for a drug or the desire to engage in a particular behaviour.

Drug therapies for the reduction of addiction

Drug treatments for nicotine addiction

After a person smokes for a while, their body gets used to getting regular doses of nicotine from cigarettes. **Drug therapy** reduces or controls the cravings that accompany attempts to abstain from smoking.

Nicotine replacement therapy

Nicotine replacement therapy (NRT) works by gradually releasing nicotine into the bloodstream at much lower levels than in a cigarette. This helps the individual control their cravings for a cigarette, improves their mood and helps to prevent relapse.

Drug treatments – varenicline and bupropion

Varenicline and bupropion are nicotine-free pills that reduce a person's craving for tobacco and help with any withdrawal symptoms. For example, bupropion works by inhibiting the re-uptake of dopamine and has been shown to be effective as a smoking cessation drug (Hughes *et al.*, 2004).

Drug treatments for gambling addiction

Opioid antagonists

Opioid antagonists (e.g. naltrexone) bind to opioid receptors in the body, blocking these receptors. This prevents the individual experiencing the rewarding response they associate with gambling. By reducing the reinforcing properties of gambling behaviour, this reduces the urge to gamble. Kim *et al.* (2002) found that naltrexone was effective in reducing the frequency and intensity of gambling urges, as well as gambling behaviour itself.

Antidepressants

There is evidence to support serotonin dysfunction in pathological gambling (George & Murali, 2005). Research suggests that gamblers treated with SSRIs to increase serotonin levels show significant improvements in their gambling behaviour. SSRIs reduce symptoms of depression and anxiety. As many gamblers report gambling as a response to the stressors in their life, reducing the symptoms associated with these stressors lessens the urge to gamble.

Evaluation

Support for the effectiveness of nicotine replacement therapy

Stead *et al.* (2012) investigated the effectiveness of nicotine replacement therapy (NRT) compared to a placebo in 150 trials involving treatment of nicotine addiction. They concluded that NRT was effective in helping people overcome their nicotine addiction, and was 70% more effective than a placebo. This was independent of any additional support provided to the individual, suggesting that quitting was a consequence of the NRT treatment alone.

Lack of blinding in NRT studies

Critics argue that clinical trials of NRT are not truly 'blind'. Mooney *et al.* (2004) found that only a minority of studies had conducted blinding assessments, and in these studies two-thirds of those in the placebo condition were 'confident' that they had not received the real nicotine patch. This means that conclusions about the effectiveness of this form of treatment are more uncertain than has been claimed.

Naltrexone can make fun activities seem 'uninspiring'

A problem with the use of opioid antagonists is the fact that they work by blocking the brain's reward system. This mechanism is a fairly general one, in that by stopping the brain from releasing dopamine, it causes some patients to lose pleasure in other areas of life while they are on the drug. This is one reason why some choose not to continue with their treatment.

Methodological issues in drug therapies for gambling addiction

Claims of the success of drug treatments are challenged by methodological limitations of research in this area. Blaszczynski and Nower (2007) claim that research studies are characterised by small sample sizes, high dropout rates and low numbers of females who are problem gamblers. Many studies fail to include control groups or randomly assign gamblers to different treatment conditions, which makes it difficult to draw valid conclusions.

Support for the effectiveness of drug treatments for gambling

Research supports the claim that SSRIs have beneficial effects on gambling behaviour. Grant and Potenza (2006) gave 13 gambling addicts escitalopram for three months. Some of these individuals were randomly assigned to either continue with the escitalopram or receive a placebo. The continuing success of the escitalopram group compared to the placebo group shows improvements were due to the effects of the drug rather than another factor (e.g. extra attention).

Apply it

Scenario. Sabrina is trying to fight her nicotine addiction. She admits she simply lacks willpower to deal with her cravings, so seeks help from her doctor. He suggests that drug therapies might be the best form of treatment for her.

Explain one advantage and one problem for Sabrina using drug therapies for her nicotine addiction. (4 marks)

Explanation. Drugs such as bupropion inhibit the re-uptake of dopamine and are believed to be effective in reducing the craving for tobacco and help with any withdrawal symptoms. This would be a significant advantage for Sabrina as she admits lacking the willpower to deal with her nicotine cravings. A problem with the use of drugs such as bupropion is that their effectiveness in the treatment of nicotine addiction is inconclusive. For example, only in a minority of studies have patients been unaware of whether they were receiving the drug or a placebo, which means that conclusions about the effectiveness of drug treatments are more uncertain than Sabrina's doctor believes.

Behavioural therapies for the reduction of addiction

Behavioural interventions try to change a person's motivation to engage in addictive behaviours. This can be achieved either by introducing a *real* unpleasant association, as in **aversion therapy**, or by introducing an *imagined* unpleasant association, as in **covert sensitisation**.

Aversion therapy

Aversion therapy decreases the undesirable behaviours associated with addiction by associating them with unpleasant sensations. It is based on classical conditioning – an individual learns to associate an *aversive* stimulus (the UCS) with an action they had previously enjoyed (the NS).

The patient engages in the behaviour while at the same time being exposed to something unpleasant, such as a drug that makes them nauseous or mild electric shocks. Once the behaviour becomes associated with the unpleasant stimulus (i.e. it becomes a CS), it will begin to decrease in frequency.

An example: treatment of gambling addiction

A brief electric shock is repeatedly paired with stimuli (e.g. pictures of a betting shop, online poker images) associated with problem gambling. The discomfort from the electric shock becomes associated with the gambling behaviour and the patient reports loss of desire and stops gambling.

Covert sensitisation

Covert sensitisation is similar to aversion therapy, but the individual only imagines the unpleasant stimulus. Rather than experiencing actual physical consequences such as pain from an electric shock, the consequences are instead pictured in the person's mind. The consequences must be vivid enough so that the individual experiences feelings of considerable discomfort or anxiety when they imagine themselves engaging in the addictive behaviour. By associating these unpleasant sensations with the undesirable behaviour, this leads to decreased desire and avoidance of the situation.

An example: treatment of problem drinking

Individuals using covert sensitisation imagine themselves engaging in behaviours associated with drinking (e.g. opening a bottle, going into a pub) and then imagine a very unpleasant consequence (e.g. experiencing intense feelings of nausea). By consistently associating the behaviour and its unpleasant consequence over and over in their mind, they eventually lose the desire to drink.

Evaluation

Research support for aversion therapy

Smith and Frawley (1993) studied a sample of 600 patients being treated for alcoholism using aversion therapy. Some patients were also being treated for cocaine dependence. After 12 months, 65% were totally abstinent from alcohol. The 12-month abstinence rate for cocaine was 83.7%. This study provides research support for the claim that aversion therapy eliminates the urge to drink or use drugs.

Ethical problems with aversion therapy

Although aversion therapy has been shown to be effective in reducing addictive behaviour, there are significant ethical concerns surrounding its use as a form of treatment, e.g. the use of drugs that cause nausea and vomiting. These effects might lead to poor compliance with treatment and high dropout rates, which decrease the potential positive impact of this type of treatment.

Support for covert sensitisation

Kraft and Kraft (2005) provided support for the effectiveness of covert sensitisation in treating a variety of different addictive behaviours such as cigarette smoking and chocolate addiction. They concluded that covert sensitisation was an effective form of treatment for the elimination of the cravings associated with these addictive behaviours in 90% of cases.

Covert sensitisation is a more ethical form of treatment

An advantage of covert sensitisation compared to aversion therapy is that it is a more ethical approach to treatment. There are no physical risks involved, such as an adverse reaction to a sickness-inducing drug in the treatment of alcohol addiction. Individuals are not required to engage in the problem behaviour, only imagine it, thus reducing the possibility of harm even further.

Problems with behaviour modification of addiction

Behaviour modification therapies fail to address other factors that might drive addictive behaviours. Treating only the symptoms of an addiction (e.g. stopping someone engaging in gambling behaviour) rather than addressing the underlying issues that led to the addiction in the first place may leave individuals at risk of developing another addiction even if the addiction being treated is eliminated.

KEY TERMS

Aversion therapy Aims to decrease or eliminate undesirable behaviours by associating them with unpleasant or uncomfortable sensations.

Behavioural interventions Work on the assumption that addictive behaviours are learned and so can be reduced or eliminated by changing the consequences of these behaviours.

Covert sensitisation Involves eliminating an unwanted behaviour by creating an imaginary association between the behaviour and an unpleasant stimulus or consequence.

Apply it

Scenario. Rosa is desperate to kick her addiction to cigarettes so decides to undergo covert sensitisation after talking to her psychologist friend.

Explain how covert sensitisation might be used in the treatment of Rosa's nicotine addiction. (4 marks)

Explanation. Covert sensitisation would involve Rosa imagining herself engaging in behaviours associated with smoking (e.g. lighting a cigarette, taking a drag on it) and then imagining a very unpleasant consequence (e.g. experiencing intense feelings of nausea and vomiting all over the floor). These consequences must be vivid enough so that Rosa experiences feelings of considerable discomfort or anxiety when she imagines herself smoking a cigarette. By consistently associating smoking and its unpleasant consequence over and over in her mind, she should eventually lose the desire to smoke and avoid cigarettes in the future.

KEY TERM
Cognitive behavioural therapy
A combination of cognitive therapy (a way of changing maladaptive thoughts and beliefs) and behavioural therapy (a way of changing behaviour in response to these thoughts and beliefs).

Cognitive behavioural therapy (CBT)

The main goal of **cognitive behavioural therapy** is to help people change the way they think about their addiction, and to learn new ways of coping more effectively with the circumstances that led to these behaviours.

CBT and gambling addiction

CBT helps gamblers identify the triggers to their gambling, challenges their irrational thinking and finds better ways to cope with the urges that prompt a gambling episode. CBT attempts to correct errors in thinking (such as the belief that the individual can control and predict outcomes), thus reducing the urge to gamble.

CBT and internet addiction

Young (2011) used CBT-IA to reduce internet addiction. The first stage aims to modify behaviour by learning to control internet usage. In the second stage, the therapist reduces maladaptive cognitions that trigger excessive online activity. In the third stage, the focus is on problems existing in the person's life that led to the addiction.

How CBT works in the reduction of addiction
Identifying and correcting cognitive biases
Clients being treated for gambling addiction are not always aware of the cognitive biases on which they base their decisions. The therapist can educate clients about the nature of cognitive biases and what randomness means, i.e. that gambling outcomes are determined by chance. The client can also be asked how effective *their* strategy has been over time (i.e. challenging the effectiveness of their beliefs).

Changing behaviour
After the individual thinks differently about their behaviour, they are encouraged to practise these changes in their daily life, e.g. gamblers are asked to visit a casino and refrain from betting. Clients are encouraged to keep a diary to record the triggers related to their problem behaviour and to record their progress in overcoming their addiction.

Relapse prevention
CBT usually incorporates some relapse prevention techniques, i.e. learning to identify and now avoid those risky situations (e.g. casinos or betting shops) that might trigger feelings or thoughts that can lead to relapse into the particular problem behaviour.

Evaluation
Supporting evidence for the role of CBT in treating addiction
A meta-analysis of CBT trials found CBT to be effective in reducing both alcohol and illicit drug addiction (Magill & Ray, 2009). Echeburúa *et al.* (1996) found that CBT yielded better outcomes than waiting list (i.e. waiting for therapy) or behavioural interventions in the treatment of gambling addiction. CBT has also been shown to be more effective than referral to 'Gamblers Anonymous' (Petry *et al.*, 2006).

Support for CBT in the treatment of internet addiction
Research has demonstrated the effectiveness of CBT-IA in the treatment of internet addiction. Kim *et al.* (2012) found that adolescents subjected to CBT-IA scored higher on life satisfaction and lower on internet addiction compared to those who did not receive CBT-IA. This provides support for CBT's ability to increase positive outcomes by changing unhealthy thinking patterns associated with internet addiction.

Advantages of CBT as a treatment for addiction
Addicts frequently suffer from negative thought patterns that contribute to feelings of helplessness. The development of more positive ways of thinking means they no longer feel overwhelmed by everyday circumstances and are less likely to engage in addictive behaviours. Addicts are particularly vulnerable to peer pressure, so with CBT they are able to learn new behaviours that make them more confident in their ability to resist pressure to engage in problem behaviours.

Irrational thinking or irrational environment?
A problem in using CBT alone as a treatment for addiction is that there is an over-emphasis on an individual's irrational thinking rather than acknowledging the stressful environments (e.g. an unhappy marriage) that continue to produce problem behaviours. This suggests CBT can be effective in reducing addiction but only as part of a wider form of intervention that also addresses the social environment in which addiction occurs.

Making the transition from use to non-use
McHugh *et al.* (2010) suggest a particular challenge to the success of CBT is that the patient is also required to make the transition to a culture in which he or she may have few skills and resources, relinquishing an addiction subculture in which there *is* a sense of effectiveness and belonging. This can make the individual ambivalent about change, and make behaviour change more difficult.

Apply it

Scenario. Despite his losses, Arno is convinced that he has the skills to make his living in the casino. Even when he tries to give up the casino he finds he can't pass a betting shop without going in to place a bet.

Explain why cognitive behavioural therapy would be an appropriate method of treatment for Arno. (4 marks)

Explanation. CBT would be appropriate for Arno because he is not aware that believing he can influence chance is an example of irrational thinking. He can be educated about cognitive biases and how gambling outcomes in the casino are determined by chance. He can also be asked how effective his strategy has been over time, and as he has lost money this would challenge his view that it is about skill. CBT incorporates relapse prevention techniques, so Arno would be taught to identify and avoid risky situations (e.g. casinos or betting shops) that might lead him to gamble again. This could be as simple as changing his route so he no longer walks past betting shops.

The theory of planned behaviour (TPB)

⊙ Main assumptions

An individual's decision to engage in a particular behaviour can be directly predicted by their intention to engage in that behaviour. Intention is a function of three factors:

1. Behavioural attitude

An individual is more likely to hold a favourable attitude towards an addictive behaviour if they believe that engaging in that behaviour will lead to mostly positive outcomes for them.

2. Subjective norms

An individual's subjective awareness of social norms relating to a particular behaviour, reflecting what they believe significant others feel is the right thing to do ('injunctive norm'), and perceptions of what other people are *actually* doing ('descriptive norm').

3. Perceived behavioural control

Refers to the extent to which an individual believes they can actually give up an addictive behaviour. The more control people believe themselves to have over the behaviour, the stronger their intention to abstain from their addiction and the harder they will try to achieve that.

⊙ Using the TPB to reduce addiction

Changing behavioural attitude

A review of the effectiveness of the ONDCP campaign to lower teenage marijuana use in the US (Slater *et al.*, 2011) attributed its success to its influence on changing attitudes towards the drug.

Changing subjective norms

Anti-drug campaigns often seek to give adolescents actual data about the percentage of people engaging in risky behaviour. This is done in order to change subjective norms.

Perceived behavioural control

Godin *et al.* (2002) examined the extent to which the **theory of planned behaviour** could explain smoking intentions and behaviours in adults intending to give up smoking. All elements of the TPB explained intentions, but perceived behavioural control was the most important predictor of ultimate behaviour.

⊙ Evaluation

TPB is too rational

A limitation of the TPB is that it is too rational, failing to take into account emotions, compulsions or other irrational determinants of human behaviour (Armitage *et al.*, 1999). The presence of strong emotions may explain why people sometimes act irrationally by failing to carry out an intended behaviour (e.g. stop drinking) even when it is in their best interest to do so.

Ignores other factors

There are many other factors that are ignored by the TPB. Topa and Moriano (2010) suggest that identification with peers could play a mediating role in the relation with addictive behaviours. Another ignored factor is motivation. Klag (2006) found that recovery was more successful in individuals who had decided themselves to give up rather than people who were coerced to do so.

Methodological issues with the TPB

Attitudes and intentions assessed by questionnaires may be poor representations of the attitudes and intentions that eventually exist in the behavioural situation, and thus poor predictors of actual behaviour (Albarracin *et al.*, 2005). A person's actual intention and behaviour may differ greatly when they are in a group of heavy smokers with all the associated sights and smells of smoking.

Predicts intention rather than behaviour change

Armitage and Conner's (2001) meta-analysis of studies using the TPB found that this model was successful in predicting intention to change behaviour rather than actual behavioural change. This suggests that the TPB is primarily an account of intention formation rather than specifying the processes involved in translating the intention into action (Ajzen & Fishbein, 2005).

The influence of alcohol or drugs

A limitation of the model is that it fails to take into account the influence of alcohol or drugs, which can produce a discrepancy between measured intention and actual behaviour. MacDonald *et al.* (1996) found that alcohol intoxication actually increased measured intention to engage in a variety of risky behaviours despite the presence of TPB variables that would otherwise predict restraint.

KEY TERM

Theory of planned behaviour An individual's decision to engage in a particular behaviour can be directly predicted by their intention to engage in that behaviour, which in turn is determined by their behavioural attitude, subjective norms and perceived behavioural control.

Apply it

Scenario. Sophie's parents are both psychologists and decide to use the theory of planned behaviour to change Sophie's digital addiction.

Explain how they might use this theory to reduce Sophie's reliance on digital technology. (4 marks)

Explanation. They could start by changing her attitude to digital technology, e.g. by providing evidence of how a reduction in digital use can make life less stressful. They could then alter the subjective norm for this behaviour. Sophie might believe that others regard spending a lot of time on the internet and checking Facebook as a good thing, but her parents may have evidence to challenge this belief. Finally, Sophie may lack confidence that she could actually reduce her reliance on digital technology (i.e. a lack of perceived behavioural control). Her parents could arrange for Sophie to have counselling to increase her self-efficacy and, as a result, her intention to overcome her digital addiction.

KEY TERM

Prochaska's six-stage model A model of addiction treatment that sees people passing through six transitional stages when attempting to change a problematic behaviour such as smoking or gambling.

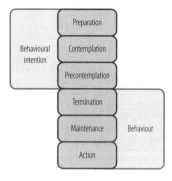

The 'stages of change' model

An overview of the model

Stage theories emphasise the gradual nature of change, and assume a transition through a series of discrete stages. **Prochaska's six-stage model** sees people passing through six stages when attempting to change a problematic behaviour such as smoking or gambling. They move through these stages in order, but may, on occasion, relapse and revert to an earlier stage before repeating the cycle again.

The six stages of change

1. Precontemplation

Individuals who currently have no intention to change their behaviour in the near future are in this stage. They may be unaware that their behaviour is becoming problematic and may only seek help because of pressure from others.

2. Contemplation

The person may be aware that a problem exists but has yet to make a commitment to do anything about it, partly because of the amount of effort it would take to give up their addiction.

3. Preparation

This stage combines *intention* to change with actual *behavioural* change. Individuals report small behavioural changes, but have yet to reduce their addictive behaviour to a point of complete abstinence.

4. Action

Individuals modify their behaviour in order to overcome their problems. They are classified as being in this stage when they have successfully altered their problem behaviour for a period of between one day and six months.

5. Maintenance

The individual works to consolidate the gains attained during the previous stage and to prevent relapse. They are classified as being in this stage when they have stayed free of the previously addictive behaviour for a period of six months or more.

6. Termination

The individual is no longer tempted to revert to the former behaviour and is completely confident that they are able to maintain the change.

The processes of change

Movement from the precontemplation stage to the contemplation stage may involve the use of *consciousness raising*, learning new facts that support the recommended behaviour change. To maintain this change, they may use *stimulus control*, removing any cues to engage in the problem behaviour.

Evaluation
Usefulness of the stage model

This model is useful because it suggests the most effective strategy to use in reducing addiction is determined by the current stage the individual is in. Haslam and Draper (2000) found that women further along the cycle of change were more convinced about the dangers of smoking during pregnancy. This suggests interventions must be tailored to an individual's stage of change to maximise their effectiveness.

Evidence does not always demonstrate *behavioural* outcomes

Whitelaw *et al.* (2000) claim that very few studies have used behavioural outcomes as a way of measuring the usefulness of this model. Much of the research evidence has tended to focus only on stage progression within the model rather than actual behaviour change. This led Whitelaw *et al.* to conclude that the strength of the evidence base for the model has been overstated.

Design weaknesses in supporting studies

Whitelaw *et al.* argue that few studies have included all the characteristics of good experimental design. Some studies have not used control groups, whereas others have used only self-selected samples. Other studies have used a variety of interventions as part of treatment, which makes it difficult to disentangle the specific effects of this approach from more generalised effects of intervention.

Research fails to support the effectiveness of the model

Recent research using random allocation has cast doubts about the effectiveness of staged intervention in the treatment of addiction. Among drinkers randomly allocated to either a staged intervention group or a control group, there was no significant difference in beneficial effects between the groups (Baumann *et al.*, 2015). This suggests that the advantages of Prochaska's model are overstated.

Social norms may influence progression through the stages of change

A limitation of this approach is that it fails to acknowledge the influence of social norms. Daoud *et al.* (2015) found that many male smokers in Arab cultures were stuck in the precontemplation stage because of the importance of social smoking. This shows that a lower readiness to quit smoking in some cultures may be a product of social pressures that limit the effectiveness of therapeutic interventions.

Apply it

Scenario. Prochaska's six-stage model is a useful approach to treatment because it suggests that the most effective strategy to use in reducing addiction is determined by the current stage the individual is in.

With reference to this claim, discuss Prochaska's 'stages of change' model in the treatment of addiction. (16 marks)

Explanation extract… There is support for the claim that the success of intervention is linked to the person's current stage in Haslam and Draper's study of women smoking during pregnancy. Women further along the cycle of change were more likely to consider the dangers of smoking while pregnant. Research has also shown that the current stage of an individual dictates the type of process that is likely to make intervention effective. For example, movement from the precontemplation stage to the contemplation stage could involve consciousness raising, where the individual learns new facts and ideas that support their attempts to give up their addiction. …

Glossary

Absorption addiction model Individuals can become psychologically absorbed with a celebrity to establish a sense of fulfilment. The motivational forces driving this absorption might then take on an addictive component, leading to more extreme behaviours in order to sustain the parasocial relationship. 38

Accommodation The process of adjusting or changing existing schemas because new, conflicting information creates disequilibrium. 50

Addiction A state characterised by compulsively engaging in rewarding stimuli despite the associated adverse consequences. 125

Adrenaline and noradrenaline Hormones associated with arousal of the sympathetic nervous system, causing the physiological sensations related to the stress response (raised heart rate, sweating, etc.). Also function as neurotransmitters. 83

Affectionless psychopathy A behaviour disorder in which the individual has no ability to experience shame or guilt, and lacks a social conscience and a sense of responsibility. This means that they may find it 'easier' to commit crimes. 118

Alpha bias A tendency to exaggerate differences between men and women. The consequence is that theories devalue one gender in comparison to the other. 21

Alternative hypothesis A testable statement about the relationship (difference, association, etc.) between two or more variables. 13

Androcentrism Centred or focused on men, often to the neglect or exclusion of women. 21

Androgyny A combination of male and female characteristics. 41

Anger management A form of CBT specific to changing the way a person manages their anger. Techniques include cognitive restructuring, skill acquisition and behavioural training. 121

Anorexia nervosa (AN) A type of eating disorder in which an individual, despite being seriously underweight, fears that she or he might become obese and therefore engages in self-starvation to prevent this happening. There are two main sub-types: restricting type and binge eating or purging type. 74

Assimilation The process of fitting new experiences into an existing schema without making any change to the schema. 50

Atavistic form An early explanation for criminal behaviour, suggesting that certain individuals are born with a criminal personality and this innate personality is a throwback to earlier primate forms. Turvey (2011) identified 18 different characteristics that make up the atavistic type. 111

Attachment theory An explanation of the formation of an emotional bond between two people (especially caregiver and child). It is a two-way process that endures over time. It leads to certain behaviours such as clinging and proximity-seeking. 38

Atypical antipsychotics A lower risk of extrapyramidal side effects, a beneficial effect on negative symptoms and cognitive impairment, and suitable for treatment-resistant patients. 64

Autism A mental disorder which usually appears in early childhood and typically involves avoidance of social contact, abnormal language and so-called 'stereotypic' or bizarre behaviours. 56

Autonomy The freedom to make decisions and determine actions without the constraints imposed by others. 76

Aversion therapy Aims to decrease or eliminate undesirable behaviours by associating them with unpleasant or uncomfortable sensations. 133

Avoidance-oriented coping A way to cope with stress by behaving in ways that distance yourself from the problem. 94

Avolition The reduction, difficulty or inability to initiate and persist in goal-directed behaviour, often mistaken for apparent disinterest. 60

Behavioural interventions Work on the assumption that addictive behaviours are learned and so can be reduced or eliminated by changing the consequences of these behaviours. 133

Behaviour modification A therapeutic technique used to increase or decrease the frequencies of behaviour using operant conditioning. 120

Benzodiazepines A class of drug used to treat stress and anxiety. They facilitate the action of the neurotransmitter GABA in quietening down neurons in the brain. 91

Beta bias A tendency to ignore or minimise differences between men and women. Such theories tend either to ignore questions about the lives of women, or assume that insights derived from studies of men will apply equally well to women. 21

Beta blockers Decrease stress and anxiety by blocking the effects of adrenaline and noradrenaline, which are part of the sympathomedullary response to stress. 91

Biofeedback A method of stress management that involves a person learning to control aspects of autonomic functioning through the use of operant conditioning. 93

Biological explanations A belief that a full understanding of thoughts, emotions and behaviour must include an understanding of their biological basis, i.e. the role of genetics, neural correlates and hormones. 62, 74, 79

Bottom-up approach A data-driven approach where statistical techniques are used to produce predictions about the likely characteristics of an offender. 110

Boundary model Considers the biological (feeling hunger, feeling satiation) and cognitive (self-imposed view of what/when to eat) boundaries influencing eating behaviour. Explains overeating as resulting, in part, from the 'what the hell effect'. 80

Calculated value The value of a test statistic calculated for a particular data set. 14

Cardiovascular disorder Any disorder of the heart (such as coronary heart disease, CHD) and circulatory system (such as hypertension, commonly known as high blood pressure) as well as strokes (restricted blood flow to parts of the brain). 84

Case study A detailed study of a single individual, institution or event. Case studies provide a rich record of human experience but are hard to generalise from. 9

Chromosomes The X-shaped bodies that carry all the genetic information (DNA) for an organism. 42

Class inclusion The relation between two classes where all members of one class are included in the other, e.g. the category 'animal' includes sub-groups such as cats and dogs, which can further be divided into breeds. 51

Coding Putting data in categories. 8

Cognitive behavioural therapy A combination of cognitive therapy (a way of changing maladaptive thoughts and beliefs) and behavioural therapy (a way of changing behaviour in response to these thoughts and beliefs). 65, 121, 134

Cognitive biases Irrational beliefs that are unhelpful, illogical and inconsistent with our social reality, and which can lead us to behave in inappropriate ways. 131

Cognitive development The process by which our mental processes change as we age. 50

Cognitive distortion Thinking that has a bias, such as what is perceived by a person does not match reality. Two examples of cognitive distortion are hostile attribution bias and minimalisation. 116

Cognitive explanations Propose that abnormalities in cognitive function are a key component of schizophrenia. 63

Cognitive priming Refers to a temporary increase in the accessibility of thoughts and ideas. For example, violent media activate thoughts or ideas about violence, which activate other aggressive thoughts through their association in memory pathways. 106

Cognitive theory When applied to disorders, this is any explanation about the way in which a person processes information that affects their feelings and their behaviour. 78

Commitment The likelihood that an individual will persist with their current relationship. It is a product of high satisfaction and investment in the relationship and low quality of alternatives. 35

Co-morbidity The extent that two (or more) conditions or diseases occur simultaneously in a patient, e.g. schizophrenia and depression. 61

Complementarity of needs How well two people fit together as a couple and meet each other's needs. 32

Concurrent validity A means of establishing validity by comparing an existing test/questionnaire with the one you are interested in. 11

Conservation The ability to understand that, despite superficial changes in appearance, basic properties of an object remain unchanged. This ability appears around the age of six or seven. 43, 51

Content analysis Analysis of data from an observational study in which behaviour is usually observed indirectly in visual, written or verbal material. 8

Control To direct or to exercise authoritative influence over events or behaviours. 76

Correlation coefficient A number between −1 and +1 that tells us how closely the co-variables in a correlational analysis are related. 17

Cortisol Hormone produced as a result of chronic stress, with both positive and negative effects (e.g. burst of energy and reduced immune response). 83

Covert sensitisation Involves eliminating an unwanted behaviour by creating an imaginary association between the behaviour and an unpleasant stimulus or consequence. 133

Crime Refers to any behaviour that is unlawful and punished by the state. It is an act that is harmful to an individual, group or society as a whole. 108

Critical value In a statistical test the value of the test statistic that must be reached to show significance. 14

Cue reactivity Objects and environments associated with a drug or behaviour become conditioned stimuli, so people experience greater craving and physiological arousal when exposed to the objects and environments associated with their addiction. 129

Cultural bias The tendency to judge all people in terms of your own cultural assumptions. This distorts or biases your judgement. 22

Cultural relativism The view that behaviour cannot be judged properly unless it is viewed in the context of the culture in which it originates. 22

Culture The rules, customs, morals, childrearing practices, etc. that bind a group of people together and define how they are likely to behave. 22, 47, 61

Custodial sentencing A custodial sentence refers to cases where the court has decided the offender is to be held in prison or some other closed community like a psychiatric hospital. 119

Daily hassles The 'irritating, frustrating, distressing demands that to some degree characterise everyday transactions with the environment' (Kanner *et al.*, 1981). 86

Daily uplifts The minor positive experiences of everyday life, e.g. receiving a compliment at work or feeling good about one's appearance. 86

Degrees of freedom The number of values that are free to vary given that the overall total values are known. 14

De-individuation A psychological state in which individuals have lowered levels of self-evaluation (e.g. when in a crowd or under the influence of alcohol) and decreased concerns about evaluation by others. 103, 119

Delusions Firmly held erroneous beliefs that are caused by distortions of reasoning or misinterpretations of perceptions or experiences. 60

Desensitisation Explanations based on this assume that, under normal conditions, anxiety about violence inhibits its use. Media violence may lead to aggressive behaviour by removing this anxiety. 106

Determinism Behaviour is controlled by external or internal factors acting upon the individual. 23

Diathesis–stress model Explains mental disorders as the result of an interaction between biological (the diathesis) and environmental (stress) influences. 68

Dieting A deliberate reduction of food intake in an attempt to lose weight. There are three basic forms: restricting total food intake, refraining from eating certain foods, avoiding eating for long periods of time. 81

Differential association theory An explanation of offending behaviour in terms of learning theory, how interactions with others lead to the formation of attitudes about crime (which may be more or less favourable), as well as acquiring specific knowledge about how to commit crimes. 117

Disinhibition In relation to eating behaviour, this is the removal of the normal inhibitions to overeating (e.g. salivation), resulting in the tendency to overeat in response to a range of different stimuli. In relation to aggression, exposure to violent media legitimises the use of violence in real life because it undermines the social sanctions that usually inhibit such behaviour. 80, 106

Disorganised type of offender The crime scene is left with many clues such as fingerprints, there is little evidence of engagement with the victim, and the offender has lower intelligence and competence. 109

Dispositional explanations Emphasise the causes of a particular behaviour as being due to the enduring characteristics of the individuals involved rather than any aspect of the situation they are in. 104

Distortions Thinking that has a bias such that what is perceived by a person does not match reality. 78

Dopamine One of the key neurotransmitters in the brain, with effects on motivation and drive. 128

Dopamine hypothesis An excess of the neurotransmitter dopamine in certain regions of the brain is associated with the positive symptoms of schizophrenia. 62

Drug therapy In mental disorders such as schizophrenia, treatment through the use of antipsychotics to reduce symptoms of the disorder. Drug therapy can also be used in order to treat addiction. Drugs interact with receptors or enzymes in the brain to reduce cravings for a drug or the desire to engage in a particular behaviour. 64, 132

Duck's phase model of relationship breakdown A model of relationship breakdown that describes the different phases that people enter during the dissolution of a romantic relationship. 36

Dyadic phase An individual confronts their partner and discusses with them their feelings, their discontentment and the future of the relationship. This is followed by the social phase. 36

Dysfunctional thought processing Cognitive habits or beliefs that cause the individual to evaluate information inappropriately. 63

Ecological validity The ability to generalise a research effect beyond the particular setting in which it is demonstrated to other settings. 11

Egocentrism Seeing things from your own viewpoint and being unaware of other possible viewpoints. 51

Electra complex A stage in girls' gender development according to psychodynamic theory. 45

Emotional support Focused on trying to find ways to reduce feelings of anxiety associated with stress. 95

Emotion-focused coping A way to cope with stress by tackling the symptoms of stress, e.g. the anxiety that accompanies stress. 94

Empirical A method of gaining knowledge which relies on direct observation or testing, not hearsay or rational argument. 12

Enmeshment Describes a family where parents are over-emotionally involved with their children but may be dismissive of their emotional needs. This can make it difficult for the child to develop an independent self-concept. The concept is used in family systems explanations of disorders such as anorexia. 76

Environment Everything that is outside our body, which includes people, events and the physical world. 24

Epigenetics Refers to the material in each cell of the body that acts like a set of 'switches' to turn genes on or off. 112

Equilibration Experiencing a balance between existing schemas and new experiences. 50

Equity theory Claims that people are most comfortable when what they get out of a relationship (i.e. the benefits) is roughly equal to what they put in (i.e. the costs). 34

Esteem support Increasing a person's sense of self-worth so they can feel more confident about coping with both instrumental and emotional issues. 95

Ethnocentrism Seeing things from the point of view of ourselves and our social group. Evaluating other groups of people using the standards and customs of one's own culture. 22

Ethological explanation Stresses the adaptive value of animal behaviours. Ethologists study the behaviour patterns of animals in their natural environments. 99

Evolutionary explanations Focus on the adaptive nature of behaviour, i.e. modern behaviours are believed to have evolved because they solved challenges faced by our distant ancestors and so became more widespread in the gene pool. 29, 70, 100

Extroversion Refers to outgoing people who enjoy risk and danger because their nervous systems are under-aroused. They are characterised by positive emotions but may get bored easily. 114

Face validity The extent to which test items look like what the test claims to measure. 11

False belief The understanding that others may hold and act on mistaken (false) beliefs. 53, 56

Falsifiability The possibility that a statement or hypothesis can be proved wrong. 12

Family dysfunction The presence of problems within a family that contribute to relapse rates in recovering schizophrenics, including lack of warmth between parents and child, dysfunctional communication patterns and parental overprotection. 63

Family systems theory Claims that individuals cannot be understood in isolation from one another, but rather as a part of their family. 76

Family therapy A range of interventions aimed at the family (e.g. parents, siblings, partners) of someone with a mental disorder. 66

Filter theory We choose romantic partners by using a series of filters that narrow down the 'field of availables' from which we might eventually make a choice. 32

Fixed action patterns A repertoire of stereotyped behaviours, which occur in specific conditions (i.e. in response to specific triggers) and which do not require learning. 99

Food preference Refers to the way in which people choose from among available foods on the basis of biological and learned perceptions such as taste, health characteristics, value, habit, etc. 70, 71

Free will Individuals have the power to make choices about their behaviour. 23

Frustration–aggression hypothesis This sees aggression being the consequence of frustration, defined as 'any event or stimulus that prevents an individual from attaining some goal and its accompanying reinforcing quality'. 101

Gates The barriers that limit opportunities for the less attractive, shy or less socially skilled to form relationships in face-to-face encounters. 37

Gender A person's sense of maleness or femaleness, a psychological/social construct. 41

Gender bias The differential treatment or representation of men and women based on stereotypes rather than real differences.In diagnosis, the tendency to describe the behaviour of men and women in psychological theory and research in such a way that might not represent accurately the characteristics of one gender. 21, 61

Gender constancy The recognition that your gender is a constant, not just across your lifetime but also in different situations. 43

Gender identity disorder Individuals experience gender dysphoria (confusion), with strong persistent identification with the opposite gender and discomfort with their own. 48

General adaptation syndrome How all animals cope with stress in an initially adaptive way, but ultimately leading to illness. The three stages are alarm, resistance and exhaustion. 83

Genetic Inherited characteristics that are passed from parents to their children in the form of information carried on their chromosomes. 62, 126

Genetic explanations The likelihood of behaving in a particular way is determined by a person's genetic make-up, i.e. it is inherited from parents. 74, 79, 98, 112

Geographical profiling A form of bottom-up profiling based on the pattern shown by the location or locations of a series of crimes. 110

Ghrelin A hormone that is released in the stomach and which stimulates the hypothalamus to increase appetite. Ghrelin levels increase when a person's bodily resources are low. 73

Grave-dressing phase Partners strive to construct a representation of the failed relationship that does not paint their contribution to it in unfavourable terms. 36

Hallucinations Distortions or exaggerations of perception in any of the senses, most notably auditory hallucinations. 60

Hard determinism The view that all behaviour can be predicted and there is no free will. The two are incompatible. 23

Hardiness A style of personality which provides defences against the negative effects of stress. The characteristics are: having control over one's life, commitment (i.e. a sense of involvement in the world) and challenge (i.e. life changes are opportunities rather than threats). 90

Hassles and Uplifts Scale (HSUP) A self-report scale. Hassles and uplifts are scored on a 3-point scale for severity and frequency. The two scores are reported separately. 88

Heredity The process by which traits are passed from parents to their offspring, usually referring to genetic inheritance. 24

Holism Focuses on the whole system rather than its constituent parts and suggests that the system is more than the sum of its individual components. 25

Homeostasis The mechanism by which an organism maintains a steady internal environment. 73

Hormones The body's chemical messengers. They travel through the bloodstream, influencing many processes including the stress response, maternal bonding and mood. 42

Hostile attribution bias When a person automatically attributes malicious intentions to another. These negative attributions then lead to more aggressive behaviour. 116

Hypothalamic pituitary-adrenal system Physiological pathway involved in the long-term (chronic) stress response, involving cortisol. 83

Hypothalamus An area of the brain which has a number of important functions, including the regulation of body temperature, hunger and thirst. 73

Identification An individual adopts an attitude or behaviour because they want to be associated with a particular person or group. 45

Idiographic approach Focuses on individuals and emphasises uniqueness; favours qualitative methods in research. 26

Immunosuppression Suppression of the immune system – a system of cells within the body that is concerned with fighting intruders such as viruses and bacteria so they cannot infect the body. For example, white blood cells (leucocytes) identify and eliminate foreign bodies (antigens). 84

Innate releasing mechanism A neural network that, when stimulated by the presence of a sign stimulus, communicates with motor control circuits to activate the fixed action pattern associated with that sign stimulus. 99

Institutional aggression Refers to aggressive acts that are found in particular violent institutions such as prisons. 104

Instrumental support When direct aid and actual material services are offered. 95

Interactionist approach With reference to the nature–nurture debate, the view that the processes of nature and nurture work together rather than in opposition. 24

Internalisation An individual accepts the attitudes or behaviour of another. 45

Inter-observer reliability The extent to which there is agreement between two or more observers involved in observations of a behaviour. 10

Intersex An individual who is not distinctly male or female due to mismatch between chromosomes and genitals. 42

Intrapsychic phase An individual broods over their current relationship and considers whether they might be better off out of it. This is followed by the dyadic phase. 36

Investigative psychology A form of bottom-up profiling based on psychological theory. 110

Investment A measure of all the resources attached to the relationship (e.g. financial, shared children), which would be lost if the relationship were to end. 35

Investment model An explanation of relationship stability that emphasises the importance of three factors (satisfaction, investment size and quality of alternative) in determining relationship commitment, which in turn predicts relationship stability. 35

Irrational beliefs Beliefs that are unhelpful, illogical and inconsistent with our social reality. Rational beliefs, on the other hand, are helpful, logical and consistent with our social reality. 78

Job control The extent to which a person feels they can manage aspects of their work, such as deadlines and work environment. 87

Learning The acquisition of knowledge, skills or habits through experience, observation or teaching. 71

Learning theory Explanations (such as classical and operant conditioning) that explain behaviour in terms of learning rather than any inborn tendencies, physiological factors or cognitive reasoning. 129, 130

Leptin A hormone that plays a crucial role in appetite and weight control. It is normally produced by fat tissue and secreted into the bloodstream, where it travels to the brain and decreases appetite. 73

Level of measurement Refers to the different ways of measuring items or psychological variables; the lower levels are less precise. 14

Life changes Events (such as divorce or bereavement) that require an adjustment in various aspects of a person's life. As such, they are significant sources of stress. 85

Life change units (LCUs) A number assigned to each life event to represent how much stress is created. The higher the number, the more stressful. 85

Limbic system A system of structures lying beneath the cortex (i.e. subcortical), including the amygdala, hippocampus and hypothalamus. The region is associated with emotional behaviour. 97

MAOA Monoamine oxidase A (MAOA) is an enzyme that, among other things, regulates the metabolism of serotonin in the brain. 98

Matching hypothesis Claims that when people look for a partner for a romantic relationship they tend to look for someone whose social desirability approximately equals their own. 30

Maternal deprivation The loss of emotional care that is normally provided by a primary caregiver. 118

Media The various means of communication, such as radio, television, newspapers and the internet, that reach or influence people widely. 47, 77

Media influences Changes in behaviour that are attributed to exposure to media such as TV or computer games. 105

Minimalisation Underplaying the consequences of an action to reduce negative emotions such as feeling guilty. 116

Mirror neuron Neurons in the brain that react when a person performs an action and also when another individual performs the same action. This means that an observer experiences the actions of another as if it were their own. 58

Modelling A form of learning where individuals learn a particular behaviour by observing another individual performing that behaviour. 77

Moral reasoning Thinking in a consistent and logical way about right and wrong, with reference to socially agreed principles. 116

Mundane realism How a study mirrors the real world. The research environment is realistic to the degree to which experiences encountered in the research environment will occur in the real world. 11

Nativist approach A theory that suggests humans are born with innate abilities. 53

Nature Behaviour is seen as a product of innate (biological or genetic) factors. 24

Nature–nurture debate The argument as to whether a person's development is mainly due to their genes or to environmental influences. 24

Negative symptoms Appear to reflect a diminution or loss of normal functioning. 60

Neophobia An extreme dislike and avoidance of anything that is new or unfamiliar. 70

Neural correlates Changes in neuronal events and mechanisms that result in the characteristic symptoms of a behaviour or mental disorder. 62

Neural explanations Involve areas of the brain and nervous system and the action of chemical messengers in the brain known as neurotransmitters in controlling behaviour. 74, 79, 112

Neurochemistry Neural processes associated with the nervous system. 128

Neuroticism Refers to people with a negative outlook who are easily upset. Their lack of stability results from an overactive response to threat (fight-or-flight). 114

Nicotine The main active ingredient of tobacco. Nicotine is known to have a number of effects, including stimulant and relaxant effects. 128

Nomothetic approach Seeks to formulate general laws of behaviour based on the study of groups and the use of statistical (quantitative) techniques. It attempts to summarise the similarities between people through generalisations. 26

Null hypothesis An assumption that there is no relationship (difference, association, etc.) in the population from which a sample is taken with respect to the variables being studied. 13

Nurture Behaviour is a product of environmental influences. 24

Obesity In adults a BMI of 20–24.9 is considered normal, 25–29.9 overweight and 30–39.9 clinically obese. A BMI over 40 is seen as severely obese. Waist circumference is a second measurement of obesity with weight reduction recommended when the waist is over 40 inches in men and 35 inches in women. 79

Object permanence A child's understanding that objects that are no longer visible nevertheless continue to exist. 51

Oedipus complex A stage in boys' gender development according to Freudian theory. 45

Offender profiling A method of working out the characteristics of an offender by examining the characteristics of the crime and crime scene. 109

One-tailed test Form of test used with a directional hypothesis. 14

Operant conditioning Learning through reinforcement or punishment. If a behaviour is followed by a desirable consequence, then that behaviour is more likely to occur again in the future. 120

Organised type of offender This type of offender commits a planned crime and may engage in violent fantasies with the victim. They are of high intelligence and socially competent. 109

Paradigm 'A shared set of assumptions about the subject matter of a discipline and the methods appropriate to its study' (Kuhn, 1962). 12

Parasocial relationship An individual is attracted to another person (usually a celebrity), who is usually unaware of the existence of the person who has created the relationship. 38

Partial reinforcement Only some responses are reinforced, compared to full reinforcement where every response is reinforced. For example, responses may be reinforced every fifth time (regular interval) or at variable intervals. 130

Peers Refers to individuals of the same age who possess common values and standards of behaviour. Peer groups tend to develop in middle childhood, when belonging to a group becomes more important for a child. 127

Personality The stable traits of a person that underlie consistencies in the way they behave over time and in different situations. 126

Perspective-taking Involves being able to view a situation or emotions from another person's viewpoint (also called role-taking). 55

Physical dependence Evident when an individual needs to take the drug in order to feel 'normal'. It can be demonstrated by the presence of withdrawal symptoms if the individual abstains from the drug. 125

Physical reasoning system An innate system that provides a framework for reasoning about the displacements and interactions of physical objects. 53

Physiological measures of stress Any method that is based on the body's physical response to stress and thus related to effects of the SAM pathway or HPA system. 88

Population validity The extent to which the findings of a study of a sample of participants can be generalised to other people outside the study. 11

Positive symptoms Appear to reflect an excess or distortion of normal functioning. 60

Pre-operational A stage in Piaget's theory of cognitive development where a child's logic lacks internal consistency. 43

Probability (p) A numerical measure of the likelihood or chance that certain events will occur. A statistical test gives the probability that a particular set of data did not occur by chance. 13

Problem-focused coping A way to cope with stress by tackling the factor(s) causing the stress, often in a practical way. 94

Prochaska's six-stage model A model of addiction treatment that sees people passing through six transitional stages when attempting to change a problematic behaviour such as smoking or gambling. 136

Psychodynamic explanation Refers to any theory that emphasises change and development in the individual, particularly those theories where 'drive' is a central concept in development. The key elements of explanations are that early experiences coupled with innate drives create the adult personality. 118

Psychological dependence Occurs when a drug becomes a central part of an individual's thoughts, emotions and activities, resulting in a strong urge to use the drug. 125

Psychoticism Refers to an aggressive, anti-social person who lacks empathy and has little regard for the welfare of others. This may be related to high levels of testosterone. 114

Quality of alternatives/comparison with alternatives An individual's assessment of whether their needs might be better fulfilled by somebody other than their current partner. 35

Recidivism This is when a person reoffends after receiving some form of punishment for previous offences. The Prison Reform Trust (2014) reports that 46% of adults and 67% of under 18s are reconvicted within one year of release. 119

Reductionism An approach that breaks complex phenomena into simpler components, implying that complex phenomena are best understood in terms of the simplest, yet complete, level of explanation. 25

Reinforcement A term used in psychology to refer to anything that strengthens a response and increases the likelihood that it will occur again in the future. 77

Reliability The consistency of measurements. We would expect any measurement to produce the same data if taken on successive occasions. 10, 61

Restorative justice A method of reducing and atoning for offending behaviour through reconciliation between offender and victim as well as the wider community. Offenders are often offered restorative justice as an alternative to a custodial sentence, if the victim agrees. 122

Restraint theory Restraint is the conscious restriction of food intake to prevent weight gain or promote weight loss. This theory proposes that attempting to restrain eating actually increases the probability of overeating. 80

Sally–Anne test A story about two dolls (Sally and Anne). Sally doesn't know that the ball she placed in a basket has been moved to a box by Anne – the audience sees Anne do this. Where will Sally look for her ball: where she left it or where it has moved to? The story is used to test theory of mind in children. 56

Satisfaction A measure of the degree to which the current partner gratifies a person's important needs. 35

Scaffolding An approach to instruction that aims to support a learner only when absolutely necessary, i.e. to provide a support framework (scaffold) to assist the learning process. 52

Schema A cognitive framework that helps organise and interpret information in the brain. Schemas are usually constructed from previous experience, and used to generate future expectations. They can be behavioural or cognitive. 44, 50

Schizophrenia A type of psychosis characterised by a profound disruption of cognition and emotion. 60

Self-disclosure When a person reveals intimate personal information about themselves to another person. 31, 37

Semiotics The signs and symbols developed within a particular culture, e.g. language and mathematical symbols. 52

Serotonin A neurotransmitter implicated in many different behaviours and physiological processes, including aggression, eating behaviour, sleep and depression. 97

Sex Being genetically male (XY) or female (XX). 41

Sex-role stereotypes A set of shared expectations within a social group about what men and women should do and think. 41

Sexual selection A key part of Darwin's theory explaining how evolution is driven by competition for mates, and the development of characteristics that ensure reproductive success. 29

Significant A statistical term indicating that the research findings are sufficiently strong to enable a researcher to reject the null hypothesis under test and accept the research hypothesis. 14

Similarity in attitudes If people share similar attitudes, values and beliefs, communication is easier and so a relationship is likely to progress. 32

Situational explanations Emphasise the causes of a particular behaviour as being due to the context in which it occurs rather than any enduring characteristics of the individuals involved. 104

Skin conductance response A measurement of the electrical conductivity of the skin, which is increased when sweat is produced as part of the sympathetic response. 88

Social cognition Refers to how our mental state (cognition) moderates our interaction with other people (social behaviour). 55

Social demography Refers to variables such as age, background and location, which determine the likelihood of individuals meeting in the first place. 32

Social exchange theory The likelihood of a person staying in a relationship is determined by an assessment of what they get out of the relationship compared to what they put in, and how the relationship measures up against what they expect and what they might achieve in a different relationship. 33

Social learning/social learning theory Learning through observing others and imitating behaviours that are rewarded. 46, 77, 102

Socially sensitive research Any research that might have direct social consequences for the participants in the research or the group that they represent. 27

Social phase Discontentment spills over to friends and family, as the distress experienced by one or both partners is made public. This is followed by the grave-dressing phase. 36

Social Readjustment Rating Scale (SRRS) A self-report scale to assess life events over a set period of time. There are 43 events on the scale, each of which is related to a certain number of life change units (LCUs). 88

Soft determinism A version of determinism that allows for some element of free will. 23

Speech poverty The lessening of speech fluency and productivity, which reflects slowing or blocked thoughts. 60

Statistical test Procedure for drawing logical conclusions (inferences) about the population from which samples are drawn. 14

Stress A state of physiological arousal produced by demands from the environment (stressors). 126

Stress inoculation therapy A type of CBT which trains people to cope with anxiety and stressful situations more effectively by learning skills to 'inoculate' themselves against the damaging effects of future stressors. 92

Superego Part of Freud's concept of the structure of the personality. The superego embodies our conscience and is our moral compass, as well as notions of the ideal self. It develops between the ages of three and six. The superego is likely to be involved in offending behaviour because it is concerned with right and wrong. 118

Sympathomedullary pathway System involved in the immediate (acute) response to stress (fight-or-flight), involving adrenaline. 83

Symptom overlap Symptoms of a disorder may not be unique to that disorder but may also be found in other disorders, making accurate diagnosis difficult. 61

Taste aversion A learned response to eating toxic, spoiled or poisonous food, which results in the animal avoiding eating the food that made it ill in the future. 70

Temporal validity The ability to generalise a research effect beyond the particular time period of the study. 11

Tend-and-befriend response An adaptive response to stress in female animals, related to protecting offspring (tend) and relying on the social group for mutual defence (befriending). 94

Testosterone A hormone produced mainly by the testes in males, but also occurring in females. It is associated with the development of secondary sexual characteristics in males (e.g. body hair), but has also been implicated in aggression and dominance behaviours. 97

Test–retest reliability The same test or interview is given to the same participants on two occasions to see if the same results are obtained. 10

Test statistic The name given to the value calculated using a statistical test. For each test this value has a specific name such as S for the sign test. 14

Thematic analysis A technique used when analysing qualitative data. Themes or categories are identified and then data is organised according to these themes. 8

Theory of mind (ToM) An individual's understanding that other people have separate mental states (beliefs, intentions, emotions) and that others see the world from a different point of view to their own. 56

Theory of planned behaviour An individual's decision to engage in a particular behaviour can be directly predicted by their intention to engage in that behaviour, which in turn is determined by their behavioural attitude, subjective norms and perceived behavioural control. 135

Token economy A form of therapy where desirable behaviours are encouraged by the use of selective reinforcements. Rewards (tokens) are given as secondary reinforcers when individuals engage in correct/socially desirable behaviours. The tokens can then be exchanged for primary reinforcers – food or privileges. 67, 120

Tolerance Means that an individual no longer responds to a drug in the same way, with the result that larger and larger doses are needed in order to experience the same effects as before. 125

Top-down approach (Also known as crime scene analysis.) Through analysis of previous crimes, a profile of the offender is created which is then used to narrow the field of possible suspects. Unlike the bottom-up approach, the top-down approach relies on the intuition and beliefs of the profiler. 109

Two-tailed test Form of test used with a non-directional hypothesis. 14

Type A personality Someone who experiences constant time pressure, competitiveness in work and social situations, and is easily frustrated by other people and becomes angry. 89

Type B personality Someone with an easy-going, relaxed and patient approach to life. 89

Type C personality Someone with extreme emotional suppression and a desire to please others. 89

Type I error Occurs when a researcher *rejects* a null hypothesis that is true. 13

Type II error Occurs when a researcher *accepts* a null hypothesis that was not true. 13

Typical antipsychotics Dopamine antagonists. They bind to but do not stimulate dopamine receptors and so reduce the symptoms of schizophrenia. 64

Universality The aim is to develop theories that apply to all people, which may include real differences. 21

Validity Whether an observed effect is a genuine one. 11, 61

Variable reinforcement A response is reinforced after an unpredictable number of responses. In variable ratio reinforcement, the delivery of reinforcement is unpredictable but averages out at a specific rate. 130

Violation of expectation research A method of conducting research with infants using their surprise as a measure of whether what they see is not what they expect to see. Thus we know what their expectations are. 53

Virtual relationships Relationships that are conducted through the internet rather than face to face, e.g. through social media. 37

Withdrawal syndrome Can occur when a drug on which an individual is physically dependent is discontinued. In such situations, withdrawal symptoms, such as shaking and anxiety, can occur, as the body attempts to deal with the absence of a drug's effects. 125

Workload The amount of effort and/or activity involved in a job. It is quite often discussed as 'job demand', i.e. the amount required for a person to do during their working day. 87

Workplace stress Aspects of our working environment (such as work overload or impending deadlines) that we experience as stressful, and which cause a stress reaction in our body. 87

Zone of proximal development The 'region' between a person's current ability, which they can perform with no assistance, and their potential capabilities, which they can be helped to achieve with the assistance of 'experts'. 52

The Research Methods Companion

- Written by leading Psychology author, Cara Flanagan.

- Practical, activity-based Student Book covers everything you need to know for the research methods part of AS and A Level Psychology.

- Designed for use with all A Level Psychology courses.

- Developed to boost your confidence and provide you with the skills, knowledge and understanding you need to get to grips with this challenging part of the course.

SECOND EDITION — for all A Level courses

Research Methods Companion

for A Level and AS Psychology

Cara Flanagan

OXFORD

Order your copy now: 978 019 835613 4

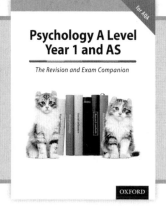

Psychology A Level Year 1 and AS

The Revision and Exam Companion

OXFORD

978-019-837640-8

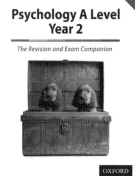

Psychology A Level Year 2

The Revision and Exam Companion

OXFORD

978-019-837641-5

Also available

- **The Revision and Exam Companions for AQA**

OXFORD   tel 01536 452620   email schools.enquiries.uk@oup.com